# The Nev
## Berksh.
## Village Book

*Other counties in this series include:*

Avon*

Bedfordshire*

Buckinghamshire*

Cambridgeshire*

Cheshire*

Devon*

Dorset

Essex*

Gloucestershire*

Hampshire*

Herefordshire*

Hertfordshire*

Kent

Lancashire*

Leicestershire
  & Rutland*

Lincolnshire*

Middlesex*

Norfolk*

Northamptonshire*

Nottinghamshire*

Oxfordshire*

Powys Montgomery*

Shropshire*

Somerset*

Staffordshire*

Suffolk

Surrey

East Sussex

West Sussex

Warwickshire*

West Midlands*

Wiltshire

Worcestershire*

*Published in conjunction with County Federations of
Women's Institutes

# The New Berkshire Village Book

Compiled by the Berkshire
Federation of Women's Institutes from notes
sent by Institutes in the County

with illustrations by Judith Fraser

Published jointly by
Countryside Books, Newbury
and the B.F.W.I., Reading

First Published 1985
Reprinted 1990
© Berkshire Federation of Women's Institutes 1985
All rights reserved. No reproduction
permitted without the prior
consent of the publishers:

Countryside Books
3 Catherine Road,
Newbury, Berkshire.

ISBN 0 905392 42 6

Cover photograph of Bucklebury
by David Short

Produced through MRM Associates Ltd.,
Reading

Printed in England by
J.W. Arrowsmith Ltd., Bristol
Printed on acid-free paper

# Foreword

It is a great privilege to be asked to write a foreword for this edition of The New Berkshire Village Book, the successor to the popular Old Berkshire Village Book of 1979.

As everyone knows, if you want detailed information about a place you button-hole the oldest inhabitant, the village post-mistress or the local publican, to answer your queries.

In this case, the majority of contributions came from a body of people equally knowledgeable – the members of Berkshire Women's Institute. They were complemented by several other equally experienced inhabitants, and all the entries show intimate and lively affection in their particular village as well as fascinating historical and topographical detail.

Berkshire is renowned for its royal connections, its history and its amazing diversity of scenery in such a comparatively small area. Its village houses display a smattering of Cotswold stone and clunch towards the west, brick and flint and some thatched roofing elsewhere, as well as some splendid large houses and churches. The rivers Thames, Kennet and Lambourn enrich its beauty, and their pretty valleys are complemented by downland, woodland and some of the finest agricultural land in the Kingdom.

It is a county which has inspired great loyalty and affection from those who have farmed, raced, shot, hunted or simply walked its ways at leisure. This attractive book, written by many hands, reflects the pride rightly felt in Royal Berkshire, and will surely receive a warm welcome from those who live here and those who visit it.

Miss Read
Shefford Woodlands
March 1985

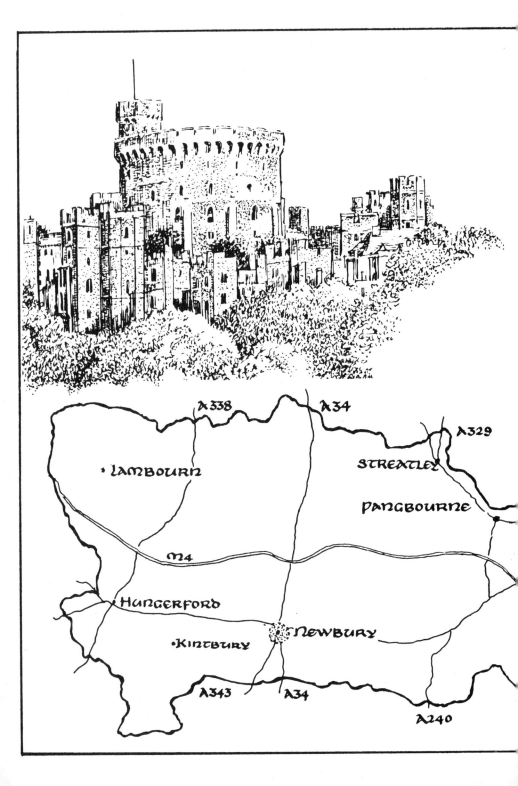

# THE ROYAL COUNTY OF BERKSHIRE

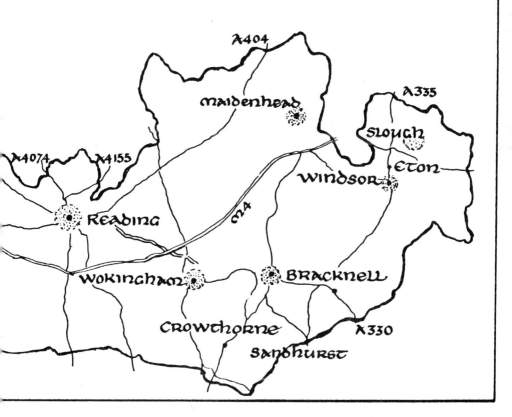

A404

MAIDENHEAD

A335

SLOUGH

A4074          A4155

WINDSOR          ETON

READING

M4

WOKINGHAM          BRACKNELL

CROWTHORNE          A330

SANDHURST

# Acknowledgements

The B.F.W.I. wish to thank all Institutes whose members worked to provide the information about their villages, and the following who also provided material:

| | |
|---|---|
| Donald Crichton Miller | (Compton) |
| Henry Farrer | (Hurst) |
| James W. Wilson | (East Ilsley) |
| Mary Eagles | (West Ilsley) |
| D. K. Wilkinson | (Padworth) |
| Elizabeth Brown | (Peasemore) |
| James Langford | (Sheffords) |
| Daphne Phillips | (Sulham and Tidmarsh, and Pangbourne) |

Judith Fraser (Remenham) for her charming picture map, and all the line drawings except those of

| | |
|---|---|
| Aaron Timbrell | (Chavey Down) |
| Mary Massey | (Sulhamstead) |
| Bernard Tomlins | (Swallowfield) |

# Berkshire

The Royal County of Berkshire has much of interest, both in its history and its beauty. The countryside is varied, from the river valleys of the Thames, Kennet and Lodden to the chalk downs to the west.

With the county boundary changes, Berkshire lost some of its more rural northern area to Oxfordshire, though much of historical interest was gained by the acquisition of villages from Buckinghamshire, while those villages which remained in Berkshire retained their particular character and charm.

It would be impossible, without going into several volumes, to record *every* interesting detail about each village. The descriptions provided by the people who live there contain the facts which they consider the most important, although, sadly, even some of these have had to be omitted for lack of space. Some of the stories are 'traditional' and cannot be absolutely vouched for, though this has been stated where necessary.

Many people have undertaken a lot of diligent research to produce this book, and without their work it would not have been possible. In a few cases where there has been no W.I., a good friend has provided material to ensure that the village is included. It may seem strange that some have been included which lie beyond the borders, but since this volume has been compiled by the Berkshire Federation of Women's Institutes, to which a few W.I.s who are just outside the county are affiliated, it was felt right to invite their contributions. History does not always take account of boundaries!

In an age of rapid change and urban expansion, those who love our heritage realize the value of recording it, and wish to share its secrets with those who may not yet know about it. Fitting easily both on the bookshelf and in the car, this book will be treasured by everyone who has an affection for the Royal County.

Christine Ingram

# Aldermaston

The picturesque village of Aldermaston lies half-way between Reading and Newbury. It is reached by turning south off the A4, when the railway station and wharf are almost immediately seen. After crossing the Kennet and Avon Canal, the road runs for 1½ miles, and the village is approached across the Iron Bridge which spans the river Kennet.

On the right stands the Old Mill Hotel, which was a working flour mill until the late 1920s. The recreation ground lies nearby, in the north-east corner of which is the village lock-up. This is said to have been used last in 1865, when a drunkard was locked up over-night; he is reputed to have been found burned to death the next morning. The Street consists mainly of red brick and timber houses, and several Elizabethan cottages with inglenook fireplaces. The post office-cum-grocery shop lies on the right. Years ago this was a saddler and harness-maker's shop. At the end of The Street stands The Hind's Head Hotel, parts of which date back to 1650. In 1800 this was known as The Congreve Arms, for in those days Aldermaston belonged to the Congreve family. It boasts a clock-tower with a gilt fox as a weather vane. Half-way along The Street is the old blacksmith's which is now the Aldermaston Pottery, exporting its wares all over the world. A little further is the Loosey or village green. A fountain at the north corner of this triangle was erected by Mr. Charles Keyser (Lord of the Manor at that time) to commemorate Queen Victoria's Jubilee. It is recorded that a maypole used to be erected on the green, to the height of 90 feet. A Roman well was discovered here in 1940, when a cow walking across the green almost disappeared.

In Church Road are two almshouses, built in 1706 by the Rev. Robert Dixon 'for the use of four widows of good character'. One house was found to be unsafe in 1906 and rebuilt, and the other in 1924; both were modernised in 1956. Details concerning them can be found in Aldermaston Church. Fifty yards further on is Aldermaston School. Here there is a tablet in the brick wall to John Stair, schoolmaster in 1770, to commemorate the fact that he produced the first William pear. On the west wall of the same building can also be seen the Congreve coat of arms.

Up the hill is the church of St. Mary the Virgin, whose churchyard is entered through a lychgate, erected in 1920 at a total cost of £270 collected from the parishioners in memory of the men who were killed in the Great War. Aldermaston Church has many items of interest: a Norman west door; 12th century stained-glass windows; an early 14th century scratch nail on the south-west buttress of the tower (used in the early days to mark the times of services); a 16th century triptych; medieval wall-paintings in the Lady Chapel; a Jacobean seven-sided pulpit with carved panels and sounding board, and a fine alabaster tomb of Sir George and Lady Foster. There is also a peal of eight bells. A large portion of the church was restored in 1898 by Mr. Charles Keyser, who also commissioned a wall painting by M. Newman.

The history of Aldermaston Court remains mostly unknown. Certainly, a manor house has been there for hundreds of years, the earliest recorded reference being a visit by Edward II in 1321. It is also known that Queen Elizabeth I stayed there in 1558 and 1601. An early manor house on a site near the church was rebuilt in 1636, and this building was destroyed by fire in 1843. Two years later Aldermaston Court was rebuilt as it stands today, and the house includes the 1636 oak panelling and carvings in the entrance hall, staircase and gallery; it also features the chimneys and much of the stained glass from the 1636 house.

One other feature to be seen in Aldermaston is Church Acre, in Fisherman's Lane. This is a tract of land which actually measures 'two acres, one rood and 33 poles'. It was bequeathed many years ago for the support of the church, and it is let by the curious custom of a 'candle auction'. Every three years, on December 13th, a meeting is called, and a horseshoe nail is inserted into a tallow candle, one inch below the wick. The candle is then lit by the Vicar, who makes the first bid, and it is up to him to keep the bidding going. The church wardens and the Lord of the Manor are expected to smoke church warden pipes all this time, and everyone present drinks hot punch. The candle gradually burns down until it reaches the pin, which then falls, and the last to bid is declared the purchaser for three years. This is practically the only remaining example of this ancient custom in England.

# Aldworth

This is a small village on the edge of the Downs at the top of two steep hills, Apple Pie Hill leading up from Compton, and Streatley Hill leading on down to the Thames. Named in Domesday Book as Elleorde, the 'Old Town', a branch of the Ridgeway runs through the parish and there is a section of Grimsdyke (Devil's Ditch) near De la Beche.

The centre of interest in the village is the church, St. Mary's, dating from the 12th century. In the church are the famous 14th century monuments of the De la Beche family, 'the Aldworth giants'. There are nine recumbent stone figures, three lying against the north wall, three against the south wall under floriated arches. The remaining three lie on stone slabs in the body of the church. Represented are three generations of one family who lived at Aldworth during the 13th and 14th centuries – the figures are very much damaged. A Captain Symonds in the time of Charles I visited the church and made notes and drawings which survive. He says: 'In the east end of the south aisle did hang a table fairly written on parchment of all the names of this family of De la Beche; but the Earl of Leicester coming with Queen Elizabeth I in progress, took

ALDWORTH

it down to shew it her and it was never brought again'. The Queen is said to have ridden from Ewelme to inspect these celebrated tombs. On the north wall lie the figures of Sir Robert, Sir John and the giant Sir Philip; those of another Sir John and Isabelle his wife lie, side by side, on a large tomb at the entrance to the chancel. Both are damaged and mutilated.

Two more figures of men lie along the south wall, and under the middle arch between them lies the figure of Joan, wife of Sir Nicholas, the most distinguished of his family. He was high in the favour of Edward III, had the charge of the young Black Prince and was later Constable of the Tower. In 1338 he obtained a licence from the King to crenellate his manor house of De la Beche and make it a castle. He died in 1345 and his figure lies in the middle of the church wearing a helmet and resting his head on a shield.

There is a legend that a tenth stone figure was buried under the outer wall of the church. Symonds says, 'The common people call the statue under the outside of the church John Everafraid, and say further that he gave his soul to the devil if ever he was buried in either church or churchyard – so that he was buried under church wall, under an arch'. In the churchyard stands the remains of the great Yew Tree still surviving despite being heavily damaged in a severe storm in 1978.

The castle of the De la Beche stood about half a mile to the south where the manor house now stands. Encaustic tiles, dating from the 13th century, were found there when the site was excavated, and in 1871 a silver seal was found which bore the name of Isabelle de la Beche.

The poet Lord Tennyson was closely connected with the village. In 1850 he married Emily Sellwood whose home was at Pibworth Manor. The tomb of her parents and grandparents is inside the railings near the church. His affection for the village was shown when he called his house near Midhurst 'Aldworth'. Another poet, Laurence Binyon, is buried in the churchyard. Today there are several people living in the village well known in the literary world.

Hikers are frequently seen treking into the village for refreshment from the Ridgeway, and the cricket club can often be seen in action on the recreation field, but the magnet that draws sightseers from all over the world to Aldworth is the collection of brooding stone giants in the church, unique in Berkshire and probably in all England.

# Arborfield

Arborfield is perhaps one of the most widely known villages of Berkshire, thanks to the thousands of servicemen who have passed through

'The Garrison', although the major part of the camp lies in the neighbouring village of Barkham. The 2,700 acres of Arborfield lie astride the busy A327 Reading to Farnborough road, five miles south east of Reading. In the centre of the village, known as Arborfield Cross from the meeting point of five roads, are two 17th century inns, the Swan, built in 1661, where George III is reputed to have taken refreshment and the Bull, where Queen Victoria changed horses when visiting the Duke of Wellington at Stratfield Saye.

The beginnings of the village known originally as Edburghfeld, however, were a mile away in Lower Arborfield, in a clearing in Windsor Forest by the river Loddon. The village's name is derived from the Saxon, meaning settlement of Eben or Heben. In the Domesday Book the 60 hides of land and woodland for 300 swine belonged to the Bishop of Salisbury, Lord of the Manor of Sonning. He was supplied with eels from the Mill Pool which existed on the site of the old manor, later to become Arborfield Hall. Osmond Bulwe of Edburghfeld was the first Norman Lord of the Manor. The name was changed to Bullock in 1331 and in 1590 Thomas Bullock sold the estate to Edward Standen for £4,000. In 1603 Standen built a beautiful manor house designed by John Thorpe. The Hargreaves and Allesbrook families lived in the Hall until the last war, when it was used by British and American forces. After demolition in 1955/6 a new house was built on the site on land which belonged to the National Institute of Research in Dairying and was named Aberleigh. This was the name given to the old Hall by Mary Mitford in her novel *Our Village*.

There was an old 'wooden chapel', dependent on the church of Sonning, in existence in 1226. It was rebuilt in 1256 of chalk and flint with a wooden tower. The present church of St. Bartholomew's was built on a site nearer the Cross and was completed in 1863. It contains a lovely 13th century octagonal wooden font and altar rails together with five of the peal of six bells from the older church, now in ruins. At that time there was a movement of population and trade from Lower Arborfield to the higher ground at the Cross and a new school was built there in 1871. A separate infant school was built in 1971 and together with the junior school caters also for children from Barkham. Likewise the Rector of Arborfield has since 1977 also been responsible for the spiritual welfare of both parishes.

Whilst still mainly agricultural, the village boasts specialist craftwork, including brick and joinery works and two small engineering works, one of which has contributed parts to both the *Queen Elizabeth II* and *Concorde*. There are two shops, two post offices and two hairdressing salons (one of each being at the Army Camp) and five horse-riding establishments. The ten-acre recreation ground provides two well-used football pitches and a children's play area, whilst the Village Hall provides a meeting place for other leisure activities which include a W.I. (celebrating its 65th year in 1984), a Wives' Group, Gardening Association, a play group and flourishing Over 60's Club. In addition the British Legion have their own hall.

Today there are many new houses and the population has risen to around 2,300, but one can, like Miss Mitford, still admire the beauty of the river Loddon flowing peacefully along, and in the quieter lanes, away from the main road traffic, between hedges garlanded with woodbine and rose-trees', hear the clip-clop of the ponies, hooves and the happy laughter and chatter of Miss Mitford and Emily, homeward bound from 'the old house at Aberleigh ...'

# Ashampstead 🌿

Known in the 13th and 14th centuries as Esshamstede, Ashampstead is situated on hilly ground in well-wooded country, 10 miles from Reading and about 9 miles from Newbury.

There is a record of a church before 1086 and the present church of St. Clement dates from the 12th century. Frescoes in the church are of the 13th century. We have always been told that monks from Lyre Abbey in Normandy built the Church and brought with them people to paint the frescoes. They lived in St. Clements (the private house next to the church) and seem to have tried out their colours on the fresco chevrons remaining on one wall. The frescoes in the church have deteriorated considerably since they were uncovered. The south wall of the nave, having been rebuilt in Tudor times, has no frescoes but from the amount on the north wall and the chancel one may suppose that *all* the walls were originally covered. The bell tower is of the 15th century and the remaining bell bears the inscription 'Henry Knight made me 1662'. The frame for the second bell is still in the tower but the bell was sold in Victorian times in order to pay for new pews to be installed in the church. Scratch dials by the priest's door have been largely worn away by bushes rubbing on the wall.

Parts of Pyt House on the road to Bradfield are of the 16th century. Here, for some years, the late Mrs. Carlisle opened her collection of miniature period furnished rooms to the public in aid of charities. In 1971 the collection was given to the National Trust. Among other older houses are the former shop situated at the cross roads in the village which is now a private residence, The Old Stores, Field House and Hartridge Farm House. Around Ashampstead Green are a few cottages, other houses and a Baptist Chapel built in 1840, now converted into a private residence. A hoard of silver coins dated in the reigns of Elizabeth I, James I and Charles I was discovered when a house was being built by the Green in 1934.

Ashampstead C. of E. school, open for almost 100 years, was closed in 1971. Parishioners used the school building from that time as a Village Hall and a playgroup was established which continues successfully. In 1979 the Parish Council completed negotiations to buy the building from the Oxford Diocese. The vicar of St. Clement's Church Ashampstead, The Rev. Sidney Edmonds officially named the building 'Jubilee Hall' on the occasion of the celebrations in the village in honour of the Queen's Silver Jubilee in June 1977.

In one of two old cottages (now one house) on Noakes Hill lived Mr. Noakes, blacksmith, who probably gave his name to the hill. The smithy was situated where a modern private garage has been built. The Village Inn once stood between Valpys and Lower Church Farm near the top of Noakes Hill but possibly lost custom when the smithy was closed. The New Inn was built opposite the land leading up to Quick's Green and its name has recently been changed to the Fleece and Feathers recalling the old droving days when stock, including geese, was driven to market.

The regular bus service through the village has been discontinued for a number of years but a 'social' bus takes passengers from Ashampstead and neighbouring villages to Reading and home again on Friday afternoons.

*The Leaflet* is published monthly, jointly with our neighbouring village Aldworth, giving local news and it is distributed to parishioners in both villages.

# Ashmore Green

Ashmore Green is a hamlet 1½ miles from Thatcham and 4 miles from Newbury and is part of the village of Cold Ash. It was first noted on a map in 1761 when it was spelt 'Ashmoor Green'. It was at one time owned by the Abbey of Reading. It lies in a fold of the hills between Henwick and Cold Ash. There are fine views towards Thatcham and Newbury. Once largely a farming community, it has attracted young professional people since 1945 who have built houses there, and has grown considerably. The village has two roads – the Ashmore Green Road leading down from Cold Ash, and Stoney Lane which goes to Shaw. These roads meet at right angles at the village green – and they are the roads along which Cromwell's men marched, singing psalms, one Sunday afternoon on their way to the Second Battle of Newbury in the Civil War.

In Stoney Lane, near the centre of the village is the Baptist Chapel which was built in 1866 from money given by villagers – none of whom were well off. The first contribution is reputed to have been given by a little girl. It was a farthing – a princely sum in those days. In the early days the preachers came by horse and buggy which they stabled at the back of the chapel during the service. So successful was the Sunday School that at one time it had 53 scholars. The chapel was closed in 1964 as unsafe. It was bought and repaired by Mr. Reginald Piper, the Ashmore Green builder, who created in it a museum of musical instruments and fair organs. This is still maintained, since his death, by his sons who still run the building and garage business in the village. There have been six generations of Pipers in Ashmore Green.

Ashmore Green join Cold Ash at church and share its organisations and Parish Council but in 1964 it formed its own Women's Insitute.

# Barkham

'An Ideal Hamlet' wrote the antiquarian Rector of Barkham, the Rev. P.H. Ditchfield of his village at the beginning of this century.

The history of Barkham, situated three miles from Wokingham at the edge of Windsor Great Forest, dates back to 951 AD when a Saxon thane gave Bloreham to the monks of Abingdon Abbey. In Saxon times it passed away from the rule of the Abbey and in the time of King Edward the Confessor was in possession of a Saxon thane named Aelmer. After the Conquest it was taken into the possession of William the Conqueror and is mentioned in the Domesday Book.

The Manor House, built in the 18th century on the site of the 16th century house, still deserves Ditchfield's romantic description – 'Nestling amid trees stands the old manor house upon the site of a much older edifice; and the picturesque mansion carries our thoughts back to Saxon, Norman and medieval times, when the lords of the manor held their manorial courts'. The gardens still contain the old Stew-Ponds, once stocked with fish for Fridays and Lent fare; now, since the beginning of this century turned into an ornamental feature.

More interesting than the manor itself are the people who lived there. The Bullocks held possession during the 14th century, and legend has it that the old inns of Arborfield and Barkham were named after the family, both being known as the Bull. The most famous family were the Balls, reputed ancestors of George Washington whose mother Mary Ball lived in Wokingham and whose direct ancestor Edward Ball lived in Barkham Manor. The present owners, Mr. J. and the Hon Mrs. J.

Clifford Wolff who bought the Manor in 1968, have maintained and improved all the beauty, with special attention to the magnificent tree, a *Plane Orientalis,* thought to be 400 to 500 years old, which stands in front of the house.

The present church was built in 1862 on the site of and from the materials from the old church. In the churchyard is a Cedar of Lebanon brought from the Holy Land and planted in the year 1788 by a member of the Leveson Gower family then living in the Manor House. The rector at that time was David Davies who being greatly concerned with the standard of life of his parishioners wrote *The case of Labourers in Husbandry* published in 1795 which gives details of the life and earnings of the villagers. There is a much battered wooden effigy of a lady in the porch believed to be that of Mistress Agnes Neville, daughter of a lord of the manor in the 14th century. There is an Elizabethan chalice bearing the date 1561, a paten 1664 and a noble flagon 1729.

The old Bull Inn has recently been modernised and the Smiths forge which has been in continual use from 1728 has now been turned into the Forge Restaurant which still contains many relics of the old Forge.

A new Village Hall has been built near the church, replacing the old Hall on Barkham Street which was too small to cater for the interests of the increased population in the Village.

# Basildon 🌿

Basildon is beautifully situated in wooded rolling country above the Thames Valley, and through the centuries has been variously known as Beorhtel's Hill, Bestleford, Bastedene and Baseldon. An entry in Domesday Book (1086) says, 'The King holds Bastedene in demesne. Aileva, a free woman, held it at the time of King Edward ... in King Edward's time as now it was worth 25 pounds ...'

It is now in the commuter belt and its worth has improved accordingly.

This village is full of interest for the visitor: at the beginning of this century the eminent architect Sir Edwin Lutyens, designer of New Delhi, made good use of the local brickworks when building some village cottages at the request of Major Morrison, who then lived at Basildon Park.

On the site of the old brickworks now stands the Tenaplas factory, one of the most modern plants in Europe for making extruded plastics, whose cables are laid under seas and across deserts, notably the Capetown/Lisbon/London telephone, repeater tube, sections of which lie in places three miles down on the sea bed.

Mr. Gilbert Beale, who died in 1967 at the age of 99, created a riverside park with a pavilion, a peacock farm, sculptures, fountains and water garden, and left it for public pleasure under the Child-Beale Trust, now associated with the National Wildlife Trust.

Lord Iliffe lives at Basildon Park, a fine 18th century mansion built for Sir Francis Sykes, who made his fortune in India. The house fell into decay during the Second World War but was purchased and restored by Lord and Lady Iliffe, who presented it to the National trust in 1978. It is now open to the public during the summer months.

The Parish Church of St. Bartholomew contains a 15th century monumental brass to John Clerk and his wife, and in the churchyard is a memorial to the famous agriculturalist Jethro Tull, author of *Horsehoeing and Husbandry*, published in 1733. The tenor bell, cast in 1621 by Henry Knight, bears the inscription:

> In True Desire For to Do Well
> The Ladi Litcot Gave this Bell

The charitable Dame Katherine Lidcott also left in her will (1623) a grant of land in perpetuation of a charity for the poor, which is still administered.

The new and handsome modern church of St. Stephen, built in 1964 with the help of an interest-free loan from Lord Iliffe, is in Upper Basildon. Its ground plan is in the form of that Christian symbol, a fish, and its modern design is of great interest to visitors.

Basildon has its ghosts ... Lady Fane, who lived in that splendid house called The Grotto, was found drowned in the well within the house, and her unquiet spirit is alleged to haunt the building. There are two other Basildon ghosts ... Nobes-on-his-white-horse, who lived at Tomb Farm, and Nan Carey, who was believed to be a witch.

Who has not heard of Basildon Bond? This popular writing paper is named after this Berkshire village. In 1911 the head of the firm of Dickinson was staying at the Park as a guest of Major Morrison, at whose suggestion the new paper was christened Basildon Bond and sent out to success all over the world.

The village today consists of about five hundred houses, some old and many relatively new. It is beautiful and well-cared-for, sophisticated rather than rural, charming to look at and a pleasant place to live in or to visit.

# Beech Hill

The village of Beech Hill, thought to have formerly been Beche Hill after the de la Beche family, has little easily discovered history, because a fire destroyed most of the archives prior to 1860.

Between 1142 and 1184 Jocelyn, Bishop of Salisbury, confirmed the grant by William de Stuteville, Lord of the Manor of Stratfieldsaye, of the Hermitage of St. Leonard of the Loddon. The hermitage became the property of the Benedictine Abbey of St. Mary of Vallemont prior to 1260.

A copse surrounded by a moat is the only evidence left of the Castle of Beaumys, lying to the east of the priory of St. Leonard, castle and priory belonging, by 1272, to Hugh de Spencer, who was deprived of them later by Edward I.

In 1444 Henry VI gave the Hermitage of Stratfieldsaye and Stratfield Mortimer to Eton College.

Beech Hill House was built in the 17th century by the Harrison family, who owned it for many years. In 1739 it was purchased by a London merchant, Henry Hunter, whose decendants lived there until 1950. After that it was for some years a home for refugees run by the Ockenden Venture.

The Jubilee reservoir was built in 1897 to commemorate Queen Victoria's Diamond Jubilee. The original pump had broken down and the well was full of muddy surface water. Donated by Mr. J. J. Ratcliffe, the reservoir held 16,000 gallons of water, thus giving the village a magnificent supply. All was not well, however! In 1905 the tap would not work, and nobody seemed to know whose responsibility it was to repair it – eventually a 1d. rate was charged for its maintenance. In 1907 it started to leak copiously – a £25 County Council loan and local subscriptions remedied it. There was back-biting too, as a motion was passed that people outside the parish couldn't draw water unless they paid maintentance; this was a pointed dig at the Queen's Head public house, which although attached to the village, is actually in the next parish. A later meeting allowed the publican to use the water.

In 1937 a severe drought dried up the reservoir, and water from an imported tank was sold off at 1d. per pail. The mains reached Beech Hill just in time for the outbreak of war, but the ornamental railings that had adorned the reservoir were turned in as 'war effort'.

Sadly, the village school is now closed, but the village green, which had deteriorated into a head-high jungle, has been cleared, flattened and re-planted, and the duck pond has been cleared and cleaned. The population is around 400.

# Beenham Valence 🪶

The village of Beenham is situated on the crest of a hill about 350 ft above the Kennet valley and is mentioned in the Domesday Book.

'Ham' is Old English for place, or home; 'Been' could have come from 'Benna', an important person from whom is derived Beenham. Another explanation is 'the ridge where beans grow' – Valence meaning 'ledge'.

The older part of the present village dates from the 17th century, and is found around the Six Bells, an inn taking its name from the bells of the Parish Church, although there are several much older dwelling places, notably White Cottage, whose barn is of 'cruck' construction dated 1500 or earlier, and other farms and cottages built in the 16th century.

There has been a church on the site of the present Parish Church of St. Mary since medieval times. this was destroyed by fire in 1794. An estimate for new bells, frame etc. was £393.7.2d. but to their credit the parishioners collected 21cwt. of melted bell metal in the churchyard and so reduced the bill to £154.4.0d.

The church built to replace it was also destroyed by fire, except for the brick tower which survived and is now the west tower of the modern church built in 1859.

Inside there is a memorial to Sir Charles Hopson, who was responsible for much of the woodwork in St. Paul's Cathedral. He was knighted by Queen Anne and lived in Beenham House. There are other memorials to families who have lived in the Manor House, such as the Carters and the Warings. The inside walls have been painted with a New Testament theme by an amateur artist, Miss Sharp, in 1900. Outside the south porch stand some interesting carved tombstones. St. Mary's stands in a peaceful setting of sloping fields, with views across small copses to the valley below.

The first school was built in 1840, a church school 'for the education of children in the principles of Christian Religion'. It consisted of one big classroom divided into two by a curtain, two small cloakrooms and two small playgrounds, one each for boys and girls. Each child paid a few pence a week and donations were made too, but by 1892 the Church could no longer afford the upkeep so it was handed over to the Board of Education and renamed Beenham Council School. It was eighteen years, however, before improvements were made to the facilities. The children still sat on long benches without backs, and learned to read by using the same book in turn.

On March 9th 1948 the school burned down during the night. The children were taught in the Victory Hall while a 'temporary' school was built – this is still in use today together with a terrapin, but a new school on another site is due to be built soon.

Beenham Post Office and General Store is now the sole shop. It was built in 1863 and previously had a bakery, and still has the oven in a room used as a storeroom, but the old shaft has been removed. There had been another shop selling, variously, sweets, vegetables and general grocery, but this was discontinued about 1952 and is now a private house.

Opposite the post office was the site of the village forge and a previous inn, The Black House, with its legend of a barmaid murdered by one of Cromwell's soldiers. The forge is no more, but the two cottages connected with it remain.

St. Mary's Farm is a lovely 18th century house which used to be the parsonage house for the church. One of its vicars was Thomas Stackhouse, author of *The History of the Bible,* written in 1792 when he was a famous theologian; today he is perhaps better remembered for his heavy drinking, patronising the Three Kings Jacks Booth, a coaching inn on the Bath Road, a convenient horse-ride away!

The Manor of Beenham existed in the 16th century and was held by one Henry Parkyns, who probably built a house on the site of the present one, quite likely a timbered and gabled mansion, no trace of which now exists. The present fine, large house, originally red brick, now painted white, was built by Sir Charles Rich, and is an impressive landmark seen from the Bath Road.

Henry Waring, the Victorian owner, improved the house, built racing stables and enlarged the gardens. In the 1920s the house became the home of the Waddell family. The last member to live there, Miss Majorie Waddell, died recently.

The Stocks Inn is a rectangular house of grey and red brick built about 1729, and is one of four small country houses of similar design, the others being the vicarage and two on Beenham Hill, The Malthouse and Hillfoot House.

The inn sign is rare, suggesting that the inn was built on the site of ancient stocks, but this is not so. It was called after its first landlord, one Donald Stocks, yeoman. It was an ale house only until 1950, when it obtained a wine and spirit licence.

There is strong evidence to suggest that it had been the local bakehouse. In the grounds was a 17th century barn, and stocks erected in deference to the inn's name, but which are not the origin of it.

Men working for Major Waring of Beenham House could claim a mild or bitter at the bar if they attended church on Sunday mornings! A famous 'regular' was one Old Charlie, an intelligent poacher who had his own special place in the bar. He had trained his dog to hide in his bicycle basket and to bark only at the approach of a policeman!

Beenham today is a village of over a thousand people, happily including many young families, and the school is thriving. It even includes a vineyard within its boundaries.

# Binfield

Binfield 80 years ago was just a quiet village with a parish nurse who lived in the village, was on call day and night and went everywhere on her bicycle. There was a village policeman, a butcher/milkman and a baker who called daily.

Now the busy A329 which provides access to the M4 runs through the southern part of the village. A more leisurely route from Windsor to Reading is the B3034 which runs through the centre of the village, but there will be few who know that they are using the old Turnpike road created in the 18th century so that wheeled traffic could journey more comfortably along the forest tracks. The formation of the Turnpike Trust to build the 'Forest Road' is commemorated by an oval stone set up by the road side at Bill Hill. Windsor Forest covered all this area and was well stocked with fallow deer for the King's hunting. The severe game laws pressed heavily on poacher and peasant alike to maintain the royal prerogative.

Binfield derives its name from the coarse grass in this clearing or 'feld' in the forest. At one time the forest was divided into 16 Walkes. The Binfelde Walke was mentioned in the 16th century under Sir Henry Neville, the keeper, who lived at Billingbear.

The centre of Binfield is only 2½ miles from the rapidly growing town of Bracknell, but the village remains rural, surrounded by carefully farmed lands. Woods with anemones, bluebells and primroses are easy to find. The village runs along a ridge that is 260 ft. above sea level. To the north is the old parish church of All Saints and to the south Amen Corner. The Corner is said to have taken its name from the congregation of a Dissenting Chapel, built in 1875, who used to say to each other as they separated after a service 'God be with you, Amen'. There are glimpses of the Chiltern Hills to the north-west. Until recently a flourishing brick and tile works at Amen Corner employed 60 craftsmen making fine, wire-cut bricks. Beehive Lane is clearly named from the old brick kilns.

Conveniently near to the Standard in the middle of Binfield is the old Working Men's Club, active since 1906. The Memorial Hall next to the Club was erected by public subscription and opened in 1920. During the 1970s it was extended and modernised.

No large-scale industry is to be found in Binfield, as it has become largely residential. Binfield Park, a fine Georgian mansion built in 1729, is now a hospital for handicapped adults, but is threatened with closure. Newbold College, a growing concern, is a training college for Seventh Day Adventists. Binfield Lodge, one of James I's hunting lodges, claims that Elizabeth I slept there and boasts that Cecil Rhodes was one of the visitors. Elm Grove in Monk's Alley has a raised bowling green, which may have been the site of ancient earthworks. White Hill, the erstwhile home of Alexander Pope, is now called Pope's Manor. It has recently been sold and, after extensive alterations and renovations, used as offices. The beautiful grounds and lake have been given to the public for leisure purposes.

Binfield Place is said to be the oldest house in the village with a history that goes back to Henry VII. It has 16th century moulded beams and a chimney marked 1702. Tradition has it that bad luck will befall the owner if a 17th century bas-relief of a lady's head is moved.

Of the many inns, the most interesting is the Stag and Hounds on the Forest Road. It was converted into an inn in 1727. William Cobbett described an excellent breakfast he had there on his way to Reading. This inn is said to mark the centre of Old Windsor Forest.

The parish church of All Saints has been much restored, but the main part dates from the 15th century. There is, however, a record of a priest of Binfield as early as 1174. The unusual open wooden porch with different carvings on both sides is 14th century and there is some fine 15th century glass. A unique hour-glass stand of hammered ironwork beside the pulpit dated 1628 is worth attention, as is the half-length brass memorial to Walter de Annefordhe, the oldest in Berkshire, to be found in the chancel under the red carpet.

The mansion behind the church used to be the Rectory which was enlarged in the last century – probably to enable the rector, the Rev. Gabell, a retired headmaster from Winchester College, to take in pupils. A new Rectory has now been built in the centre of the village.

The churchyard of All Saints has become a wild flower sanctuary. At least 23 different species grow here and all can enjoy the snowdrops and primroses that carpet the ground, and the smell of the sweet-scented roses. Birds, too, nest and sing undisturbed. Saint Mark's Church, at the other end of the village is a Chapel of Ease built in 1867. It has been rebuilt after a fire destroyed it in 1958.

The addition of several small estates and a modern shopping precinct with a large parking area have ensured the continuing life of the village.

# Bisham

Bisham village is of Saxon origin and in the old days was known as 'Bustleham'. It was originally the home of the Knights Templars and is mentioned in the Domesday Book.

Situated as it is on the Berkshire side of the Thames, one mile upstream from Marlow towards Temple, it has a beautiful location, some 4 miles from Maidenhead, and with the backcloth of the famous Quarry Woods.

The main road to Marlow runs through the village between picturesque brick and timber cottages, some as early as Tudor in origin, and these together with the local inn, now enlarged and modernized, make up a delightful model village setting, unfortunately somewhat spoilt now by the speeding cars which rush through the village instead of using the by-pass. This was built in the early 1970s and literally cut the village and the farms in two. However, it has done some good by protecting it from the ever-increasing heavy traffic.

The main part of Bisham's history lies in the famous Bisham Abbey

BISHAM. THE CHURCH OF ALL SAINTS

and Estate, which at one time extended to 5,000 acres, and which is now one of the leading sports centres in the country. Bisham Abbey was the Manor House in the past and has the reputation of being the most haunted house in England. It also has many connections with royalty. Queen Elizabeth I stayed there and Queen Victoria was reputed to have called whilst out driving in her carriage. She found no one at home to greet her and was so indignant she ordered her coachman to drive back to Windsor Castle immediately!

The Abbey has been the family home of two great families since the 16th century, the Hobys and then the Vansittart-Neales. As in so many sad instances, the male side of the family was completely wiped out by the deaths in military action of the two heirs to Sir Henry Vansittart-Neale's Estate in 1942 and 1944, namely Berkley Paget and Guy Paget, his grandsons. In 1947 their aunt, Miss Phyllis Vansittart-Neale, in answer to a letter to the *Times* by the late Lord Astor, on behalf of the Central Council for Physical Recreation, offered Bisham Abbey to be used by the young as a memorial to her nephews, and on her death her sister, Mrs. Elizabeth Paget, sold the Abbey to the Sports Council in conjunction with the C.C.P.R., thus perpetuating the use of the building and grounds for the youth of England.

It is fortunate that this acquisition by the Sports Council has enabled the Abbey to be maintained and kept up to the highest standard, thus preserving part of the heritage of Britain, a task so costly these days, and which for private families is now an almost impossible burden. New buildings have been erected of the highest calibre and the new blends with the old reasonably well. It is well worth a visit to see how this fine old building is being used to such advantage. This can usually be arranged by appointment.

The 12th century Church of All Saints at Bisham could not have had a more tranquil setting, standing as it does on the banks of this superb reach of the Thames. It has been maintained and kept in wonderful condition by the loyalty and dedication of successive vicars, churchwardens, parishioners and benefactors. Within are interesting memorials to various local residents of the past, including the Hoby Chapel, commemorating that family who resided for so long at Bisham Abbey from the 16th to 18th century; and of course the Vansittart-Neales. Then there is the Williams Chapel, now restored and in use, to the memory of General Owen Williams, former resident of Temple House, now demolished, and aide-de-camp and friend of King Edward VII, who used to visit him there.

Bisham is a well scattered community, stretching up to Quarry Woods and Cookham Dean and to the south as far as the Henley Road and Burchetts Green; also to Temple Island upstream, where there is now a modern development of houses and marina on the island, which was formally a paper mill.

Over the by-pass beyond the cottages known as 'Under the Wood' is the famous Ice House, a cavern where ice used to be stored for the preservation of food at the Abbey. This has recently been restored and is an historic part of Bisham's past. Running through Temple Park Farm is a stream which continues its way past Town Farm out into the Thames by Quarry Woods below Marlow Lock. In close proximity to this stream is a spring which is known as Queen Elizabeth's Well, and the tale goes that during her three year stay at the Abbey with the Hobys, the Queen used this water for her bath for it was reputed to have healing properties.

A further interesting feature of the village is the War Memorial in memory of the dead of both world wars. This was designed by the famous sculptor, Eric Gill and was erected at the southern end of the village at the junction with Temple Lane.

Despite many changes, Bisham has preserved its character through the centuries and is still one of England's most picturesque villages, retaining its excellent school and shop, but sadly having lost its post office.

# Boxford 🦋

Boxford is situated in the Lambourn valley in an area of outstanding natural beauty. It is as old as it is beautiful. Evidence of the stone age has been found: eight flint scrapers, a flint saw and hoe have been unearthed at Westbrook and Ownham farms. Iron Age man left traces of his presence in the shape of earthworks at Wyfield Farm, and an Iron Age settlement on Boxford Common.

The site of a Roman Villa was excavated off the Boxford and Winterbourne road, and pottery and coins were found. Potsherds of Romano-British origin and Roman roof tiles were found at Huntsgreen Farm, and a bronze bracelet and a spindle-whorl of clay at Wyfield. A pot, narrow-necked and 12 inches high, holding 800 coins was found, stamped with the heads of five emperors, all of whom reigned in Rome in the 4th century. This is now in Newbury Museum. A Roman glove was dug up locally, and Miss Highfield of Westbrook owns a Roman brooch found in Boxford.

Mr. Harold Peake, the archaeologist who lived at Westbrook House, believed the Boxford of the 14th century was situated opposite the present church. This building, now St. Andrews, dates from 1225. The tower was added in the 16th century, and has since been rebuilt twice, the last time in 1802. There are traces of a wall fresco above the chancel arch, probably of a coat of arms. Fine craftsmanship in oak in the shape of an organ screen, bishop's chair and magazine table can be seen. These were made and gifted by the Rev. Legh Beauchamp McCarthy, Rector of Boxford from 1965 – 74.

A Wesleyan Chapel, built in 1809, was one of three in the country with a thatched roof. Sadly, owing to lack of congregation, it is no longer a place of worship, is privately owned, and its thatch has been replaced with slate tiles.

The village school, which stood for about a hundred years, and educated the children of the village, suffered the sad fate of closure in 1971, and now on the site are two executive-type houses, overshadowing the thatched cottages nearby.

The Rectory at Boxford no longer houses the rector. He lives at Wickham Rectory and has the care of four parishes, including Boxford.

In spite of changes such as these, much of the old character of the village remains. Many homes in Boxford have withstood rain and sun for 300 or 400 years. A number are thatched cottages, which once housed workers on the land and in the mill, blacksmiths, carpenters and thatchers, are now privately owned, having been restored and modernised. Some are 'week-end' cottages and, with easy access to the M4 motorway, quite a few residents commute. Julian Pettifer, well known in the world of television, lives in River Cottage, once a bakehouse; and the wife of the late Bernard Schlesinger, father of John, the film director, lives at Oliver Cottage. This was once a saddlery, and where Oliver Sansom, the famous and persecuted Quaker of the 17th century, dwelt. However, descendants of the old inhabitants of Boxford remain in the area, and names like Baylis, Chandler, Dean, Huntley, Johnson, Mundy, Pocock and Snook are still familiar.

The Bell Inn, which dates back to 1300, by law had to feed guests and afford accommodation. Recently, the new purpose-built post office and village stores has closed and, by coincidence, is now re-sited at the Old Post Office, where Olive Creese, postmistress for many years, lived. A Victorian post box remains in the wall of the old parsonage opposite the church, and an oak gate into the churchyard has recently been dedicated to the memory of Olive Creese.

Boxford has been known over the years for its great interest in music and drama. In 1905 Mrs. Charlotte Peake, wife of Harold Peake, began writing and producing the Boxford masques, with music composed by her cousins Geoffrey and Francis Toye. These were performed every year on the last Wednesday in July, in what became known as the Woodland Theatre, with the audience sitting in successive tiers cut out of a bank, with a wonderful view of the Lambourn Valley below. This theatre is now on land owned by the Pocock family. Mrs. Rosina Pocock, at 96, has been a W.I. member for over half a century, and is the oldest inhabitant of Boxford.

Mr. and Mrs. Peake also started the Glee Club which was in being for 60 years, and won many certificates and banners in the Newbury and Winchester Music Festivals. The Boxford Mummers regularly performed their play which originated from Hoe Benham, and is 800 years old. It was produced by the W.I. as recently as 1966.

Alas, times have changed with regard to entertaining ourselves within the village, although the 18th century barn in the centre of the village is occasionally used for a barn dance or barbecue. Another such barn, where Berkshire waggons were built, has recently been converted to a private dwelling, as has that at Westbrook House.

During the summer of 1984, the village sadly lost a number of true Boxfordians, among them Nancy Stancliffe, the founder-President of Boxford W.I., and a dedicated worker at national level for many years. A Denman College bursary to her memory is being administered.

People of Boxford are rightly proud of their village, and will endeavour to preserve its character and beauty for ever.

# Bradfield 🦢

The original village of the Broad Field, with church, mill and manorial Bradfield Place (remnants now incorporated in the College), stands around the Pang chalk stream, noted for its Blue Pool a mile or so up stream, where springs keep the sandy bottom fuming with miniature volcanoes, while a trick of light in the transparent depths produces an intense blue. These springs have never failed, even when droughts have dried out the upper reaches of the Pang.

The 7th century royal charters quoted by Abingdon Abbey's *Chronicle* suggest that there may have been some temporary grant of land here to that Abbey at the time of its foundation. But apart from a delightful legend of Bradfield monks sallying forth to oppose a detachment of William the Conqueror's army approaching from Theale, and the survivors being suffered to retire to the mother house at Abingdon, there is no word of any monastic site. The so-called Monastery Wall, with Tom o' Bedlam's Hole, are relics of a much later Bradfield Place.

For three centuries the history of the nation left little mark here until, in October, 1644, a letter to the Parliament announced that "My Lord General quartered all night at Bradfield ... Great bodies of the enemyes Horse are in view, but whether to face or engage we know not".

Elias Ashmole, whose collection formed the nucleus of the Ashmolean Museum at Oxford, came to Bradfield at this time, bent on marrying the rich widowed lady of the manor, despite the attempt of one of her sons to murder him. The unhappy couple (she was twenty years his senior) soon moved up to London, leaving Bradfield Place to decay. All was sold to a London merchant, who built himself a brand new mansion which has totally disappeared, leaving its name to Great House Wood and its site carpeted with snowdrops.

Bradfield Hall was then built in 1763/4 for the Hon. John Barrington, natural son of George II. His successor presented the parish with the block of four two-storey almshouses that bears his inscription of 1811.

But the vital history of Bradfield began when the manor came into the possession of Henry Stevens, whose great-grandson, Thomas, was to change its face completely. This remarkable man dominated the local scene for nearly half a century after becoming "squarson" in 1842. He virtually rebuilt the 14th century church, one of Gilbert Scott's first commissions, of which he always felt specially proud. With the idea of founding a choir school for this enlarged church, Thomas Stevens opened a school in what remained of Bradfield Place. The school grew rapidly, as new buildings were added year by year. Amongst other activities the founder was a pioneer of steam-ploughing and milking machines; he also started a mineral water factory at St. Andrew's Well. An authority on the Poor Law and contributor to its reform he was instrumental in establishing the local Workhouse, which now functions as a hosptial for mentally handicapped women and children. Unfortunately his energies and enthusiasms were not controlled by financial judgement, so that his many activities led to his being declared bankrupt. Since he was by far the largest landowner and employer in the parish, a great deal of hardship ensued. His College, however, had been taken over by a Governing Body, and has gone on growing in size and reputation, famous for its Greek theatre.

Meanwhile the parish has also increased and prospered, developing right away from the old village (which has become largely College property, including its one haunted house) on to the higher ground at South End. Although the total area of alluvial valley and plateau gravel supports some sixteen farms, its agricultural labour force has thinned away. The great majority of the present inhabitants are employed outside the parish, except for a recent development of joinery works.

In the 1970s vineyards were established at Frogmore farm, and are now producing table wines.

South End has a church of its own, and the primary school, whose 1866 premises in the village were long ago relinquished to the College, is also at South End, as are the village hall, playing fields and social club. There too stands a most impressive war memorial. Its exceptionally fine setting was designed by George Blackall Simonds, the name of whose only son is among those inscribed on it.

In the old village the outstanding addition has been a restoration and expansion of the riverside group of Old People's Homes, which is an absolute masterpiece.

Most recent innovation of all, the M4, has sliced the parish in two with its lordly swathe commanding the finest scenery for miles around, but taking trouble to treat rights of way with proper respect. A few footpaths have been lost, out of the large number possessed by this parish and jealously tended by its Parish Council.

# Bray 🐚

Bray is situated at a bend of the Thames, a mile from Maidenhead and within easy access of the M4 motorway and the A4. The name 'Bray' was generally taken to mean 'a marsh', and it is certainly not a 'dry' village.

There are five inns all in close proximity to the centre of the village. The Hind's Head came into being in the 16th century, and has grown from a small ale-house to a hostelry which has been patronised by royalty and famous people over the years. The Queen has brought her party here in traditional horse-drawn carriages several times for lunch during Ascot week. Burned into the wood of the fireplace there is the following inscription: 'Fear Knocked at the Door. Faith Answered. No One was there'.

Just off the banks of Thames lies Monks Eyot, originally the property of the Abbey of Burnham. This was acquired by Charles Spencer, third duke of Marlborough, who built a fishing lodge there in 1739. This has been extended and modernised over the years, and is now the Monkey Island Hotel. A French artist, commissioned by the Duke, used frescoes of monkeys on the domed ceiling of the entrance hall of the lodge, and this room, known as the Monkey room, has been preserved to the present day.

The Waterside Restaurant (which was originally called the George Inn) is situated on the banks of the river on the opposite side of the Ferry Road. It has had a chequered history, and in the early part of this century it was notorious for its riotous parties, when the licence was withdrawn. Since then, it has changed hands several times, but the licence has been retained, and today it survives as the Waterside Restaurant which possesses an Egon Ronay award and a 2-star rating in the Michelin guide – a far cry from the early days of disrepute.

The Parish Church of St. Michael is the dominating feature of the village, and dates from Edward I, but only the Perpendicular tower remains to remind us of its long history. It was built in 1293 on the site of the original Norman church, and has many beautiful and elaborate examples of 14th, 15th and 16th century brasses. Simon Alwyn, who changed his religion rather than give up his parish, was famous as the celebrated *Vicar of Bray*. His tombstone lies in the middle of the nave. The Lych gate was built in 1448, and was once a 'Priest's home'. It spans the churchyard's original entrance, where for centuries mourners halted with their coffins to await the minister.

In the High Street stands Jesus Hospital, a Grade A listed building. These ancient almshouses were built in 1627 by the Worshipful Company of Fishmongers pursuant to the will of William Goddard, a statue of whom stands over the entrance to the hospital gardens, which inspired the artist Frederick Walker to paint a picture which now hangs in the Tate Gallery. It is aptly named *The Harbour of Refuge*. There is also a beautiful little chapel where services are conducted regularly by the resident chaplain. Thirty minutes before each service the 'Bonnet' bell is rung; a legacy from the days when the old people needed time to dress for chapel. The name 'Hospital' is very confusing, but in bygone days it meant almshouses, schools, etc. The houses and grounds comprise a total of 6 acres, with lawns inside the quadrangle of these delightful little houses, the exteriors of which have been preserved to retain their original appearance. The interiors, however, have been modernised, and there are plans for further alterations. Talk to any of the old inhabitants of Bray, and you will always be told about the Great Flood of 1894 when the whole village was awash, and a fish was caught in the high street. The dangers of such flooding happening again has been alleviated by the re-routing and enlargement of the Cut (originally called Public Drain No: 1), and has become the Maidenhead Relief Channel.

The following year, in 1895, there was the Great Freeze when the river was frozen solid. Parties were held, and stalls selling roast chestnuts, sausages and oranges were set up on the ice.

Bray Lock is noted for having received the prize for the best kept lock for many years. One Hetty Slack, an eighteen year old girl was drowned in Bray Lock, and is buried in St. Michael's Church, where her ghost is still supposed to walk.

Bray Marina is a comparatively recent amenity, with easy access from the Windsor Road. There is space for around 700 boats, and a good parking area for cars.

Bray Village has been judged the best kept village of its size in Berkshire in 1982, and again in 1984.

# Braywood 🦋

When people are invited to visit organisations in Braywood, unless they are given careful directions by their hosts, they often have difficulty in finding their destination because, according to most maps, Braywood does not exist.

Yet it has a very long history. As might be expected from its name, the first mention of it as Bray Wood (the last remnants of which were cut down in 1917 and auctioned) occurs in the Domesday Book and for centuries it, and the villages or hamlets of Oakley Green, Fifield and Water Oakley, were part of the Manor of Bray and then in more recent times the Parish of Bray. It is difficult to separate these hamlets as for about 50 years almost all the land in them belonged to one family and for nearly a century this area constituted the Ecclesiastic Parish of Braywood.

This happened because Sylvain Van De Weyer, the first Belgian Ambassador to England and a great friend of Queen Victoria, built New Lodge on the Drift Road, high above the villages and bought most of the land from New Lodge right down to the river and covering most of Fifield, Oakley Green and Water Oakley. He built cottages for his workers in various places on the New Lodge Estate and each cottage had the Van De Weyer crest built into its wall. The crest is still to be seen on many houses in the area – it is not unlike the Volkswagen emblem. One of the houses, now called Braywood Linn, used to be Braywood Inn so it seems likely he provided for the employees' leisure time as well.

As part of the New Lodge Estate, Braywood Church was built on the hill known locally as Sparboro, and Queen Victoria agreed in 1871 to create the new Parish of Braywood. This was virtually an Estate church and all the employees and their families were expected to walk up the mile drive from the Lodge Gates on Oakley Green Road to the church. This was also the route taken by the Van De Weyer family to New Lodge, and the children of employees were expected to line the drive and curtsey or bow as their coach went past.

The New Lodge Estate was broken up and sold in 1911 and the report of the sale made the front page of the *Maidenhead Advertiser*. After this New Lodge became a clinic and wounded soldiers were taken there during the First World War. Amongst other owners have been Dr. Barnardo's and British Rail and it is now owned by a firm called Barbour Index.

In the late 1950s the Rev. Daniels, the Vicar of Braywood, died and Braywood church was deconsecrated. A new wooden church was built next to Braywood School and the Parish was reabsorbed by Bray. The attendance at the new church was poor and now it is used as the school annexe. After the old Braywood church was deconsecrated it was used in 1960 by Hammer Films for the christening scene in *The Curse of the Werewolf* and the six-week-old granddaughter of one of the villagers was used as the baby.

Braywood School, a Church of England school, was opened in 1857, and is typical in design of the schools of that period. Originally all the local children were taught there from 5-14 years old, but now children leave at 9 years old and go to school in Windsor. Before the M4 was opened, the children at Braywood School had the four days of Royal Ascot off, rather than the whole of Whitsun week, because of the volume of traffic going to Ascot. Now there is no need, as few racegoers use the village roads.

The School House, which for many years was the home of the Head of Braywood School, is now a private house. Along the Oakley Green road visitors will find Braywood Cottage, Braywood Lodge, Braywood Cottages – these are all, according to the road signs, in Oakley Green, Windsor (but many have Maidenhead telephone numbers) – but where is Braywood Memorial Hall, the home of Braywood W.I? Well, that's in Fifield, Maidenhead, on the corner of Fifield Road and Forest Green Road. And Braywood House? Well, that's what used to be Braywood Vicarage and, according to the telephone directory, is in Windsor Forest, Windsor. It is reached by a long drive off the Drift Road, opposite New Lodge itself, which is now in Winkfield. So, if you're ever asked to visit anywhere in Braywood, make sure you get clear directions.

# Brightwalton 🐑

Nine miles from Newbury and six from Wantage, on the edge of the Berkshire Downs, lies Brightwalton. At first sight, it seems a village untouched by time: indeed, for very many years, the population has remained at just under 300. But the doctor, three shops and the post office have all gone. The nearest post office and the nearest inn, The Ibex, are both in neighbouring Chaddleworth. There is, however, still a thriving primary school, with children coming from a wide area around.

The village was once owned by the Wroughton family of Woolley Park, but most of the property was sold to pay death duties. There are many picturesque houses and cottages, with well-tended gardens, especially those clustering round the church, and Brightwalton has twice been the winner in its section of the Best Kept Village competition.

It was once essentially a farming community, but with the changes in farming methods has come a change in the working population, and many residents now commute to Newbury, Wantage or even further. The village community spirit remains, however, and this is vouched for by the Misses Bracey, who live at Brightwalton Green, in a cottage close to Green Farm where they were brought up. Some years ago, when a new village hall was needed, the residents led by Miss Ivy Bracey (Chairman) and Mr. Higgins, set about raising funds, with a village fete and other events. Hard work eventually achieved the hall, and this project won the Jubilee competition organised by the Berkshire Association of Local Councils, and they have a plaque to show for it. More recently, in 1980, a total of £441.90 was raised by the village for the Ken Thomas Scanner Appeal. To this was added another £157.97 given to Miss Ivy Bracey for this purpose when the Youth Club closed down. Fund-raising to repair the old part of the Village Hall continues, and they are hoping for a grant.

Where there were once small meadows with cows, there are now giant fields for corn. The footpaths are ploughed up, but the Parish Council have signposted them, thus ensuring that their routes will be marked and remembered in the future.

Brightwalton had many wells: that on the Green was 283 ft. deep, but now for safety's sake, they are almost all filled in. Facing the Green, on an angle between two roads, stands a thatched cottage, owned and used as their business headquarters by H. G. Wells, builders. Once it housed wheelwrights and carpenters.

The people of Brightwalton are determined to retain the character of the village as it is – but they would like just a handful of bungalows built for the older residents to move into, to ensure that houses with more ample accommodation are available for families with young children, thereby guaranteeing the continuity of the village school and of the village community.

# Brimpton 🦡

The village of Brimpton lies on the Hampshire-Berkshire border, bounded on the north by the river Kennet and for some distance on the south by the river Enbourne. The greater part of the village lies at the end of a ridge.

The village has always been an agricultural community, but in the past twenty five years there has been an influx of residents who work outside the village. It has a church at its centre, one village shop, a post office, one public house in the village and a garage. There is a Baptist chapel on its outer fringe. The present population is about 500. Brimpton Common is also regarded as part of Brimpton.

The name Brimpton evolved over a period of several hundreds of years, with numerous variations. In 944 it was Bryningtune, in 1086 Brintone, in 1167 Brinton, in 1275 Brimpton Douile, in 1412 Brympton and in 1420 Brumpton.

There was almost certainly a pre-Roman settlement in, or near the village. Evidence to support this comes from five burial mounds, or barrows, just inside the parish at Brimpton Common. Two are bell type and three are bowl barrows. They vary in diameter from 60-90 feet. Canon Greenwell who excavated them in 1880 thought that they had existed since the Bronze Age.

There is evidence of Roman occupation of Brimpton. A hypocaust was found behind the present Forge Stores, and a Roman urn of baked earth, containing bone, ashes and flesh coloured dust, was found in one of the peat grounds.

There is virtually nowhere in the village where the spire of the Parish Church of St. Peter's cannot be seen. It is situated at the end of a ridge and is a landmark for miles around.

The present church was built between 1869 – 1872 in the 14th century decorated style. The architect was John Johnson and the church was paid for by James Blyth of Midgham House.

In the grounds of Manor Farm is the Knights Templars' Chapel of St. Leonard, a 14th century building still in very good repair.

Further north is Brimpton Baptist Chapel which was built in 1845. Baptisms at one time took place in the river Kennet.

In the days before social security, village charities met the needs of the poor. Brimpton had several charities. In 1854 the Countess of Falmouth built the St. Peter's Almshouses for aged couples and widows. There were seven almshouses each containing a boarded living room with a bedroom above. £3,000 was left by the countess for 'repair, maintenance and support'. Today the almshouses have been altered to provide flats for those who may need them.

The Earl of Falmouth gave a small piece of land on which was built the Parochial School, supported partly by voluntary contributions and by an endowment of £20 per annum from £644. 13s. 4d. left for this purpose by the Countess of Falmouth. In 1861 the school was enlarged and a master's residence built on. James Blyth gave the extra land needed. In 1883 it had provision for 94 pupils. Today Brimpton School is still a C. of E. School with about 30 pupils.

A trout farm was established at Hyde End at the turn of the century on the site of a former water mill. An attractive brochure offers 'Brown trout 3 - 4 ins at £1. 4s. 0d per hundred and Rainbow Trout 3 - 4 ins at 19s 6d. per hundred. This was the first farm of its kind in Berkshire. The trout were fed on maggots from the decaying carcases of horses suspended over the tanks.

The Hyde family who gave Hyde End its name, possessed the mansion, now Hyde End House, from the 16th - 18th centuries. There is a family vault in the churchyard. Anne Hyde, the wife of James II is reputed to have lived there in some secrecy for a time. The house was rebuilt after a fire 200 years ago. During the Second World War the house was the headquarters of the Great Western Railway.

The present Forge Stores, the Brimpton village shop, was formerly the home of Duncan McClean, who came there in 1920. He was blinded in the First World War. He was a basket and net maker and poultry farmer. Later his wife started the village shop. Glebe Cottage was once known as The Brimpton Refreshment Rooms.

Like all villages, Brimpton has its quota of stories. One stormy night a carriage taking a party of young people to a Hunt Ball in Newbury were driving down Brimpton Lane going via Able Bridge. But the old wooden bridge had been swept away in the storm. The carriage and horses plunged into the river and all the occupants were drowned. A ghostly carriage and pair is said to travel down Brimpton Lane on a certain night in January.

The late Israel Sieff, who lived at Lane End Cottage, also once the home Aneurin Bevin, took as his title Baron Sieff of Brimpton. He gave a Sports Pavilion and Recreation Ground to the village. His son Marcus, is now Lord Sieff of Brimpton and still lives here.

Today, social events in the village are mainly connected with the various village organisations. In spite of being in the heart of 'Silicon Valley' and midway between the Atomic Research Establishment at Aldermaston and the Cruise Missile Base at Greenham Common, the village is still very much a country village.

# Bucklebury- cum–Marlston

Burghild, an Anglo-Saxon princess, gave her name to a small village on the banks of the river Pang. Recorded as 'Borchedeberie' in the Domesday Book, there were several variations in the spelling before Bucklebury became the accepted form in the 18th century.

The village itself remained small as the river frequently overflowed and most of the villagers preferred to build their houses on higher ground, leaving the church of St. Mary the Virgin to watch over the few who remained in the valley.

King Henry I granted the manor to Reading Abbey and the abbot found it so attractive that he built a house just above the village. The five fishponds made to ensure a fresh supply of fish for his table remain to this day.

Additions to the early Norman church included the beautifully carved south doorway in the 12th century. A chest brought from Reading Abbey still remains in the church.

At the Dissolution the manor was bought by John Winchcombe, son of the famous clothier, Jack of Newbury. He replaced the Abbot's house with a fine Elizabethan mansion but died before it was completed. His son, another John, finished the house in which he is thought to have entertained Queen Elizabeth I.

The Winchcombes left their mark on the church. An oak beam above the chancel records '1591 Francis Winchcom Esquire Build This'. In 1701 Sir Henry Winchcombe extended the chancel and added the manor pew above which can be seen the 'fly' window. Its sundial and realistic fly remind us that time flies. The magnificent portrayal of the crucifixion in the east window, and the nativity window in the north aisle are the work of Sir Frank Brangwyn. The latest renovation in this ancient church was the full restoration of the peal of eight bells in February 1984.

Bucklebury acquired notoriety in the early 18th century when Frances Winchcombe, the eldest daughter of Sir Henry Winchcombe, married Henry St. John (later Lord Bolingbroke) in 1701. Two years afterwards she inherited the manor and the rising politician and his beautiful wife entertained lavishly. Dean Swift, Alexander Pope, John Gay, John Arbuthnot and, probably, Queen Anne were among their guests. This happy period was shortlived. By 1713 Lord Bolingbroke had deserted his wife and he fled to France in 1715 to escape impeachment. Lady Bolingbroke died, broken hearted, three years afterwards.

Unfortunately the Elizabethan manor house was extensively damaged by fire in 1830 and was later demolished, apart from one wing. This was restored in recent years and the present lord of the manor again lives in the house of his ancestors. The Tudor dovecot stands in the courtyard.

Bucklebury is proud of its fine oak avenue. The first oaks were probably planted to commemorate the visit of Elizabeth I, others to celebrate the victories of Marlborough, and, a century later, the Battle of Waterloo. In 1972 young trees replaced old when Queen Elizabeth II visited Bucklebury and eight years later Princess Anne planted a tree to commemorate the eightieth birthday of Queen Elizabeth, the Queen

Mother.

At the end of the avenue stands the Blade Bone Inn so called because its copper sign encases the bladebone of a mammoth found in the Kennet valley in the 17th century.

Further along the Pang lies the village of Marlston with its 13th century church built by Geoffrey Martel to serve his family and dependants although they were obliged to attend the parish church at Bucklebury on all major festival days.

The little church was extensively restored in the 19th century but still retains its Norman doorway, its Norman holywater stoup and an ancient bell. This was cast by Peter de Weston, a bell founder of London in the early 14th century.

The Rt. Hon. George Palmer, of Huntley and Palmer of Reading, acquired the Marlston estate in the late 19th century and built Marlston House, now a boys' preparatory school. He also founded Marlston Club to provide recreation for his employees.

The parish of Bucklebury-cum-Marlston has an abundance of footpaths. Some lead to charming thatched cottages built in bygone centuries. Many were made by men trudging to work at the village foundry and manor timber yard, once the two principal places of employment. Other tracks were worn by cattle and sheep searching for fresh pastures. Domestic animals, apart from dogs, are rarely seen on the Common nowadays, but foxes, badgers, and deer still walk stealthily at dusk along secluded pathways. It was a different scene less than a century ago when Commoners were thankful to graze their livestock on the open land. They were grateful to John Morton, a farmer and wayside preacher, who travelled to Westminister in 1835 and successfully opposed the enclosure of Bucklebury Common. He eventually became the first pastor of the Congregational Chapel erected in 1840 on Turners Green.

Here the bowl turners once worked at their ancient craft. When George Lailey, the last of the turners, died in 1958 Bucklebury lost a great character.

Times change. The building of the Memorial Hall in 1961 and All Saints' Church a year later provided for the needs of a growing population, especially in Upper Bucklebury, but the extensive Common and thriving farmlands of Bucklebury-cum-Marlston should ensure that the parish remains a rural community.

# Burghfield

In the reign of Edward the First, Mathew de Burghfelde built a bridge over the marshy flats of the Kennet to enable the peasants to reach

Reading. There is a unique double bridge over the Kennet and the old Great Western Railway line at the site. A skirmish between Prince Rupert's cavalry and Roundhead forces, then lying at Newbury, took place at Burghfield Bridge.

Much of the land was owned by the Earls of Shrewsbury , and two alabaster monuments in Burghfield church have been identified by their armorial bearings as Richard and Alice Neville; their eldest son was Warwick the Kingmaker.

The present church was built in 1868 on older foundations. It contains the 14th century wooden effigy of Sir Roger de Burghfield, stolen in 1978 and later recognised in Belgium, in an antique market. The cost of recovery was £10,000, raised by public subscription and worldwide donations. Sir Roger was restored to the church in May 1982, and now sleeps in a secure display case.

When the original Mrs. Bland's School became overcrowded because of development, new infant and junior schools were built. After housing the county library, the site was sold to the District Council, who, in 1975, built flats for retired persons. The building also houses the Anderson Hill Day Centre, a memorial to one of our original doctors, whose son still practices in the village.

Burghfield also has a thriving Volunteer Bureau. Due to the foresight and generosity of our forebears, parishioners can benefit from Trust Funds set up from their donations.

Holiday House is another building no longer standing. Presented to the working men of the village in 1913, it was declared unsafe in 1979 and was replaced two years later by a new Village Hall, the home of our W.I. which was formed in 1917, and since the closure of Hurst, is the oldest Berkshire W.I.

In 1981 Burghfield Scouts built their new headquarters on the Old Recreation Ground. The same year saw the closure of H.M.S. Dauntless, the initial training ship of all W.R.N.S. The site dated from the Second World War when it housed hundreds of women working at the Royal Ordnance Factory. After the war the Navy took over the site for W.R.N.S training.

From two all-age schools, the village now has nursery, infant, two junior and a large comprehensive schools; the latter houses the Adult Education classes.

Burghfield and District Horticultural Society held its first show in 1870, and has continued with only two breaks during the wars.

The old Three Firs Inn was pulled down in the early 1950s to make way for a housing estate, and another rural tradition died. The Boxing Day meet of hounds on the common opposite, and the mummers play of *George and the Dragon* are now no more.

Birch broom making was a former Burghfield industry. Farming always was, and still is a major occupation with sheep re-appearing. There are two light industrial workshops, one on the site of the old forge, but another smithy, barns and riding stables have fallen to the housing. We are well served by shops, and have been lucky to keep our post office. There are still some old residents living here: one kept *the* original Village Shop, which still exists; and others tell of the carrier who would take your order to Reading and return with it in his horse and cart. They also tell tales of days spent fishing for tiddlers and newts, of scrumping for apples, and of other schoolboy pursuits.

Burghfield will be subject to massive developments over the next few years, and from a small village with gravel tracks through the pinewoods to Reading, it is likely to exceed a population of 10,000.

# Burchetts Green

Burchetts Green is a small village with a population of about 400. Many of them work in Maidenhead or commute to London. The village stands rather uneasily astride a busy main road connecting two even busier trunk roads, the Maidenhead-Henley and the London-Bath roads. The houses edge the Common and the Green, or straggle along the main street, and are surrounded by woodlands, fields and farmsteads. It has no parish church divided as it is between the three ecclesiastical parishes of Stubbings, Hurley and Littlewick.

The noble manor house of Hall Place is now taken over by the Berkshire College of Agriculture. It is approached by a magnificent avenue of limes. It is recorded that Hurley Priory owned Hall Place, until the Dissolution of 1535. In 1728 it was purchased by William East of the Manor House, Kennington, who pulled down the old house and built the one standing today. It remained in the family until after the last war, when it was sold to the Berkshire County Council. The old mansion stood in a great deer park of some 130 acres. Descendants of this herd now roam wild on Ashley Hill. Interesting out-buildings include a bee-house and an ice pit, and in the gardens can be seen the remains of a cock-fighting ring.

Stubbings Farm, in the centre of the village, boasts a barn reputed to be 400 years old, and old maps mark Stubbings Heath to the south. It is believed that the road through the village was made by Lord Salisbury, for his personal use. As his health was poor he journeyed from his home at Hatfield to take the cure at Bath, and went this way to avoid the highwaymen lurking on Maidenhead Thicket. The milestones on this stretch give the distances to these two towns. Alleyhill Coppes, now

Ashley Hill, dominated the scene then as it does today.

Woodlands Cottage, 17th century, was formerly a Quaker Meeting House. Stubbings House, half a mile to the east of the village, was the home of Queen Wilhelmina of Holland during the last war when her country was invaded by the Nazis.

Among the legends and ghost stories of the neighbourhood is that of Claude Duval, the famous highwayman who is said to have carried out his expeditions in this area. Both Woodlands and Burchetts Green House are said to be haunted, the latter by Druids! Hall Place is no exception and students claim to have seen a coach and horses crossing the lawn at the back of the house. The ghost of a coloured servant has also been seen at Black Horse Lodge. More recent anecdotes of the Clayton East family include their driving to Ascot in their horse-drawn carriage and, if the day had been profitable, scattering their winnings to the servants lining the drive, on their return. It is also said that unless Sir Gilbert could see across country to the spire of Shottesbrook Church the gardeners were in trouble for not keeping the trees trimmed back.

Within living memory a well in the centre of the village supplied the villagers with water, geese grazed on the Green and an old warhorse was tethered there, a far cry from today's busy restlessness.

# California 🌿

Once forming part of Windsor Forest, California today still has many trees, silver birch and pine predominating, with their colonies of birds: tits and finches of all kinds and a current invasion of jays, magpies and collared dove. Leafy lanes and fields where moles and foxes are constant visitors and extensive gardens are a proud heritage of the pioneers who, between the two World Wars, built their own houses, dug their own wells and who lived and worked by the light of oil lamps and candles. Ever increasing settlements of new houses replace the expanses of heath and woodland where children used to build their hide-outs and play undisturbed during the long summer holidays.

The name California is derived from the land surrounding California Lodge, once a hunting lodge on Nine Mile Ride which was one of many rides through Windsor Forest long ago. At the turn of this century much of the area was included in the Bearwood Estate, owned by the Walters family. After the First World War the land was sold and this was the beginning of the development of California.

It is now centred where Nine Mile Ride crosses the Finchampstead Road and extents for roughly two miles north and south, covering part of Finchampstead, Barkham and Wokingham Without parishes. From the 1920s onwards there has been fluctuating interest in the official recognition of California as a village but this has never materialised and it remains an area, though many years ago the County Council did agree to the name being used for the Post Office. Under local government reorganisation in 1974, California was designated a ward in the area covered by Wokingham District Council and returns two council members.

California may lack the status of a village but is nevertheless a neighbourly community with many of the features of a recognised village. Until the late 1950s the flourishing Ratepayers' Hall was just a small hut but, as a result of local effort, it has over the years been enlarged and improved until today it is a substantial brick building accommodating many lively groups. Among these are the vigilant Ratepayers' Association, the Gardeners' Club which some years ago was host to the radio programme *Gardeners' Question Time,* the Women's Institute now nearly nineteen years of age, the Art Class, Flower Club and the local branch of the National Pensioners' Association. Regular calsses are held for young dancers and in the vicinity several play groups are run for pre-school children. Older children attend Gorse Ride infant and junior schools and the older established Nine Mile Ride primary school; at eleven-plus pupils go on to secondary schools outside the area. The recently built Gorse Ride Community Centre caters for social activities and a fortnightly Mobile Library is provided by Berkshire County Council.

The doors of St. John's Church in Nine Mile Ride, built in the early 1930s, are now closed but under the guidance of the Rev. K. G. Humphreys the parish of St. Mary and St. John has emerged, and services are at present held in Gorse Ride School and at the Vicarage.

California Country Park with its sixty-five acres of woodland and six-acre Longmoor Lake is now owned by Wokingham District Council and a nature reserve has been set up to protect its wetland habitat. Here can be seen the wild orchid and other interesting plant and animal life; nature trails and walks are arranged together with fishing competitions. Fifty years ago young visitors enjoyed a summer swim in the lake, now it is devoted to fishing and is a reserve for aquatic life – swans, ducks, and recently a flock of Canada geese. An unobtrusive caravan park replaces the holiday chalets popular in the 1930s.

# Charvil 🐝

Largely a product of the post World War Two era, Charvil was almost entirely agricultural in origin. Part of Woodley and Sandford parish until 1970 when it was constituted a civil parish in its own right. Part of the ecclesiastical parish of Sonning, that is the church mostly used by the people of Charvil.

Around 1925 there were about 20 houses in Charvil, now the population numbers around 1700. There is no church, no school, two public houses and one shop, but many flourishing organisations. The village magazine *Charvil Chimes* produced three times a year, is full of interesting information on local activities. There has been much controversy recently on the proposed building of 100 houses in the vicinity.

St. Patrick's Hall is the meeting place for residents of Charvil and there is talk of a new village hall being built in the hopefully near future.

There is a suggestion that the name Charvil may derive from 'Cheorivil' the settlement of the churls or villeins, the semi-free peasants of the manorial system. More about this can be found in *Understanding English Place Names*. Sir Wm. Addison.

# Chavey Down

Chavey Down is in the Parish of Winkfield and is one of Berkshire's 'babies'. It lies on the southern edge of the Thames valley between Ascot and Bracknell and was formerly a tract of land in Windsor Forest. Chavey Down was at one time surrounded by an estimated 100,000 acres of wild heathland. By an Act of Parliament dated 21 July 1813, King George III vested in himself all the commonable land within the Forest and disposed of large areas. Chavey Down being common land at that time was enclosed. From that date the old Forest laws ceased to exist. After enclosing land a Deed of Award empowered Commissioners to allocate land to various persons for a nominal sum to defray the expenses of Parliament for the Enclosure Act. John Davis of Bloxham in the County of Oxford was duly appointed a Commissioner and was responsible for awarding or allotting land in Winkfield, of which Chavey Down formed part.

The area known as Chavey Down Hill was allotted to the Reverend Samuel Sewell and after various wills and bequests the land finally came into the ownership of Charles Sewell. The area was divided into two roads, North Road and Church Road with building plots on either side. These plots were sold to local builders who erected cottages which were soon filled with working class families. The first house to be completed was Rosemount on the corner of Church Road and Priory Road and as the date on this is 1879 it is reasonable to suppose that the village dates from then. The village became known as Chavey Down and the inhabitants formed a close knit community. Several traders opened

*Artist's impression of the Windmill at Chavey Down.*

small shops in the village which soon boasted a grocer, two bakers and haberdashery store.

The oldest known building in the Chavey Down area is Chavey Down Farm, parts of which are over 400 years old. This was probably originally a miller's cottage, as old plans and documents refer to 'The Windmill' which was thought to have been on the apex of the road junctions, Longhill Road, Priory Road and Locks Ride. The date the windmill was demolished is not known but Rocques Map of Berkshire dated 1761 shows the windmill very clearly. Chavey Down at one time comprised part of the Manor of Winkfield and Mr. C. C. Ferrard was the last known landowner of that manor. The Manning family owned Chavey Down Farm for many years and provided a very comprehensive service to the new village, not only with farm produce but also by hire of waggons and carriages for local weddings. Mr. Manning also allowed the villagers to play cricket and football on one of the farm fields and one of his barns was regularly used as a venue for village entertainment. The property was sold to the late Mr. R. W. Sharples in the mid 1940s and as a compliment to the village he named his racehorse 'Chavey Down'. His only son became the Governor of Bermuda and was tragically assassinated in the early 1970s.

The earliest development (prior to the village) was the building of Ascot Priory in Priory Road, Chavey Down. Dr. Edward Bouverie Pusey purchased a large tract of land in 1861 and was responsible for the first unit of the Priory of Jesus Christ and the Hospital of the Holy Cross and Passion. Priscilla Lydia Sellon was for 30 years its Superior. This was later known as The Society of the Most Holy Trinity Devenport (later Ascot). The sisters founded an orphanage, a ward for sick children and ran a private school known as St. Augustine's which was on the corner of North Road and Priory Road at Chavey Down. The Sisters also visited the poor and the Priory employed many people from the village.

As the village began to develop various people in the area contributed to the building known as St Martins Church. In 1900 the new chancel was built and village funds were raised to pay for this. In 1905 the village received an 'Iron Room' which was delivered by horse and cart. This acted as a Village Hall, Sunday School and a meeting place for boys' clubs and other functions. In March 1974 St Martins church was closed for extensive repairs and the 'Iron Room' was demolished as it was found to be unsafe. The Church reopened a year later and a new Village Hall adjoining the church was also opened.

The area surrounding Chavey Down is still very rural, although it is under constant threat from development now that the New Town of Bracknell is expanding in its direction.

# Chazey Heath & Mapledurham ☙

Chazey Heath which forms part of the Civil Parish of Mapledurham (just within the bounds of Oxfordshire) and the lovely village of Mapledurham itself lies at the foot of a long hill leading down from the main highway nestling alongside the river Thames.

The village is still feudal in spirit and is dominated by the Manor House which looms behind the church of St. Margaret. The church was restored in the middle of the last century but is ancient in origin and is notable for the 14th century south chancel which to this day remains the private property of the Lords of the Manor and has thus been continually in the hands of Roman Catholics since it was built nearly six hundred years ago. The Manor House has also been restored and is open to the public, although the Lord of the Manor occupies it with his family.

The village also has a very lovely water mill recently restored and in working order. It dates back to the 16th century and lends its own particular charm to the village as do the two cottages recently converted but which were once six Almshouses and inhabited as such until recent years.

Alexander Pope, the celebrated poet, often visited the village to see Martha Blount, the daughter of a 17th century Lord of the Manor and it is said that this friendship was the nearest thing to a love affair which the poet ever had. Another notable resident of the village was Lord Augustus Fitz-Clarence, son of William IV and the actress Mrs. Jordon. Lord Augustus was Vicar of the Parish between 1829 and 1854 and was generous in his benefactions to the parish particularly when the restoration of the Church was taking place.

John Galsworthy's *Forsythe Saga* featured Mapledurham in that Soames Forsythe owned a house there so the village became known in a fictional sense quite widely. More recently the shooting of the film *The Eagle has Landed* brought Mapledurham a wider audience. But they might not have recognised it as such as it was meant to depict a village in East Anglia!

Chazey Heath itself derives its name from the Manor of Mapledurham Chawsey or Chausey as it was known in the Middle Ages. It is now largely farmland but there stands within its bounds a farmhouse known as Chazey Court. It is mainly 15th century in construction but it has earlier features possibly dating back to the 13th century thus making the farmhouse of some architectural and historic importance.

# Cheapside 🦋

Cheapside in the parish of Sunninghill, was once the market site for Windsor Forest and derives its name from the old English for market-place. It lies along the eastern edge of Windsor Great Park. The area of Sunninghill Park which forms the northern boundary to the main triangle of the village had been part of Windsor Forest as a Royal deer park and the first house was built there in 1486. Later it was owned by the Nevilles, one of whom was Gentleman to the Chamber of King

Edward VI and an important figure in the reign of Elizabeth I. During the Second World War it was taken over by the American Ninth Airforce as a hospital before it was returned to the Crown in 1947 for the then Princess Elizabeth, but unfortunately the house was burnt down that same year.

The village lies on the route of the Royal Procession to the Royal Ascot races and every year in mid-June the pageantry of the procession makes its way from Windsor Castle, by way of the Great Park, down Watersplash Lane, which lost its ford before the last war, and on to enter the racecourse near the top of the village by the modern gates built in 1955 for the new 'straight mile'. The old Golden Gates, their cast iron magnificently restored black and gilded, were built, probably in Glasgow, in 1877 when the racecourse was under the patronage of Edward Prince of Wales. Queen Victoria disapproved of this addiction to 'the turf' and always spent June in Scotland.

Cheapside was surrounded by large country houses and estates which gave employment to the villagers. Many such as the Georgian Buckhurst Park, advertised in 1798 as 'a modern an excellent family house,' still survive as private houses while others are divided into flats. Up to the end of the Second World War the village consisted of one straggling row of mostly small cottages with a few others along one side of the other two roads which form the main triangle which still looks mainly outwards from the centre. Although much infilling of modern houses has taken place, enlarging the village to take its place in the commuter belt, the village still keeps its feeling of isolation.

At the end of Pump Lane the old pump which used to water the once unsurfaced road still stands in its original place. Few historic buildings survive in the village. The one church a Wesleyan Methodist Chapel built in 1862 was pulled down in 1970, but the one remaining public house still functions. Although called the Thatched Tavern it is slate roofed. The present building dates from 1780, which in its turn replaced one of much greater antiquity. But the true hub of the village is the Village Hall which was built after a true community effort in fund-raising (in which the then seven year old W.I. played a very active part), in 1970 to replace a nissen hut transferred from the American Airforce establishment in Sunninghill Park in 1945.

# Chieveley

Chieveley is a lovely Downland village about 5 miles north of Newbury, its name having derived from the wild chives growing all around.

Walk along its main street and you will find many beautiful cottages and several notably fine large houses of Queen Anne and Georgian architecture. A lovely Regency verandahed house behind high walls has particularly fine gardens, and is modestly called The Cottage! The Manor House looks out over superb views of the rolling Downs towards Winterbourne.

Once a self sufficient village with shoemakers, wheelwrights, blacksmiths, bricklayers, carpenters, an undertaker and a shop 'that sold everything', Chieveley now follows the prevailing pattern ... the craftsmen have mostly gone but the village still boasts an excellent bakery, a general stores with Post Office, a butchers and three Public Houses; The Hare and Hounds, being well known for its old character and skittle alley, The Wheatsheaf and The Red Lion.

On the outskirts of the parish is the Blue Boar Inn, a free house and a most lovely thatched building that sits high on the Downs with magnificent views towards Newbury. The inn sign, a life size stone Blue Boar, is alleged to have been brought by some of Cromwell's men from Yorkshire, and left at the inn when they camped on North Heath, during the Civil War.

Although Chieveley is an established village of considerable character it is changing with the times with modern properties being built in styles to compliment the old. With the growth of the village, the old village school has seen considerable change and has had to expand, and the doctors surgery likewise has expanded and been modernised. The Village Hall and playing fields is more commonly known as Chieveley Recreational Centre which is well patronised by local clubs, groups and societies; catering for all age groups, thus still encouraging the well known community spirit of Chieveley.

With a beautiful rural setting, good shopping at the nearby town of Newbury, and fast access to London and the west by motorway, Chieveley is a village which combines all the advantages of modern day living.

# Cold Ash

Cold Ash is a straggling village of 1881 acres in area, rising to over 500 feet above sea level. There is no village square, no picturesque stream, but it is built on the hillside which falls to the Kennet valley, with houses spread spider-like along the roads and tracks of the village. In 1900 it was a small and typical rural community with a population of about 800. The village had four public houses, four general stores incorporating the post office and the bakery, two shoe repairers and one smithy, and various other smallholdings and workshops, mostly long since gone.

Few people travelled outside the village for work. Today the population is 2,800 and still increasing.

St. Marks church was designed by C. N. Beazley and built by Hollis of Windsor in 1865 and is of local red brick with bands of stone. It has an unusual stone pulpit and some fine stained glass. Rev. W. S. Grindle was vicar of the parish for 55 years from 1873-1928. He was chairman of the Managers to St. Marks School and also chairman of the Parish Council for a number of years, and records show that he enjoyed verbal battles with other members of those bodies. Another fine character and the subject of many local tales was Rev. R. S. Podd who came to Cold Ash in 1959 and stayed until his retirement in 1980. In 1981 Cold Ash joined five other villages into one team ministry.

Next to the Church one finds the village school which was erected 1873 and Caroline Handcock entered on her duties as first Mistress of the School on 2nd March, 1874. Many generations of the older village families received their only education in this building. Teaching in this building ceased in 1981 after a new single storey building had been erected on land opposite.

Cold Ash once had a Children's Cottage Hospital and a Church of England Children's Home. The hospital was opened in 1886 by a private benefactress for crippled children. In 1917 it was granted a certificate for teaching of children on the premises, and a governess employed. The village was grateful for the employment provided by the hospital which also received great support from the parishioners. The hospital closed in 1968, and soon after the children and nurses had left was demolished and Sewell Close was built in the grounds. St. Mary's Home was closed in 1980 and was purchased by a local consortium and preserved for posterity by conversion to four large country houses. The external appearance remains practically unaltered since the turn of the century.

Two other large establishments still flourish in Cold Ash. Downe House, a large public school for girls, came to Cold Ash in 1921 from the village of Downe in Kent, with Miss Olive Willis as Headmistress. The building had been erected during the First World War for a religious organisation known as The Order of Silence. The second establishment is St. Gabriel's Convent, which houses a large number of Roman Catholic nuns. At one time they were virtually self supporting with produce from their farm, and made a pretty picture when working in the hayfield in their black and white habits. Their numbers have now dwindled and the premises serves the local community firstly as a place of worship for Catholics, a primary school for the children and as a conference centre for the County.

The Spotted Dog Inn was saved from closure by four of its customers, and after extensive renovation, was re-opened as one of the first free houses in the Newbury area. The Castle, originally owned by Simmonds Brewery and later by Courage, has recently been modernised and a car park provided for customers. The Fir Tree and the Pheasant, which were both owned by Simmonds Brewery of Reading, were sold and converted to private dwellings over twenty years ago.

Cold Ash was for a great number of years the home of the Acland family. The Village Hall which was erected by local builders, H. Burgess in 1925, on land donated by Sir Reginald Acland and with money raised in the village, was named after its chief benefactor. Although now over fifty years old, it is still well appointed and is greatly in demand.

Another hall exists in the village, the timber frame building, clad with corrugated iron situated opposite the church and known as the Parish Room. This building was erected by the menfolk of the village on land donated by Lady St. Helier of Poplar House.

Unfortunately, many of the larger houses in the village have been demolished and replaced wih large numbers of modern buildings. The Shop House, on Cold Ash Hill was replaced with six houses, Collaroy House, the home of Rev. J. M. Bacon the pioneer of hot air ballooning was replaced by five large houses, although the cottage was retained. The Children's Hospital which is mentioned elsewhere, and Red Lodge were demolished, and permission has been granted for five dwellings to be erected on the site. The Methodist Chapel was closed for worship and after demolition a bungalow was erected on the site. Campbell Cottage, home of the Walters family was demolished and eleven houses erected in the close known as Walters Close.

# Colnbrook

The early history of Colnbrook can only be guessed. It was probably started by a settlement on either side of a safe river crossing between three manors on the Colne Brook. This river formed the old Middlesex and Buckinghamshire border. The village grew to have a watermill grinding corn, and inns to accommodate the travellers on their way west to Bath and Bristol from London. Gradually, it expanded to become a town, with its own market, but no church. The inhabitants north of the street were expected to go to Langley Marish, and those on the south side to Horton church, for the parish boundaries ran down the centre of the High Street until early Victorian times. With the growth of the population, a Chapel of Ease was built, and administered from the church at Horton. Much later, St. Thomas church was built, and a new parish formed in late Victorian times.

While the coaches plied the roads of the country, Colnbrook flourished, but when the railways were built, it gradually died, and is now more like a suburb of Slough. Yet it still retains a village atmosphere, and several interesting buildings remain, including several old inns, a small museum which houses the village fire engine, and a clock which was put up in the village to commemorate the coronation of King Edward VII, taken down during the 1930s, but recently restored.

Colnbrook is situated on the eastern border of Berkshire, becoming so with the boundary changes in the 1970s. It now has, within a mile along the Old Bath Road, four boundaries: the Berkshire / Slough Borough boundary, Iver Parish and Buckinghamshire, Spelthorne Borough Council and Surrey County boundary, and the London Borough of Hillingdon.

Physically, Colnbrook has to the west and north the M4 motorway; to the south, reservoirs built to supply water for the west of London, and to the east, the nearly completed M25 motorway, with Heathrow Airport beyond it.

# Compton

No English village is genuinely old which does not appear in Domesday Book. Compton is fully recorded: there were two manors, that at East Compton being the greater. Both were given to supporters of William the Conqueror, but later they came into the possession of churchmen, including the Bishop of Bath and Wells.

Compton, on the Berkshire Downs, is steeped in English history. Perborough Castle, an Iron Age fort, lies less than a mile away to the south, whilst to the north, at a similar distance, is The Ridgway, one of the oldest tracks in Britain. A little further is the Icknield Way.

A church almost certainly existed in the early Middle Ages, on the site of the present St. Mary's and St. Nicholas'. The oldest part was the chantry of St. Nicholas, which was torn down in the Reformation but the lower part of the tower is Norman, and the font mid 12th century. Additions, rebuilding and restoration have been made ever since. The tower contains a peal of six bells, cast by Pack & Chapman of London, in 1775.

The Manor House and farms eventually came into the ownership of the Loyd family, who finally sold them to sitting tenants. The land which is now the recreation ground was donated by Lady Wantage.

The Berkshire Downs were once extensive sheep-grazing lands, but gradually fell victim to the enclosure movement, and smaller tracts gradually came into private ownership, as they are today. Now, with modern fertilizers, much of the farming is arable, and there are cattle, too.

In the 19th century a local railway line was built, running from Didcot to Newbury, and Compton became a staging post for the sheep fairs at Ilsley, with rows of sheep pens at the station sidings. The railway was closed in the 1960s.

The occupational character of the village has changed too, from sheep farming and agriculture, and there are not the number of racehorse training stables that there were. Some years ago the Institute for Research in Animal Diseases was established and, more recently, Her Majesty the Queen opened some additional buildings there. As well as laboratory work, the Institute manages a vast area of land, formed by the amalgamation of four large farms.

In the 19th century a small foundry flourished in the village, owned by T. Baker and Sons, and famous for its village pumps and water carts. It was a successful company for 120 years, becoming in turn the 'Moist and Crane' business, and then Jones Cranes. Sadly it is no more, and the factory is being rebuilt.

Many of the agricultural workers who tend the farmlands are descendants of former farm workers in Compton.

There is now a fine comprehensive school, providing education for students from 13 villages in the area, and there is still a primary school for local needs.

Several estates, both private and council, have been built on the outskirts of Compton, bringing in more residents; but, curiously, many of them work outside the village, at Harwell Research Institute or even further away, whilst many of those who work in the village live elsewhere.

It is to Compton's credit that the newcomers are soon made welcome, and become part of the flourishing community.

# Cookham Dean

Each season of the year there's beauty to behold,
The blossom in Spring, Summer so green, Winter so cold.
The colours of Autumn, so sweet and so still,
The view you can have when you're on Winter Hill.
The lanes, the fields and the village green,
This place of my birth called Cookham Dean.

(Nellie West 1961).

The parish of Cookham Dean on the Berkshire bank of the Thames is made up of two hills and the valley between. Until the reign of George III it was part of the Royal Manor of Cookham which was sold by the King in 1818. Mrs. A. M. Vansittart of Bisham Abbey who bought the manor in 1843 was so horrified by the vice and ignorance of the inhabitants that she obtained permission under an Act of Parliament to enclose a portion of the Waste for the erection of a church. The size of the site was 1 acre 10 poles, and £5 was paid to the churchwardens of Cookham as compensation for the loss of Rights of Common. The church of St John the Baptist is in the Early Decorated Style of the 13th century and was built to the plans of R. C. Carpenter of the Ecclesiological Society. At the laying of the foundation stone in 1844 the vicar of Cookham who preached said 'The distance from the Parish Church (Cookham) to the main population of Cookham Dean has led to a desecration of the holy day of rest. I may say a kind of hereditary Sabbath-breaking has prevailed on this place descending from parents to children and Sabbath-breaking has led to the lowest level of ignorance and vice.'

The church was followed very quickly by a school for children of all ages on the site of the Dean Garage, but in 1899, when the building became too small, permission to enclose a further piece of Waste was obtained and a school for infants was built at the top of Bigfrith Hill.

A chapel near the top of the Chalkpit Lane was built by the Primitive Methodists in 1843 and was last used in 1973. It has now become a private house and the head-stones of the graves have been moved to an enclosure next door.

The War Memorial was designed by F. C. Eden and records the names of those who died in the two World Wars.

The Village Hall was rebuilt in 1980 on the site of the old Drill Hall dating from the Boer War which later became the Young Men's Club. The small hall next door belongs to the Women's Institute who use it for many activities: monthly meetings, weekly art and keep-fit classes, craft afternoons and entertaining; it also provides a meeting place for the Brownies and local societies.

Successive owners of the manor, absentee landlords, sold off the manor farms for development and many large houses with extensive grounds were built until the First World War. Today the lovely houses have generally been sub-divided and several smaller houses have been erected in the grounds. The commons are the only part of the manor still remaining and are maintained by the National Trust. There is still a considerable acreage of farmland in the centre of the village in private ownership, much of it used for fruit growing – cherries, apples, plums and soft fruits. In springtime the blossom is a picture, while in autumn the beeches of the Quarry Woods on the northern boundary are a magnificent sight.

Many artists have painted in Cookham Dean – Dewey Bates, E. J. Gregory, Sir George Clausen, Stanley Spencer. Kenneth Grahame lived here as a child with his grandmother and returned with his wife and young son. Quarry Woods and the Thames below Winter Hill provided much of the background to *Wind in the Willows*.

The Flower Festival in June with concerts in the church, and the Village Fair in September attract many visitors, and every weekend parties of walkers, either families or ramblers, may be seen exploring the footpaths which link the village to Cookham, Marlow and Maidenhead.

# Cookham on Thames 🌿

There is evidence that Cookham was in existence as an Iron Age settlement in 100 AD. It was occupied by the Romans and afterwards by the Saxons, proof of which lies in the old field and place names of this area. In medieval times it became a Royal Manor, and this title was retained until 1818.

Less than 60 years ago Cookham High Street was free of cars, children played there with their tops, bowling hoops and marbles. Everything one needed could be obtained within this one short street. The apothecary, the butchers shop – with its traditional glazed tiles – the forge, the leather mill, a shoe-maker, a dairy and even an undertaker. Life in the village was gentle and pleasant. The beautiful 12th century Norman church was the centre of the community and the river provided the main summer attractions of boating and swimming. However, 'the past is another country, they do things differently there'. Gone is the peace and quiet, gone are the facilities. The twentieth century, with its noise and bustle has encroached on the village, and crossing the road has become a hazard, even for the residents.

Nevertheless, the beautiful and historic old buildings remain. The church of the Holy Trinity is still the heart of the village, with a large congregation and a lovely peal of bells. There is always a welcome for the many visitors of whatever denomination, either to take part in a service or to just sit quietly and absorb the atmosphere.

Hostelries abound in the area. Bell and the Dragon and the Kings Arms are respectively 15th and 17th century inns. The former was originally called The Olde Bell, but, although the older of the two, the Kings Arms – at one time The Kings Head – has the distinction that a resident, during the reign of Charles II, one Martha Spott, had her own special coinage for use only in the village, and a framed specimen of a half-token may be seen in the inn.

Oveys Farm is proof that farming was carried on in the heart of the village – within living memory – and Tannery House and The Maltings were both part of a large brewery. Two 17th century houses form an elegant backdrop to the High Street: Wistaria Cottage and Eastgate. When Wistaria Cottage had to have a facelift, each brick was numbered and replaced exactly in its original position. One whole day's work had to be taken out and rebuilt, due to one solitary brick being missed out. Thus we preserve our heritage.

Cookham has always attracted famous and interesting people but, perhaps the two who will be best known to the general public, and both of whom are natives of the village, are Sir Stanley Spencer RA and John Turk MVO.

Many of the historic buildings are preserved for posterity in the Spencer paintings. At the corner of Sutton Road and High Street stands a simple building which, more than any other in Cookham, provided the initial impetus for Spencer's artistic genius. At the turn of the century it was a Weslyan Chapel to which Mrs Spencer marched her nine children every Sunday. Today it is a gallery, housing a significant collection of Spencer's paintings, and is high on the priority list for visitors to the area. A copy of his work *The Last Supper* hangs in Holy Trinity Church.

John Turk MVO was honoured by H.M. the Queen in 1977. He holds the appointment of Her Majesty's Swan keeper and Waterman, a personal appointment and one which his father, Frederick Turk, held before him. One of the few pageants still held on the Thames is the Annual Ceremony of Swan Upping. This dates from time immemorial and takes place in July. The ceremony consists of taking up the swans and marking them for their owners, H.M. the Queen, the Worshipful Company of Dyers and the Worshipful company of Vintners. Six boats, two for each owner, carry out the marking, the officials wearing the traditional colourful uniforms and carrying banners. The Queen's swans are unmarked. One mark on the beak denotes those belonging to the Dyers and two marks those of the Vintners. Boats of the Uppers are easily recognisable, scarlet uniform in the Royal boat, white in the Vintners and blue in the Dyers.

A stone 3½ ft high, 4 ft long and 2½ ft thick is known as the Tarry Stone. It was formerly called the Cookham Stone. Originally it served as the boundary stone to the property of the Abbot of Cirencester. It has had many moves over the years but has now come to rest at the corner of the Dower House, formerly Bridge House. In its earlier days, when it rested at the east end of the village, it was a meeting place for the younger members of the community, before deciding whether to go walking, courting, or to just sit and talk. So it is today, thanks to Mrs Briggs who, in 1942, asked to be allowed to erect a seat behind the stone in memory of her son, Pilot Officer Briggs. In spite of its travels the stone is now very nearly in the same position as it was in the 15th century.

# Cranbourne

The parish of Cranbourne has been formed comparatively recently, cut out of the parishes of Winkfield, Old Windsor and Sunninghill. The Gothic Victorian Church, built by Benjamin Ferrey in 1850, is of flint and stone. It was dedicated by Bishop Wilberforce, who argued fiercely against Darwin over the *Origin of Species,* and was known unkindly as Soapy Sam. Some of the stained glass windows are designed by William Morris. The Alexander Chapel is in memory of Field-Marshal Earl Alexander of Tunis, who died in 1969. His house was not far from the church where he worshipped.

One of the oldest schools in Berkshire was founded at Cranbourne in 1709 by Richard, 1st Earl of Ranelagh for 'twenty poor Protestant boys and twenty poor Protestant girls'. It became known as the 'Green School' as a uniform rather like the more famous Blue Coat School was provided for the children. Every Whit Monday they paraded outside Winkfield Church to receive a new set of clothes. The number of admissions increased over the years and in 1880 a larger shcool was opened in Lovel Road called Winkfield Cranbourne Ranelagh C.E. School. The original school building is now called Cranbourne Hall.

When the Grammar School in Bracknell was opened in 1908 it was named Ranelagh School. Cranbourne School then dropped the name Ranelagh but retained part of Lord Ranelagh's coat of arms on its badge. Today it is known as Cranbourne Primary School and caters for children of infant and junior age.

Lovel Road takes its name from the family who were important landowners in Norman times. Plaistow Green Farm, built in 1569, said to be originally a hunting lodge, has associations with the Jacobite Trust. An inscription on one of the walls reads:

```
                    C
1569  O U M D      *      1716
                   1 E
```

The six-pointed star is a Jacobite emblem. C 1 E refers possibly to the old Pretender, James Edward Stuart.

St. George's stables once housed the winter quarters of Billy Smart's Circus. The circus has 'left town' now, and several applications from developers for building permission have been made – so far unsuccessful.

On Sundays, the premises are buzzing with activity, when regular car boot sales and mini antique markets are held there.

# Crazies Hill
# & Cockpole Green

Crazies Hill is an outlying hamlet in the north ward of Wargrave, and leads on to Cockpole Green in Hurley Parish. It is thought that both their curious names can be accounted for thus: Crazies Hill was almost certainly named because 'crazies' is an old country name for buttercups, whilst on Cockpole Green there was once a cockpit, where cockfighting took place.

The hamlets formerly had a large number of inns for the small population, but now only the Horns (which stood on the edge of the old Windsor Great Park) and the Hatchgate remain. The Four Horseshoes, Fox Steep and Hurdlemakers (where hurdles were indeed made) were all inns at one time. Springlands for many years housed a hand laundry, and there were many wells in the village. Rebecca's Well remains as a local landmark.

During the Second World War land at Upper Culham farm was used as an R.A.F. airfield, and the factory at Warren Works started in disused hangars.

Thistle House, on the top of Crazies Hill, was built in 1930-31 as a convalescent home for children by Sir Campbell Rhodes in memory of his wife Eleanor Wemyss, after whom it was originally called. It closed in the 1960s, and was then bought by David Greig, the butcher, whose emblem is the thistle, and who used it as a training college for a time; but it is now a private house.

In Victorian times there was also a brick kiln, and the old claypit is now a haven for foxes and badgers. Three ash trees in the meadow at Kiln House are said to mark the site of the kiln.

It is well-known that 'The Crazies', which stands opposite the Mission Hall, has the Georgian front of the old Henley Town Hall as a facade.

# Crowthorne

The village of Crowthorne owes its existence to the proximity of Wellington College and Broadmoor Hospital, round which the village has grown. Wellington College, built about 1859, is a national memorial to the Duke of Wellington, whose name and those of his generals find echoes in the titles of roads and inns of the neighbourhood, e.g. Duke's Ride and the Iron Duke.

Broadmoor Hospital was built about the same time on a high spur of the ground near Caesar's Camp. According to an old resident, the former inhabitants of the district were known as Broom Squires or Broom Dashers, whom he described as 'good-living people, having a semi-underground life, all of whom had an altar of sods with bits of glass stuck in the top'. Such were the 'Aborigines' of Crowthorne.

The Devil's Highway, a Roman road, crosses the village and two Roman milestones are in existence still. Although most buildings are modern, one Tudor cottage remains in the woods towards Owlsmoor. Crowthorne would appear to have wider boundaries than is expected, being bounded on one side by Owlsmoor, formerly called Newfoundland after an original squatter called New with numerous progeny; and on the other by California.

Crowthorne, once part of the Parish of Sandhurst, acquired its name because the postal authorities wished to give it a name to facilitate deliveries from Wokingham, instead of York Town, Surrey (which with Cambridge Town became known as Camberley). 'Albertonville' had been suggested in honour of the Prince Consort, but luckily the suggestion of 'Crowthorne', after some thorn trees at Brookers Corner, at the top of the village, was adopted. In Domesday Book, Crowthorne Farm appears as a separate holding in the Royal Forest of Windsor, although the present farm holdings do not date back to the days of William the Conqueror.

Three men who died in the Crimean War at the famous charge of the Light Brigade are buried in the old churchyard.

Since 1950, the population of Crowthorne has greatly increased, due partly to the setting up of the Road Research Laboratory and also to the building of quite a number of very attractive housing estates, and, as part of the evolution, some of the smaller shops in the High street have disappeared, to be replaced by supermarkets. The village also has an excellent community hall, the Morgan Centre, with good parking facilities, which houses many of the events and activities run by local organizations.

# Curridge 🌿

Woods with primroses, anemones and bluebells make Curridge a place of much natural beauty. Its history can be traced back to 953 AD, when King Edward granted Custeridge to his thane, Affwold.

The settlement is reputed to have been visited by King John, and it is known that Oliver Cromwell once stayed at the thatched farmhouse Lanolee Farm. More recent history is commemorated in names: Chapel Lane, where a small chapel, now a dwelling house, once existed; Kiln Terrace, a reminder of the brick making that was carried on until the last war; Church Lane, where services were held in one end of the school building until 1965, when the church was closed, and moved to the ecclesiastical parish of Hermitage.

The school has an interesting history. Much of Curridge land belonged to the Church Commissioners and, in the mid 19th century, just over one acre of land was bought by members of the Wasey family to build 'a school room and master's residence'. After their deaths the buildings and land were given to the Chieveley School Board in 1886, with the proviso that the vicar and his successors should have 'exclusive use of the school buildings for the whole of every Sunday, Christmas Day and Good Friday, and on Wednesday evenings and Friday evenings after five o'clock'.

The cartoonist H. M. Bateman once lived in the house still known as the Old Parsonage.

The W.I. hall is built on land for which they paid a peppercorn rent to the Church Commissioners, until members and other residents of Curridge raised enough money to buy the land.

Curridge covers a wide area, from the A34, with easy access to the M4, to the B3004 to Hermitage, so houses are scattered. There is only one shop, and Newbury is the main shopping centre.

The W.I. hall, with its attractive woodland setting, is the venue for meetings, and new residents are welcomed there by the W.I. and the Horticultural Society.

# Datchet 🌿

Datchet (or Daceta as it is named in the Domesday Book) still preserves its character as a village. To the south it is bounded by the Thames and to the north by the M4 motorway whilst the Queen Mother Reservoir lies to the east and the playing fields of Eton to the west. From early days the traffic from London came through Datchet via the London Road

*January day in Datchet.*

past the church, then across the Green to the Manor Hotel, down the High Street and over the old river bridge to Windsor. The Southern Railway line from Waterloo which cuts through the village originally had its terminus at Datchet until 1849 when the extension to Windsor across the Home Park was agreed to by Queen Victoria. In 1851 the two bridges, Victoria leading to Windsor, and Albert to Old Windsor, were built and the old bridge at the end of the High Street was taken down.

The noble spire of the church of St. Mary the Virgin dominates the village. Part of the present building dates from the 13th century but in 1857 it was largely rebuilt, and extended in 1864. Inside are various memorials to benefactors of the village and the churchyard contains interesting old headstones. Next door stands the Royal Stag originally the home of Robert Barker, printer to Elizabeth I. He bequeathed the revenue from five acres of land and his house to the village in 1644. The front of the building was added about 100 years ago but the wall alongside the churchyard is of Elizabethan structure. The charming interior contains old beams and antique furnishings.

On the other side of the Green stands St. Mary's C. of E. School which was founded in 1844 for the education of the poor. Between the shops and the post office there is an arched approach to a fine Hall built by George Scott and given by him to the Datchet W.I. On this side of the Green also there are the Manor cottages and the Manor Hotel, parts of which date from the 15th century. In 1742 the Datchet Manor was sold to the 2nd Duke of Montagu who also acquired the estate of Ditton Park (now the Admiralty Compass Observatory).

The High Street leading over the railway crossing to the Thames contains a number of Georgian houses terminating in the Post House, a charming Regency building. The river front is very pleasant with grassy slopes shaded by chestnut trees and presenting delightful views towards Windsor and downstream. We return to the village Green via Queen's Road and 'Mays' crossing to find on our right hand the 17th century Morning Star inn with its bricked-in window and the hardware shop which stands on the site of the blacksmith's forge.

On the Green opposite there is an oak tree planted by Lord Montagu of Beaulieu to commemorate the award to Datchet of the best kept village in Buckingham in 1966. The large spreading oak tree on the grass triangle near the Manor Hotel was planted in 1887 in honour of Queen Victoria's Jubilee. The market cross also there was erected by Mrs. Crake, a great benefactor to the village, for the Diamond Jubilee in 1897. On the main Green, rising from a bed of roses, is a splendid memorial inscribed with the names of the Datchet men who fell in the two World Wars.

Before 1900 much of the centre of the village was occupied by a large pool which overflowed when the river rose. In 1894 severe flooding was recorded and again in 1947 when the water level was over the top of the white posts which surround the Green and residents were supplied with food and a doctor by boat. Since then steps have been taken to prevent another such happening.

Datchet is fortunate in possessing a fine Recreation Ground situated along the Horton Road comprising playing fields, tennis courts and a small children's play area. It was obtained largely due to the efforts of Charles King, Chairman of the Parish Council at the time and it was opened by H.R.H. Princess Margaret in 1951. Later an imposing brick built village Hall was added together with an Old Folks Day centre and library.

Among famous people who have resided in Datchet are Sir William Herschel, the astronomer, William Corden, R.A., painter of scenes of the village, Watson Watt, the inventor of radar, Billy Cotton, Stanelli,

Gordon Harker, Donald Pleasance, Laura la Plante and Billie Whitelaw. The village is also a port of call in the well-known book of *Three Men in a Boat* by J. K. Jerome.

Today's residents include TV Sports Commentator Barry Davies and Giles Smith, TV Industrial Reporter. Datchet W.I. Hall is also the venue for a lively group of morris dancers who, with the members of the W.I., aim to preserve the traditions of our village.

# Earley

The name derives from Anglo-Saxon, Earn – eagle, and leah – a wood – Eagle wood.

Domesday mentions two main manors – Erlegh St Bartholomew, later known as Erlegh Court, and Erlegh St Nicholas, later Erlegh White Knights – so named because of chapels dedicated to these two Saints on the two manors. Neither had font nor bell, but a wooden cross erected in an enclosed space on which palms were hung on Palm Sunday.

The de Erleghs held the manors for some centuries; one John de Erlegh in 1292 was known as The White Knight – hence the re-naming of the manor. The leper hospital of Reading Abbey owned lands at Earley White Knights, the revenue of which was devoted to lepers.

Earley nowadays is not a village in the true sense of the word. It is an extended area of Reading with its boundary only two miles from the town centre. It covers an area of approximately 2000 acres and has a population of over 13,000, and has lost all traces of its ancient history. The size and population does not include that of the rapidly expanding area of Lower Earley which will eventually extend to the M4.

The old Dreadnought public house, once the only one in Earley, is used as a Sailing Club House by the University of Reading, who have also built a large Hall of Residence in Earley.

The Parish church of St Peter was completed in 1844. At this time, looking towards Wokingham, Hungerford Lodge could be seen and one or two cottages where Earley Station now stands, but for the rest it was open country.

The Manor of Maiden Erleigh was formed in the 14th century, and after many changes of ownership through the years, it was purchased in 1903 by the millionaire Solly Joel, well known in horse racing circles, who in fact had a race course on the Estate. He donated a piece of his land to the village to be used for sporting purposes, and this is well used to this day. It was opened in 1927 by the Duke of York (later King George VI) and is known as the Solly Joel Playing Field.

The ancient Estate of Bulmershe Court once belonged to the Abbey of Reading. In the eighteenth century it became the home of Henry Addington, first Viscount Sidmouth, Statesman and Prime Minister. The house has now been pulled down and Bulmershe Teacher Training College occupies the site. The excellent Bulmershe Girls' Choir is well known in the locality, and has made several broadcasts on the radio.

# Eastbury 🌿

Eastbury lies between Great Shefford and Lambourn, in the green and winding Lambourn valley. The stream runs between parallel roads, on either side of which are timber-framed, thatched and tiled roofed cottages and barns, plus larger houses of brick and flint, while footpaths lead up to and over the Berkshire Downs to the ancient Ridgeway on one side and to the Roman road, Ermin Street, on the other.

Eastbury is a fairly compact village, with most of the houses built along the river banks which in many places are planted with flowering shrubs and bulbs. The river rises in Lambourn and has the unusual feature of flowing in the summer and being dry for three miles or so for 3 or 4 months in autumn and winter. The stream is crossed by two road-bridges and three footbridges joining the two roads which traverse the village: Gumbletons, then Top Arch by Eastbury Manor, Church Bridge, somewhat wider than the other footbridges to accommodate the hand-cart hearse used in earlier days, leads from the Old Vicarage to the church of St. James the Greater, then Pigs Bridge, and lastly the stalwart road bridge, Bottom Arch. Nearby is Pigeon House, early 17th century, used in medieval times as a retreat for the Black Monks of Wallingford, where they hunted and fished, as portrayed on a fine carved arch in Lambourn church. Close to the Pigeon House is a fine octagonal dovecote, dated 1620, where beautifully fitted chalk blocks form nesting spaces for 999 pairs, and a self-propelled spiral stairway made egg-collecting easier. Unfortunately, after several changes of ownership and the dividing up of the Pigeon House fields and buildings, the dovecote is not so well cared for nowadays.

At the Lambourn end of the village is the splendid Manor, dating from before 1429, and added to over the centuries to form the gracious mellowed brick and stone building with gables and interesting clustered chimney stacks which we see today, backed by its cornfields and woodlands. A manor has stood there from the date of the Norman Conquest in 1066 (the date that everyone knows!) and must be mentioned in the Domesday Book.

The Church of St. James the Greater was designed by G. E. Street and built in 1851 at the instigation of Robert Millman, Rector of Lambourn. It is a flint and stone structure consisting of chancel and nave, with a very steeply pitched tiled roof and a small bellcote for two bells at the east end. Opposite the North door is the window Laurence Whistler engraved to celebrate the lives of the poet Edward Thomas, killed in action at Arras in 1917, and of his wife Helen, who lived in Eastbury for the last twelve years of her long life. The design shows chalk downland and woods, with the village of Steep in Hampshire, where the Thomas family lived for some years, and a thatched gamekeeper's cottage in Hodson Bottom, near Swindon, where the couple spent a short honeymoon. Across the landscape lines from several poems are engraved. Since his death the works of Edward Thomas have become more and more widely known and Helen's book *As it Was – World Without End* tells the poignant but triumphant story of their life together. The window, an idea of their younger daughter Myfanwy, who taught at Lambourn School for 21 years, retiring in 1975, was made possible by the generosity of nearly 700 people from all over the world and from all walks of life. It was dedicated in 1971, when Lord David Cecil and Professor R. George Thomas spoke of the poet and his wife and read from their works.

In the small square opposite the church stands the Prayer Cross of St. Antoline where, up to as late as the 19th century, itinerant preachers, trade union agents and others stood upon the steps to harangue and be heckled by those who came to listen. As far back as the 16th century processions took place to and from this Prayer Cross to the Cross standing before the church at Lambourn and to Wodebury Cross at Shefford Woodlands.

There are some interesting charities in Eastbury. In 1791 John Sarjent gave his garden and orchards to provide education for 25 poor children. In 1776 under an act for the enclosure of Eastbury, 10 acres of land in Sheep Down were allotted to the Lord of the Manor for raising furze or other fuel for the use of the poor. This charity is still known as 'Poor's Fuzz'. The land proved unusable and by order of the Charity Commissioners it was exchanged in 1911 for three acres in Eastbury on part of a larger field at Pound Farm. A trust financed by a former resident of Pigeon House provides homes known as The Hermitage for retired professional people.

As the average age of the population grew greater, the need for a school became less, and the village school was eventually closed, and the children in the village attend schools at Great Shefford, Lambourn and later Hungerford or Newbury. In the same way, with the popularity of road transport, the single track railway from Lambourn to Newbury was considered unnecessary and the line was closed and some of the track built on or incorporated into farmland.

One of the chief industries of the neighbourhood is the training of racehorses, and many famous trainers have their establishments at Lambourn and nearby.

Chalk-loving wild flowers abound in the woods and downland and some rare species have been found here. There are many beautiful walks, where the keen countrylover need hardly see a main road.

Like a number of villages these days, with the nearness of the M4 many of the cottages are bought and modernised by weekenders and commuters, and the quality of village life is very different from what it was even 25 years ago. But there are still several villagers who can recall with nostalgia the 'old days'.

# East Garston ✍

East Garston lies in a dip in the chalk downs of the Lambourn valley surrounded by farmland. It is in an area of outstanding natural beauty. The name, Esgar's Tun, has varied considerably over the ages and was pronounced Argasson, locally, until settling to its present form. In Saxon times the Esgar was the staller who looked after the king's horses. The Esgar fought on the side of Harold at the Battle of Hastings and his Tun was forfeited to a Norman lord. The village used to provide a knight and a vanguard when the king or his justices travelled through en route to Wales. There are still many horses in the village today including two racing establishments.

The river Lambourn rises from springs at Lambourn early in the year and the river bed dries between October and February. When it rises it has been known to flood the village road and planks were placed on bavins to ensure dry feet. At the turn of the century it also flooded into the cottages.

All Saints church, 1100 AD, cruciform in shape and built from flint and stone has Norman features. A carved south doorway in the 16th century porch, a blocked north door and fine pillar piscina. Before the Reformation the church was rich in furniture, vestments and ornaments but became so neglected that it required complete restoration between 1876-82. More recently in 1980 fund raising provided £10,000 necessary to repair the roof and the fabric of the building.

The 18th century manor house is next to the church and has a beautiful roof of patterned tiles. Goldhill House in the centre of the village was mentioned as far back as 1469 and was originally a farmhouse within the manor grounds and was granted to John of Estbury. The village also had two mills but the site of these is unknown.

In 1898 the railway came to the Lambourn valley and passed through East Garston. The line was closed in 1959 and bungalows now occupy the site of the station. The Society of Friends built a new meeting house on the site of the old one in 1979 and it is quite well attended by Friends travelling from nearby towns. The original building was used as an artist's studio before becoming the meeting house with an extension added. The village hall was once a chapel, bought and removed from another village and still used with extensions added.

The village still has a parish council, post office, shop, pub, village hall and social club. The school closed in the 1960s and the children are transported daily by coach to Hungerford and Great Shefford schools.

Since the forge closed many years ago, thatching is the only old craft left in the village and David Brown carries on in Great Shefford now in the tradition of his father who died in 1983. He is in great demand over a very wide area. During the past twenty years, newcomers have brought other crafts to the village such as pottery, painting and sculpture.

Disused farm buildings in the centre of the village have provided premises for an agricultural engineering business which is planning further expansion. One of the cottages was used for the filming of *Quiet Weekend* and others have been featured in women's periodicals. The cottages are in great demand as the M4 has put residents within easy daily travelling distance of London and Heathrow Airport.

With the decline of the bus service and the last bus passing through the village at 6.15 p.m., residents rely on their own transport and help those unable to get to the surgery in Lambourn. Realising the need of a convenient service to suit shoppers, Eastbury and East Garston W.I. were the instigators of a Wednesday bus which collects people from the four villages between Shefford and Wantage and allows one and a half hours shopping time in Wantage.

# Easthampstead

Although much of it has been enveloped by Bracknell New Town, and therefore it is no longer strictly a village, Easthampstead is an ancient parish. In the Domesday Book it is referred to as 'Lachinstede' which is of Saxon origin. By the beginning of the 13th century it had become Easthampstead. Roman remains have been found, to the south of the area, but Caesar's Camp, within that part – a fine place for dog-walking! – is misnamed, for this was the site of an Iron Age fort.

The Manor House in Easthampstead Park, on the Wokingham side of the parish, began life as a hunting lodge in Windsor Forest. This was incorporated in the old mansion, which was pulled down in about 1860. The present Victorian mansion, built shortly afterwards by the Marquis of Downshire, remained with that family until 1954, when it was sold to the Berkshire County Council and became first a teacher training college, and later a centre for further education. There is also now a secondary school in the grounds.

The Downshire family were great benefactors to the village. Lady Downshire was responsible for the complete rebuilding of the parish Church of St. Michael and St. Mary Magdalene, whose windows were designed by Sir Edward Burne Jones and executed by William Morris. The church stands on a small hill, and its high tower can be seen from quite a distance.

The parish originally extended further to the north, joining Warfield and Winkfield, but the creation of the new Parish of Bracknell in the 19th century separated and reduced all three.

The second Marquis of Downshire rebuilt eight cottages opposite the church for the poor of the village, parts of which were incorporated in the Infirmary which later became the Union Workhouse. Today this is Church Hill House Hospital, providing care for mentally and physically handicapped patients, most of them permanently residential.

Another interesting mansion is at South Hill Park, on the opposite side of the parish. The present Edwardian house, built by Lord Haversham, stands on the side of one built in 1760 by William Watts. During the Second World War it was taken over by the Royal Sea Bathing Hospital of Margate. After their departure it fell into neglect, and was rescued by the Ferranti Company, who rented it for their administrative department, from the New Town Development Corporation. Now it is the Arts Centre, and recently the ambitiously designed Wilde Theatre has been built alongside.

Although Easthampstead has many housing estates in its midst, some green areas remain, and it is still possible to find peace in the woods and fields on the outskirts.

# East Ilsley ✤

East Ilsley lies in a fold of the Downs, midway between Abingdon and Newbury. It is a village of great charm and antiquity; there was settlement here in Saxon times and probably earlier. The name Ilsley is derived from the Saxon 'Hilde - laeg', meaning battlefield.

The village is peaceful now, safely distanced since the by-pass came in 1963 from the heavy traffic thundering along the A34. Running across the top of the Downs north of the village is a road, unlike the A34, of peace and isolation, the Ridgeway, used as long ago as Neolithic times, over 4,000 years ago. Along it came traders, specialist craftsmen in due course such as bronze and iron smiths, and armies marching to battle, complete with war chariots in the Celtic period, from 500 BC. If we add the cattle and sheep which were moved along the Ridgeway, it must have been a lot busier than it is today. The movement of sheep has a direct connection with East Ilsley. As it was close to the Ridgeway, 'Market Ilsley', as it was once called, became the centre for sheep sales, and its great Sheep Fairs can be traced back to medieval times. The fairs received a charter from James I in the 17th century, and with the exception of Smithfield, Ilsley became the greatest sheep market in England. Many of the sheep were fattened for the London market. The fairs declined with the coming of modern transport, the last one being in 1934, but in 1975 the tradition was revived. A commemoration stone was set up on the site where the sheep were penned, and now a fair is held annually on the auction site, Pen Meadow. Instead of sheep selling, there are demonstrations of sheep-shearing and sheep dog skills, and craftsmen and women come from the surrounding district to show that English craft traditions are very much alive, even in the modern mechanised world. A copy of a tape-recording of inhabitants' memories of old Ilsley, made for this 1975 revival, is held at Reading Museum.

The training of racehorses is a notable feature of East Ilsley. There are three stables here, and the trainers are following a long tradition, as the Duke of Cumberland, brother of George II, had a stable at the foot of Gore Hill in the 18th century, and trained the famous *Eclipse* there.

East Ilsley used to be an important centre for the administration of law and order with a police station, complete with resident sergeant, cells, and a courtroom where local sessions were held. The station was pulled down in 1962, and replaced by the present Police House.

Though it no longer has its own rector and doctor, as it had up to the 1950s, East Ilsley is luckier than many villages. It has a generous provision of churches and inns, a primary school, a combined post office and grocery store, a new delicatessen (on the site of Dudden's old shop), and a saddler's shop with a long tradition. In 1956, Stan Ward succeeded Harry Pearce in the saddlery trade, and Harry had in turn succeeded his father. Stan Ward was a highly skilled craftsman whose leatherwork was in great demand over a wide area well beyond the village. Sadly, he died in 1984, and the future of the business is uncertain.

The three inns which remain of the thirteen or more which existed in Sheep Fair days provide welcome refreshment and entertainment for village folk and visitors.

Despite being proud of its historical traditions, the people of East Ilsley are not content merely to dwell in the past. There are several active societies catering for the present, and looking to the future too. One of these is the Conservation Society, inspired by European Conservation Year in 1970, which has performed sterling work in the village, especially by improving the pond (for which it won a County award). The 1977 Jubilee seat, shaded by the pretty Jubilee Maple tree, is almost continuously occupied in summer by picnic parties of all ages, who come to see and feed the large variety of water birds which the society has developed here. One of the longest established functions in the village is the Flower Show, founded in 1945, and held most years since then. There is a well-established football team, keep fit classes are currently being held, and in 1983, two village groups won awards in the Berkshire Community Services Village Enterprise Competition. One of these was for a plan to allow part of the school to be used as a Community Room, a most useful achievement, as the village had been without a hall for holding events since the demolition of its 'Old School' in 1968.

# Emmbrook

Emmbrook is to the west of Wokingham, and is, in fact, a part of the town, yet still retaining its community spirit. Until about 1964, it was only a small hamlet, but a great deal of development took place, a large comprehensive school was built and two primary schools.

Emmbrook W.I. was started in 1936 in a building which was erected in 1867, and was affectionately known as the 'Tin Hut'. The W.I. had a 25 year lease on the hall but, in 1976, with the help of the local council a management committee was formed and, with a considerable amount of voluntary help, a new hall was literally built around the old one, complete with new kitchens and cloakrooms. This has done wonders for the village community and, apart from the schools, is now very much the focal point of the village. A play group is held there daily, and some church services and Sunday school classes, though the congregation has grown so much that services are often held in the senior school.

The village's name is derived from the Emm Brook, which flows through the centre of the area to join the River Loddon. Recently the brook was polluted by effluent from a nearby factory, and many fish and wild life were killed. Happily, the problem was cleared, and the brook is now being re-stocked.

# Emmer Green 🍃

The name of the village is believed to derive from an old Saxon word Eamere meaning 'a lake beside a stream'. The once sizeable lake is now but a pond. The stream could be 'the swillies', which runs from the west side of the pond down to the river Thames.

Before piped water came to Emmer Green at the turn of the century, villagers relied upon the springs for their drinking water. One of these, Chalybete Spring in Surley Row, was reputed to have healing powers, especially for the eyes, and the water was regularly bottled and sold. Villagers drew water from the pump opposite the pond, and carried it home with the aid of the yoke.

The stone dragon over Emmer Green Post Office was originally over the blacksmith's shop on that site, and was made at Emmer Green Brick Works. The blacksmith's shop, in an ideal position for travellers to and from Reading, probably dated back to the 16th century, and undoubtedly was one of the busiest spots in the area before the advent of the motor car.

The early 16th century White Horse Inn has Elizabethan oak beams and floor boards. Until the 1920s groceries were sold over the counter and beer drawn from the barrel; skittles and quoits were the regular pastimes of the locals there of an evening, right up to the end of the First World War. In the late 1800s and early this century, firemen had their headquarters in the yard of the early 19th century Black Horse Inn opposite. Several residents still remember the firecart being pulled out by hand and, with much shouting and encouragement from the onlookers, charging off down the road.

Within living memory, it was the custom at a funeral for six pall-bearers to carry the coffin on their shoulders from Emmer Green all the way to St. Peter's Church, Caversham, with a change of pall-bearers halfway. Old survey maps show a right of way from the pond, across the fields to Bottle Cottage in Surley Row, then down Rotherfield Way. Fortunately for the pall-bearers the foundation stone of St. Barnabas Church was laid in 1924 and the finished church was consecrated five years later.

Though largely an agricultural area, a brick-kiln was built in about 1654 on land known as Homer's Field, then under Sonning Manor. The Brickwall cottages were originally offices and stables for the horses used on the brickfield.

During the last war the Reading archives were stored in underground caves in the area, as were the cardboard coffins ready for possible gas victims — praise be, they never needed to be used! The caves are very large, extending from the old brick-kiln, under Kiln Road, and beneath woods on the other side. They came into being when chalk was quarried for agricultural purposes.

Rosehill House, standing in 14 acres of ground, was once part of Caversham Manor, the first building being erected in 1791. Martin John Sutton, of Sutton's Seeds, lived there, the house then being called Kidmore Grange. In 1923 it was bought for the Oratory Preparatory School; then from the outbreak of the last war until 1958 it served as the Salvation Army Headquarters. The house has since been converted into flats and a housing estate built on the grounds.

St. Benet's Home, which was built and maintained by Dr. Powell of Derby Road in 1902, was a Church of England Home for young boys. They attended the local village school. This building has now been demolished and is the site of another sheltered housing complex.

There are a number of springs, now underground, in the area, and over the years swallow holes have appeared. In 1955 people noticed an unpleasant smell at a pond in Camp Wood. There was a sudden loud noise and the pond soaked away! But that was not all, for three hours later, with an explosive roar, four fully grown trees disappeared into the ground in a matter of seconds, sending up a great water spout. Sixty-five years before, near Brickwall House, locals had been enjoying themselves at one of the regular dances that were held in the small hall. They made their way home unaware how near they had been to tragedy. By the next morning the hall had disappeared into the ground!

Surley Row is a very ancient, narrow, winding road, along which are a number of interesting houses, including Caversham Hill, c.1810, the Tudor Old Grove House, and No. 46 Surley Row, which used to be the 18th century Gardeners' Arms. The garden of 164 Kidmore End Road appears to be a virtual treasure trove, having yielded, amongst other things, a 150 million year old Coxcomb Oyster, prehistoric hand axes, Roman and 16th century coins and medieval pottery.

Nowadays, only by a stretch of the imagination can Emmer Green be called a village, so linked up with Caversham and Reading has it become, though it is still only a few minutes walk out into the countryside.

# Enborne
# & Hamstead Marshall ஜ

Enborne, a rural and scattered village three miles from Newbury, has a 12th century church dedicated to St Michael and All Angels, built on land once owned by Romsey Abbey. It has a Saxon font with emblems of the Passion, a fresco painted by an Italian monk from Sandleford Priory, a bell cast in 1260 (making it one of the oldest in England), and in 1984 it was proved to have a very rare species of bat, which must be protected, in the belfry.

There is much history of battles fought in the area during the Civil War in 1643; in fact a part of the churchyard was used to bury some of the war dead.

There are two notable houses that have survived from an early period, namely, Wheatlands and Biggs Cottage which was built in 1540.

The Rector has recently compiled a history of the church and has found several instances of letters between the then rectors and Henry III and Edward III who were both in the habit of visiting the Earl Marshal at Hamstead Marshall Manor.

The Enborne river runs south of the district forming the county boundary between Berkshire and Hampshire. It crosses the Andover road at Wash Water, a place name derived from where sheep, being brought from the downs, were cleaned before going to Newbury market.

The Inner London Education Authority run a special boarding school for boys at Enborne Lodge, a large house that used to belong to the Valpy family.

After a lapse of many years, The Garden Society and Flower show has been revived in the summer of 1984.

The local inn is the Craven Arms.

Hamstead Marshall village was first mentioned in the Domesday Book, and named by Richard III who often visited the shooting lodge in the 700 acre park which was originally the home of the Earl Marshal.

The first Earl Craven was granted ownership of the estate in 1620 and it has remained in the family for 364 years, but owing to several lots of death duties and the tragic death of the 6th Earl in 1983, it has been sold to private buyers.

The church, dedicated to St Mary, on the west side of the park is interesting, it has an early English chancel arch, some box pews and traces of a rood screen. In 1983 two parishioners took time off from their profession as airline pilots to completely re-roof the church.

The village is bordered on the north by the river Kennet and the Kennet and Avon canal, which has become popular for barge trips. The old corn mill stands by the bridge which, along with Biggs Cottage in Enborne, is depicted on our Women's Institute banner.

The village is mainly agricultural and used to consist of many small farms. Now the farming is managed on a larger scale and the old farm houses have been modernised and occupied by non-farming people, also quite a number of new houses have been built causing a change in the life style of the village.

The Canine Defence League has a headquarters at Plumb Farm and there is an Agricultural Research Station. The local inn is the White Hart.

The school was disbanded in 1954 so the children now go to the C. of E. school at Enborne which celebrated its centenary in 1983. The old school house has been turned into the Village Hall and is of great benefit to the community.

# Englefield 🌿

Englefield lies six miles west of Reading with a population of 170. The single road through the village is known as The Street. The outlying farms and cottages make up a very small part of the 1,200 acre Englefield Estate, the hub of which is the mansion, the residence of Mr. W. Benyon, M.P., and his family. Previous occupants of Englefield House include the original owner, Sir Francis Englefield, the Earl of Essex, Sir Francis Walsingham and Sir Henry Benyon, Lord Lieutenant of Berkshire. Each played an important part in the history of Englefield.

The house overlooks the deer park with its head of 200 fallow deer and the now dry Cranemoor Lake. The water birds and wild life which once haunted the lake will hopefully return when water is restored in the near future. On summer weekends cricket matches are played in the park, which is also the scene of other activities such as Rolls Royce Rallies, pony jumping and equestrian events. The pleasure gardens with a wonderful display of rhododendrons and azaleas in the spring, are open to the public each Monday throughout the year from 10 a.m. until dusk, and on two Sundays in May when teas may be obtained in the Long Gallery.

The Church of St. Mark's rests in a well kept churchyard. The memorial on the left before entering the church is dedicated to the large number of children who died, and for 'merciful deliverances' during two measles epidemics in 1890 and 1893. The church contains some interesting relics. A stone figure of a knight and a wooden effigy of a lady are both 13th century, whilst the canopied memorial to Thomas Englefield is now used as a communion table.

The Church of England primary school of 1865 was saved from closure in the early 1970s by merging with children from Sulham and Tidmarsh school. There are approximately 70 pupils now from mostly outside the village. At one time, the numbers were as few as 17, but in the early part of the century 126 pupils were taught in the original small school. A scholar of that day tells of pupils being sent to look at the date inscribed on the wall of the cottage opposite the shop to see how many yards there are in a mile, namely 1760, the date the cottage was built.

There is no public house in the village but a thriving social club exists to satisfy the thirsts of the local population and those from outside the area. The club, built in 1880 was originally a reading room for men only. The football club had its beginnings here and the first minutes were read at the committee meeting in 1884. The social club, despite its Victorian exterior has been completely modernised inside and its members enjoy today's benefits.

The brick building, half way along the street, with its high gabled roof and wide doors, is the Old Fire Station. It once housed a powerful horse drawn steam engine, which is now with the Berkshire and Reading Fire Brigade and can be seen on special occasions at County Shows. The building is now being renovated to serve as a Community Centre for the village.

Adjacent to the Fire Station is the Estate Yard where most of the men of the village were once employed to maintain the Estate. Modern methods have caused the depletion in the numbers of workmen. Water is pumped from here to a reservoir serving the whole village. In the Blacksmith's shop some fine old engines are kept in tip top condition by the Thames Valley Steam Engine Society. They can be seen working each October when the sound of the old fair ground hurdy gurdies can be heard and the steam engines take to the road in full 'steam up'.

The people of Englefield were honoured and delighted to receive a visit from the Queen Mother during her 80th birthday year in 1980, and were also proud to win the Best Kept Village award in 1983.

# Eton Wick & Boveney

Eton Wick lies on the north bank of the Thames immediately west of that most famous of English public schools, Eton College. To the north west can be seen the cooling towers of Slough Trading Estate and to the south east the facade of historic Windsor Castle. The exact beginning of the village is not known, though by the early 13th century it was an established community known simply as The Wick; and archaeologists excavating in a field opposite the church in 1984 discovered Bronze age pottery, bones and flints and pinpointed a burial mound and long barrow, indicating occupation in the late Stone Age.

For at least seven centuries Eton Wick, in the County of Buckingham, was part of the parish of Eton. With the 1894 Civil Parishes Act Eton Town became an Urban District and the remainder became the civil parish of Eton Wick. Already, however, the village had spread beyond the parish boundary into Boveney, giving rise to a new community known as Boveney New Town though it was more than a mile from the tiny riverside village of Boveney. When Eton Wick & Boveney Women's Institute was formed in 1933 Eton Wick and Boveney New Town were still separate parishes though they shared the same churches, school and village hall. In 1934 both were taken into the Urban District of Eton and, except for ecclesiastical purposes, the remainder of Boveney was merged with Dorney Parish. It continues so today in Buckinghamshire while in 1974 Eton Wick and Eton Town were incorporated into the Royal Borough of Windsor and Maidenhead and transferred into Berkshire.

From its founding in 1440 the influence of Eton College in the village has been considerable. The Provost was Rector and College Chapel the parish church. The College was an important landowner and employer and, within living memory, boot and shoe making, tailoring and laundering were undertaken in many village homes. Today many village people work in the boys' houses, laboratories, playing fields and offices. In the past wives of College masters played a major role in running village welfare and social activities, but this link now seems largely to have been severed.

The oldest building in the village is Bell Farm House, built about 1360 and still has most of its original timber-frame walls. Four more timber-framed houses survive – Saddocks Farm, Crown Farm, Little Common Farm and Long Close. Wheatbutts Cottage and the Three Horseshoes Public House were built in the 18th century and many rows of 19th century cottages still stand.

The foundation stone of the Church of St John the Baptist was laid in August 1866 by Provost Goodford. Prior to this a room of the village school was licensed to hold services. The site for the new church, plus £100, was donated by Queen Victoria. The Methodist Chapel was built in Boveney New Town in 1886, with money raised from subscriptions, under the inspiration of Mrs. Tough, a formidable lady who had great influence in the village. In 1964 the Roman Catholic Church of St. Gilbert was built opposite the old recreation ground.

The first school was built in 1840 on a site now occupied by the Post Office shop, but by 1880 the schoolroom was so overcrowded as to be 'unwholesome' and the present school was built in 1888 on land given by the Crown, on which Lammas rights were relinquished. The school was enlarged in 1958 and again in 1965.

The Village Hall was given to the inhabitants of Eton Wick and Boveney in 1906 by former Eton College housemaster Edward Littleton Vaughan – a great benefactor to the village who died in 1940. His widow, on her death in 1951, bequeathed a stained glass window in the village church in memory of her husband.

An important feature of Eton Wick is its Commons and Lammas Lands, the rights of which have been jealously guarded over the years. The term 'lammas' usually applied to meadows used as common pasture after the hay was cut, but here it also embraced the open fields over which the village hayward grazed the horses and cattle after Lammas Day or as soon as harvest had been gathered. In so many parishes these common lands were lost through enclosure, but in the 19th century Eton College as tithe owners, and the Crown, supported the villagers and commoners of Eton Wick in their opposition to the Inclosure Bill which John Penn, Lord of the Manor of Eton and of Stoke Poges, tried to push through Parliament. The defeat of the Bill in 1826, celebrated by the town and village with bonfires and feasting, has enabled farming to survive in Eton Wick.

It is interesting to note that when some lammas land was sold in the 19th century to the GWR for the Slough-Windsor branch line, the money paid as compensation for loss of lammas rights was used to buy the old Recreation Ground for the villagers. However, confirmation of the rules and regulations of the Commons and Lammas Lands at the Manor Court held in Eton College Hall in 1948 made it impossible to take such land for building. Lammas rights could not be extinguished, but transferred from land needed for development to other land in the village.

In 1965 the Commons and Lammas lands were registered under the Commons Registration Act and this should mean that only by another Act of Parliament can the land be released for building. Further large scale building developments should now be impossible in Eton Wick and the village should be able to retain its rural atmosphere and privacy, combining the pleasures of village life with the convenience of its proximity to London and Heathrow Airport and to the employment and shopping facilities of the large towns surrounding it.

# Fifield 🦢

Fifield is a small village or hamlet about a mile south of the A308. It is built around a triangle (known to locals as 'the circle') of three roads; Fifield Road, Forest Green Road and Coningsby Lane, with a short 'leg' in each direction before the junction of the roads, according to the signs, belonging to Fifield. Although small, Fifield is an old village being recorded in 1608 as consisting of 12 acres.

Opposite Coningsby Lane is the Old Cottage which dates back to the

17th century, and next to the cottage is Fifield Chapel, a wooden building. The visitor should take a good look at the chapel before turning into Coningsby Lane. This is a narrow lane, much favoured by walkers and their dogs, and horse riders.

Grove Farm House is where, in 1867, the Fifield Village Mission was founded by Thomas Reynolds, the owner of Grove Farm. At first the mission was held in a barn, but later a wooden chapel was built. A later owner of Grove Farm preferred its room to its company so in 1897 the chapel was moved on rollers to its present site. Naturally, everyone turned out to watch this extraordinary feat. Mr. Nathanial Micklem of Fifield House paid for the removal.

All the farm land on the right of Coningsby Lane belongs to Coningsby Farm – the farmhouse being opposite Yew Tree Cottage. The farm land on the left belongs either to Grove Farm or, further on, to Ledgers Farm, the farm house of which is in Forest Green Road. There is little of Fifield to the right other than the Horse Rangers' base, from which come some of the horses often met in Coningsby Lane.

On the corner of the Fifield and Forest Green Roads stands the Braywood Memorial Hall built in memory of those killed in the Great War. Captain Brittain at that time lived opposite at Fifield House and he played a large part in the building of the Hall. Until recently, the owner of Fifield House was always a Hall Trustee. There has been a Fifield House since before 1591 when 'William Norreys, Black Rod of the Order of the Garter and Comptroller of Works at Windsor castle, died, aged 68, at his home, the House of Fifield'. It is believed that the present Fifield House is not built on the site of the original house.

Travelling along the Fifield Road, back towards Fifield Chapel, the visitor will pass (or stop and visit) the White Hart, one of Fifield's two public houses. This is quite an old house, which has recently been tastefully extended. Next to the White Hart are some turn of the century cottages and then comes the driveway to Deep Meadows. This is an old cottage, much improved and extended, where 'Teasy Weasy' (Raymond, the hairdresser) lived for many years until he recently moved to Pinkneys Green. The houses on the other side of Fifield Road from Fifield House to the Hare and Hounds (the village's other pub) are fairly modern and include the post-war Council estate of Meadow Way. The Hare and Hounds is quite old and has been extended and modernised, but the extension is at the back and does not spoil the look of the pub.

On the left of Fifield Road, after passing the entrance to Deep Meadows, there is a modern estate with the two village shops (there were no shops in Fifield until 1955) and then the row of pre-war Council houses. Opposite the Hare and Hounds is Fairview Cottage, once two cottages belonging to the New Lodge Estate which has, under the creepers, the Van De Weyer crest. Back in the early 1950s, Diana Dors and her then husband, Dennis Hamilton, were frequent visitors here. A few more yards and the visitor is back at the start of Coningsby Lane and has walked (or driven), as do many of the villagers on a fine Sunday afternoon, 'round the circle'.

# Finchampstead

The village is blessed with distinct traces of its early history – part of the Roman road from London to Bath, via Silchester (Calleva Atrebatum), runs right through the parish, marked on the map as the Devil's Highway.

Entering the parish as Roman Ride, it may still be traced past the Queen's Oak, to the left of White Horse Lane, through Webb's Farm fields, on to West Court built on the road itself, then across Arborfield Road. In 1841 a Roman milestone was discovered in Six Acres field and removed to the garden of Bannisters.

Some walls and the very fine font of St. James's Church are the original, possibly Saxon. An oak tree facing the churchyard entrance was planted on June 21st, 1877, commemorating Queen Victoria's Golden Jubilee.

The original manor probably stood on Church Hill, divided, about 1290, into the east and west moieties of the Manor of Finchampstead. Sir William Banastre left the manor and advowson of the church between his two daughters, East and West Courts becoming their respective homes.

A certain Banastre apparently betrayed Sir Henry Stafford, Duke of Buckingham, to his death in 1483. The present house, Bannisters, was built in Charles II's reign on the site of an older property.

The Manor of Finchamestede Mill, in Domesday Book, yielded to the King 7s. 6d. The well-preserved, very old 'Thatched Cottage', now a private house, was once the smithy, reputedly haunted.

In 1858 Mr John Walters of Bearwood, owner of East Court for 45 years, provided the first school buildings. In 1971 Mr W. R. van Straubenzee, MBE, MP, opened the latest extension, paid for in part by people of the parish. John Walters was also responsible for the Sequoia Pine-lined road over the Ridges to Wellington College Station, opened to the public in 1863.

The Ridges, National Trust property since 1913, command a view over the Blackwater Valley to Hindhead, south-west to Cottingham

FINCHAMPSTEAD - *The church in snow.*

Clump, and west to Inkpen Beacon, now somewhat obsured by tree growth. To these Ridges Henry VII is said to have ridden with Prince Arthur, to meet Katharine of Aragon after her arrival in England, as the Prince's bride. Spanish custom forbade a bride to be seen by the groom till after the marriage ceremony, but Katharine lifted her veil to face Arthur. We can picture the stately procession, next day, to Chertsey; little did that young Spanish girl know what lay ahead of her during her eventful and tragic life in England.

Dozell's well, on Fleet Hill, in the 10th and 11th centuries, was said to have possessed marvellous curative properties, especially for eye diseases. It was described in the *Anglo Saxon Chronicle* as 'boiling up with streams of blood, whose waters made red all others where they came, to the great amazement of the beholders...' This occurrence was regarded as a sign of impending national calamity. The well was accidentally distroyed in 1872, by deepening of the ditch, but there is still a constant trickle of water on the spot. An adjacent property is named Constant Spring.

In the village live the Misses Bramwell-Booth, daughters of the founder of the Salvation Army. Catherine, the eldest daughter, reached her 100th birthday in 1983, and two seats to commemorate both her centenary as well as that of Lady Lidell were presented by the village and are sited for weary walkers near the War Memorial Cross, close to the Finchampstead end of Wellingtonia Avenue.

The village has an active social life, the Finchampstead Society organising local events, several of which are held in the Memorial Hall, built in 1960. Adjacent to the Hall is a fine park and sports field.

An annual fete is held here, which is popular with everyone in the village as well as countless people from the surrounding towns and villages who enjoy the natural amenities of Finchampstead.

# Frogmore Green 🐸

Frogmore Green W.I. serves the area of Frogmore and Darby Green. The village stands on the south bank of the River Blackwater, which divides it from Berkshire and Surrey on the north. Until quite recently a deep ford made a natural barrier, except for a small footbridge. Very often floods covered the fields, and hundreds of yards of the road.

An ancient road from Yateley connects the two parts of the village, although Darby Green seems to be the older part, being marked in the 17th century registers, and some 16th century timber and brick houses still remain.

The area was settled in Saxon days along the fertile river valley, although remains of Stone Age and Bronze Age man have also been found.

On our doorstep, to the south, we have the beautiful Yateley Common, where there are hundreds of acres of heather, gorse, broom, wild flowers and wild life; it has been an ideal setting for a Sunday afternoon walk for many a year, and local residents exercise their dogs and horses there daily.

The old road, now Darby Green Road and Rosemary Lane, once used by stage coaches, presently serves a busy community of over 3,000 with a bus service from Reading.

Frogmore Park was once the home of Sir Almeric Fitzroy, a well-known Victorian, at one time clerk of the Privy Council under Queen Victoria, King Edward VII and King George V. A later occupant was Sir Charles Denniston-Burney who was concerned in the design of the famous airship R. 100, which was seen to do a 'dip of honour' over the house. The popular novel *The Woman in White* by Wilkie Collins, was also set in Frogmore Park.

In the last 20 years the area has been built up considerably with housing developments, schools and shops filling the once open spaces.

Originally the community was served by the C. of E. school at Hawley, but today there are infant, primary and comprehensive schools in Frogmore, the latter school now used also as a Community Centre, providing a much-needed service, catering for all tastes and all age groups.

The church of St. Barnabas was started by Dr. John Mills around 1883, and was first established in the taproom of the disused Yew Tree inn. This was a little beer house whose reputation had gone down and was threatened by closure when the brewers hurriedly built on a taproom to try to save it. However, the licence was withdrawn, and it closed. The taproom juts out at the side of the old building.

The small St. Barnabas church in Darby Green Road was built in 1901 on a site close to the Yew Tree Inn, and has since been rebuilt, modernised and improved as necessary; but the community has now outgrown the little corrugated church building and today uses the drama hall of the Comprehensive School for its main meetings and Sunday services.

In the garden of the Yew Tree inn still stands the famous yew tree where a highwayman, Parson Darby, was once hanged, and left hanging as a stern warning to those entering Yateley. Children today still talk of the ghost that haunts this dark creepy lane.

Although the Yew Tree inn has long been closed, the Greyhound (renamed Spennys in August, 1984) and the Bell flourish.

On Frogmore Green is the Darby Green and Frogmore Social Hall. A magnificent tribute to the local inhabitants who raised funds and built the hall themselves. The hall is in constant daily use by various organisations and clubs, and its value to the community cannot be estimated.

# Grazeley Village ❧

Grazeley Village was part of the Kingdom of Wessex in the time of King Arthur. In 1086 William the Conqueror held Hartley Dummer, and early history from then centres on three Manors in Hartley, Diddenham and Grazeley, which was variously spelt Greyshull and Griesley, and formed part of the Manor of Sulhamstead Abbots. In the 13th century, the Manor of Grazeley came into the possession of Reading Abbey and a Luke de Grazeley also held land. The rent in 1539 was £9.15s.10d. per annum and in 1541 when the land was granted to Sir John Williams, the rent due to the Crown as 19s.11½d.

In 1525 during the reign of Henry VIII, a Samuel Woodcock lived at Moor Place Hartley, and Woodcock Lane exists to this day. Samuel Woodcock's daughter, Mary Spiers, left money to enable local children to be taught to read the Holy Bible and the school still benefits from the bequest. In 1834 a Charity School was built beyond Gravelly Bridge, as a result of a sermon preached by the Reverend G. Hume, to carry out the terms of Mary Spiers' will. The present Parochial Church School was built by Mr Merry of Highlands in 1860 to replace the original and also endowed by him to provide twenty boys with boots and twenty girls with cloaks, the buttons being marked 'G.S.'. Money was also provided by Mr Merry for a Nursing Trust.

The New Parish of Grazeley was established in 1860, due to the efforts again of the Reverend G. Hume of Shinfield who was concerned at the long distances his parishioners had to travel to his church in Shinfield. With local help, particularly that of Mr Merry, he raised the necessary funds to build Holy Trinity Church. Mr B. Ferry, a famous church architect, was engaged in 1849 and the completed flintstone church was consecrated by Samuel Wilberforce, Bishop of Oxford, on 18 September 1850. The east window, by the firm of O'Connor, showing the crucifixion and the four evangelists, was dedicated to the memory of the Reverend Hume, who died in 1845. This window is mentioned in the late John Betjeman's *Berkshire Architectural Guide*.

Many inhabitants still remember the village pump, the hump-backed Gravelly Bridge in Mereoak Lane, now the busy Mortimer Road, the weekly visits of Mr Double to shoe horses and hearing of the Workhouse in Great Lea. Also remembered was a successful Grazeley Ladies Cricket XI playing in their long skirts and straw boaters.

GRAZELEY VILLAGE. " a successful Grazeley Ladies Cricket XI."

Edward VII acquired Hartley Court sometime during the late 1890s or early 1900s and it is remembered that one of his favourites, to whom he granted the title of Lady de Bath, better known as Lillie Langtry or the Jersey Lily, the actress, lived in Hartley Court for some years before her death.

Mary Mitford, author of *Our Village* whose father bought Grazeley Court, after winning £20,000 in the Irish Sweepstake, wrote 'wandered down a winding lane amidst green meadows, all alive with cattle, sheep and beautiful lambs in the spring'. Grazeley Court was rebuilt by Dr. Mitford, renamed Bertram House and is now sadly demolished, but Mary Mitford could still take her long walks today and see and write about these features, even perhaps, come across the brown snakes which startled her.

The Village lies south of Reading and junction 11 of the M4 and may be drastically changed in the future, with the prospect of a mini-town to be built within the parish boundaries.

# Great Shefford

Mentioned in the Domesday Book, Great Shefford could still be called a downland parish area, but has changed greatly since 1900, when the Marquis of Downshire – an absentee landlord – owned the greater part of the village, and most of the land. The village community which at that time was largely orientated toward agriculture, and with a strong Methodist tradition, has changed to commuting business people of many types – and the chapels have closed.

The church also was strong, and the rector lived in the biggest house, surrounded by a substantial area of glebe land. He now lives at Wickham, and cares for four parishes.

The Marquis of Downshire lived at Hillsborough House, County Down, at present the residence of the Governor of Northern Ireland. The Marquis also owned the Berkshire house and estate of Easthampstead Park, of late years a Berkshire college. The family parted from Shefford in 1905 after a century as Lords of the Manor. Previously this position was held by the Browne family, and a tablet to Sir George Browne in St. Mary's Church is dated 1673.

All these changes have accelerated since 1971 because Junction 14 of the M4 is just two miles to the south of the village. Much building development in the main village area caters for the new population.

The parish is in lovely country with two main hamlets round the central village ... East Shefford and Shefford Woodlands. The Lambourn stream, with useful trout fishing, flows between chalk hills with

*Little or East SHEFFORD. Church of St. Mary.*

a clay cap. Although the heyday of the grey partridge went with the red clovers, roots and grasses of the pre-1939 days, there is good pheasant and other mixed shooting.

Along the valley from West or Great Shefford is East, or Little Shefford, originally a separate parish, but now joined both civilly and ecclesiastically. Down in the water meadows is the redundant church of St. Thomas. The walls are of early Norman date, and hold splendid tombs of the Fettiplace family from the 15th and 16th centuries. Nearby an Anglo Saxon burial ground was found when excavating for the now defunct Newbury to Lambourn Railway. The modern church of Holy Innocents, built around 1870, was totally demolished some 12 years ago; since then, the parish church of St. Mary's suffices.

Southwards up the hill from Shefford village is found the east/west Roman road known as Ermin Street, and on it the hamlet of Shefford Woodlands – residences, farmhouses, a small church and a pub, with woodland bordering the modern motorway. The church of St. Stephen contains oak panels and carving, mostly done in the early half of the century by Arnold Burmester. It was enlarged into the present church from a previous Methodist chapel in 1911.

The population of Shefford Woodlands in 1900 was almost certainly greater than it is today. Noticeable differences would be the narrow roads with banks and a hedge on top, so that heavy snow would isolate the community for weeks on end. There was no electricity, telephone or water supply. The only clean water available was from the deep chain-and-bucket wells of the farmhouses which supplied drinking water. All other water – for the people and animals – relied on rainwater tanks. In dry seasons the farmers ran a service of water carts to Shefford, where water was dipped from the ford – a crossing of the Lambourn stream near the Swan Inn. Just about 100 years ago one of the boys ferrying an empty water cart to Shefford hit the roadside bank as he went down the hill. The cart tipped over, breaking the shafts, and the horse ran home to Templars Farm. After considerable search for the boy, someone at last went to examine the water cart, and a small voice from inside called 'I be in here!' Relief – and, no doubt, some laughter! About the same date a toddler of the Allen family, out in the field with other families and children harvest working, as usual, wandered into the corn on Fishers Farm, and was not missed until too late in the evening. Unhappily he died of exposure.

# Greenham 🐚

Little sign remains of Greenham's 'village' given to the Knights Hospitallers during the reign of Henry II; nevertheless it is a large parish of much interest, past and present. The rivers Kennet and Enborne form natural boundaries with much of Newbury's Wharf included, where once stood in Stephen's reign (12th century) the castle of Newbury of which remains no trace except that it features in the Borough's Coat of Arms. Also here stood the Greenham Preceptory of the Order of St. John of Jerusalem built by the Knights Hospitallers.

Nearby Greenham Mills, the 'first true cloth factory in England with 200 looms and employing 1,000 men, women and children' was built by Jack of Newbury, alias John Winchcombe, at the beginning of the 16th century. It was here that one John Coxeter accepted a wager of a thousand guineas from Sir John Throckmorton that 'at eight o'clock in the evening of the 25th June 1811, Sir John would sit down to dinner in a well-woven, properly made coat' from wool shorn at 5 o'clock that morning. Sir John brought to Greenham his shepherd and two sheep by daybreak; the coat was completed with more than two hours to spare. The now famous 'Newbury Coat' is in the care of the National Trust at Coughton Court, Warwickshire.

Newbury's famous race-course is in Greenham parish; a magnificent avenue of poplars leading the way to it through the serenity of Stroud Green with, on two sides, attractive houses and cottages of character, old and new. A Samian (Roman) vase, coins and pottery of the second and third centuries have been found here.

Up the steep hill, the Parish Church of Saint Mary, built in 1875 to replace a much older church, has a 'Jesse' window made in 1618 of Flemish glass; the interior wall and roof paintings are also of special attraction.

Greenham Lodge, (built also in 1875) was the home of the Lord of the Manor, Mr L. H. Baxendale; Mrs Baxendale was Greenham W.I.'s first President; her husband presented a plot of ground for a meeting place to be built – fondly called The Hut where now a charming bungalow stands. During the war, Greenham Lodge was occupied by the evacuated Jewish Carmel College, now at Wallingford. The house is now in the hands of American servicemen.

The ancient earthworks, Bury's Bank, lie today beneath several feet of concrete runway, but much still remains graced with lovely wood-lands, homes and gardens and the fine golf course. Greenham Common, within steep walking distance of Newbury, was a favoured place for picnics, walking, horseriding, so it was a sad day in 1940 when an airfield swallowed up most of it as a base for American Gliders; reconstructed in 1954 to a N.A.T.O. airbase and today, American Cruise Missiles are based there.

Also on high ground is Sandleford Priory, founded c. 1200 for 40 enclosed nuns but was occupied only by three Agustin Canons without Abbot or Prior and there followed a period of disrepute.

In the latter half of the 18th century the Priory was the country house of Mrs. Montague, the centre of literary society and founder of the Blue-Stocking Club; guests at her frequent parties included Dr. Samuel Johnson, Oliver Goldsmith, Burke, Dr. Stillingfleet, whose odd attire, it is believed, prompted the name Blue-Stocking. Also, among many others, would be Sir Joshua Reynolds who painted the lady's portrait. The extensive gardens were set out by Capability Brown and are still very beautiful today.

The name Greenham is derived from the Anglo-Saxon 'Green Meadows'. Not many years ago the steep hillside overlooking the race-course was just this; now a vast estate of modern dwellings where all roads have been named after famous race-courses – Windsor Rise; Ascot Close; Aintree Close ... A large area, however, has been acquired by the Nature Conservation Trust and much of Greenham's natural beauty will be preserved.

# Hampstead Norreys 🦋

In a green hollow of the Berkshire Downs lies the village of Hampstead Norreys, with its ancient church, Manor farm, old cottages and a few modern houses filling odd corners.

A pre-Roman trackway, the lower Icknield Way, skirts the western side of the village on its way to join the Ridgeway near Compton. Perhaps the earthworks immediately south of the church, concealed in woodland and covered in bluebells and primroses in spring, belong to that time also. There amongst the trees is a small steep-sided circular mound, perhaps either a miniature motte or a tumulus of considerable size.

Recorded in Domesday Book, by the 13th century the village was Hamstede-Sifrewast; by 1367 it had become Hampstead Ferrers, eventually coming into the great estates of Sir John Norreys of Yattendon in 1450, thereafter being Hampstead Norris or Norreys.

The church stands back at an angle from the village street, next to the Manor House, a stretch of grass edged with lime trees in front of the building being part of the old village green. The church is a simple building with a massive flint tower, Norman doorways and a fine Jacobean roof to the nave. There is in the churchyard an extraordinary tomb of the Lowsley family, a stepped pyramid of cast iron, made at Bucklebury Foundry in 1855 from disused farm implements.

The railway came to Hampstead in 1882 as part of the Didcot, Newbury and Southampton Railway and disappeared again in 1964, leaving a track now clothed in shrubs and wild flowers, haunt of many wild birds, butterflies and the occasional fox, nowadays a popular walkway.

The river Pang, a winterbourne tributary of the Thames winds its way through the village, alongside Water Street, through gardens and orchards towards Bucklebury. Sadly, nowadays the amount of flow is diminished as a result of water being pumped from the underground 'aquifers' to Didcot and London, but in most years there is some water, with attendant moorhens and the occasional wild duck.

During the Second World War, an airfield was constructed on the top of Folly Hill, originally as a satellite aerodrome for Harwell. Here Wellington Bombers were first based, and later wooden-constructed Albermarles and Horsa gliders left on D-Day landings. Later still the Admiralty claimed the airfield as an ammunition dump, but today, where formerly some 500 personnel lived and worked a large pig-farming unit exists.

Some of the older villagers can remember using the Parish well, one of the few remaining in Berkshire, given to the village by Harry Weber of Hawkridge (near Frilsham), in 1903. This stands under a tiled roof, surrounded by wooden palings, with heavy iron machinery still intact for raising water, and with stone horse troughs, now filled with flowers in summer.

Today Hampstead Norreys is a flourishing rural community still, fortunate in having a working farm at its centre; two village pubs, a village shop and an expanding village school – a very pleasant place in which to live.

# Hare Hatch ❧

Visitors to this part of Berkshire often remark at the number of place names in the locality which include the word 'bear'. Many people are under the impression that our woods were at one time full of wild bears or that there is a connection with the bear baiting which was known to take place in Maidenhead Thicket.

A study of older maps reveals that during the Napoleonic wars and in the period shortly after, many place names or at least the spelling of them, was altered. At about this time 'bare' became 'bear'. It was the Saxons whose farming method was to cut down and burn the woodland, and the crop planted on the bare ley became known as barley and was used to make their beer and feed pigs. The sense of this can be demonstrated today; barley grown on the site of a wood fire is better than the surrounding crop.

These bares, the cleared woodland, were sometimes named after their owners, hence Billings Bare, now spelt Billingbear.

The bare in which Bear Place is built has an unusually shaped edge to the wood above which has remained for centuries. Bear Ash was probably named after a large leafless or bare ash and there are still one or two giant sized very old ash trees nearby.

Bears Corner is an exception to the general rule as its proper name is A'Bears Corner, called after the Norman family of that name who were the owners. The last of the A'Bears is said to have died in Australia earlier this century but a relative still lives in Bix.

# Hawley ❧

In the centre of the bridge, over the river Blackwater, the boundaries of three counties meet; Berkshire, Surrey, and to the south Hampshire, in which lies the parish of Hawley, (in the old records it is spelt Halle). Formerly an outer tything of Yateley, it was just a collection of small farms and cottages reached by gravel tracks and surrounded by vast open desolate stretches of heather-covered commonland, or great wooded areas – part of the Forest of Windsor.

Sir Francis Dashwood, notorious politician and statesman of the 1740s and founder member of the Hell Fire Club, stabled his many racehorses at Hawley House and used the house as a resting place when he was on one of his wild racing sprees. The clock on the stable-block, which is still in perfect working order, is dated 1743. At the turn of this century Field Marshal Sir Linthorn Simmonds resided in this house. He had had a brilliant millitary career and was 'a real Christian gentleman'. He helped with the arrangements to bring the ex-Empress Eugenie of France to come and live nearby. They were great friends and the Empress kindly allowed the villagers to hold their Horticultural Shows in the grounds of Farnborough Hill. Few people know that in 1922 Princess Mary and her husband Viscount Lascelles spent a fortnight of their honeymoon in Hawley, at the home of Lord Revelstoke.

Another resident was Admiral Sir Charles Denniston Burney, who invented the paravane (a device for protecting ships against mines) which brought him a great fortune. He also helped design the airships R100 and R101.

By far the oldest part of Hawley parish is the village of Blackwater. At one time it was called Duddas brook, the explanation being that 'dhu' means black, 'dwr' is water. The Saxons would not doubt have spoken these words phonetically and they would have become Dudda – Blackwater.

For centuries the famous Blackwater Cattle Fair was held annually in November on the wide open spaces of commonland around the great cross-roads. It was listed in Old Moore's Almanac as the largest cattle-fair in the south of England. Horses would be brought up from the New Forest, with them came the blacksmiths with their bags of shoes and anvils. Some of the cattle were driven hundreds of miles from Wales and the West Country, moving about ten miles a day. At the fair travelling musicians supplied the entertainment, while cheap-jacks and gypsies sold their wares. After two days of buying and selling came riotous jollification at the Pleasure Fair, the stalls and booths being set out along the roadside.

It seems that Blackwater has always been well provided with drinking places, being situated on the highroad from London to Exeter. It boasted two ale-houses and three large coaching inns in days gone by, welcome havens where passengers could rest while the horses were changed. Travelling was a perilous experience and there was need of the formidable blunderbuss carried by the guard, as highwaymen and robbers roaming the wild desolate heathland often relieved the passengers of their money and jewellery. In 1746 a reward of £200 was offered for the capture of a highwayman who held up and robbed a mail-coach at Blackwater.

The coming of the railway in 1849 opened up a whole new way of life and before the Great War there was a staff of fourteen men and a boy at

Blackwater so it must have been a very busy station.

Over one hundred years ago Hawley contained many elegant houses set in beautiful grounds. The pine filled healthy air attracted people to settle in the area and the village folk were employed in the stables, gardens and in domestic service; the church was well supported and in the local school a very high standard was always found when H. M. Inspector made his annual visit to examine the children in all subjects – indeed in 1895 Hawley was the first school in the locality *not* to be inspected, yet full grants were given. The following words penned in 1894 are as appropriate today as they have been throughout the years, 'the popularity of Hawley School continues to grow in favour, not only with parents in this parish but with our neighbours also.

Inevitably the village grew in size as the years passed by, and since the Second World War the London overspill has greatly increased the population and diminished the fields and open spaces. Due to many residents having connections with the military establishments nearby we now have a 'moving population' – people come and people go, but Hawley goes on for ever.

# Hermitage & Oare

Although only three miles from the M4, Hermitage is surrounded by delightful woodland walks, most of the land belonging to the Palmer Trust or the English Forestry Association, and lucky walkers may catch a glimpse of the shy muntjac deer. A stroll to the ancient earthworks of Grimsbury Castle with an 18th century battlemented tower which is still inhabited, is a faviourite pastime.

Being on a bus route to both Newbury and Reading, the village has lost some of its shops, but is well served by a sub post office and a butcher, as well as three thriving inns. A fourth one is now a private residence, but used to cater mainly for the workers of Pinewood Brickworks which closed in 1967, the last in the area to cease working.

The church was built in 1835 by the vicar of Hampstead Norreys who was the personal chaplain to Queen Adelaide, the wife of William IV. She often visited the area and took a great interest in the building of the church and as well as contributing to the over-all cost, she presented it with a set of silver communion plate.

An old school building was purchased by a group of residents in 1962 and was rebuilt to form a Village Hall which is in constant demand for all the local organisations and children's groups, as well as outside functions.

The novelist D. H. Lawrence was probably Hermitage's most famous resident, living and writing for a time in a farm cottage. Devotees from home and abroad occasionally arrive on its doorstep asking to be shown the room that he worked in.

The presence of a hermit living in woods near a well which was said to have curative properties is reputed to have given the village its name.

'A Victorian gem set in the Berkshire countryside' was how John Betjeman described the little church at Oare, and the hamlet has probably changed little since St. Bartholemew's was built.

Now with only one farm and a handful of private residences, the single winding lane is off the beaten track, and only the hum of traffic from the hidden motorway reminds those who reach it from across the footpaths from Hermitage that civilisation is not far away.

King Edgar gave Orha to the great Abbey of Abingdon in 968 AD and it is said that a Priory was built there as a resting place for travellers from Abingdon to Winchester. Certainly there is a pond in what is called Chapel Meadow, where it is reputed that carp for the monks were kept.

# Holyport 🦢

Situated south of the M4 on the Maidenhead to Ascot Road, Holyport is an attractive hamlet whose centre and principle feature is its extensive green. Rumour has it that the name Holyport was derived from the fact that groups of religious people stopped regularly at one of the local farms en route to London.

It is believed that there has been a settlement in the area since Roman times and Roman artifacts were found during the building of the M4. There is also evidence of Roman roads in Moneyrow Green and Stud Green which are part of Holyport.

The main settlements date from the time of William the Conqueror. In 1208 the ruling manor was Philiberts originally owned by Hugh de St. Philibert who died in 1248 after which time the estate came into the hands of the de Cressewell family. During the following centuries the estate changed hands regularly and the house was rebuilt at least three times. One of its most famous visitors was Charles II who called upon Nell Gwynne whose residence it was for some time. The manor house of Philiberts no longer exists as it was demolished some time after the First World War. Other important old properties still in existence include Chuffs owned by William Chuff in 1426 and Gays (originally Geys) owned by John Gay in 1455.

Three more recent properties of note are Bourne Bridge Lodge, the seat of Sir Robert Sidney during the last century; The Lodge, which possesses one of the few Real Tennis Courts in the country; Linden Manor, once the home of the Marquess of Milford Haven whom Prince Philip visited regularly in his youth.

The name Foxley occurs in some form on several properties in one area of Holyport. The Manor of Foxley was owned by John de Foxle in the 14th century and he was granted a licence to make a park. It left the de Foxle family in the late 15th century. In 1925 the late Col. A. E. Marnham MC, TD, DC, JP bought part of the original de Foxle estate, and it stayed in his family until 1976 when the greater part of the estate was split up and sold.

It was at Cadogan Riding Stables, now a housing development, that the Queen and Princess Margaret, when children, received riding instruction from the owner, Mr. Horace Dayer-Smith. The manager of the stables for some time was the father of Dick Francis, champion rider and thriller writer.

There were three ponds on the green but only the one outside the Belgian Arms remains. The others were in front of 'Rails' on the west side of the green and to the left of 'Pamela Row'. The derivation of the name 'Rails' is assumed to be in connection with falcons. It has always been understood that falcons were kept in the house during the 16th century for use by hunting parties from Windsor Castle.

A Wesleyan Chapel was built in 1835 on the west side of the green. Prior to that the congregation had met in an upper room of the Belgian Arms in Holyport Street. The Chapel is now sadly derelict.

The Belgian Arms pub has an interesting history. There has been a beer house on the site for 200 years. The Henley Brewery took it over in 1896 when it was called the Eagle. During the First World War there was a prisoner of war camp in the grounds of Philiberts and the German soldiers were marched past the pub on their daily exercise and would stop to salute the eagle, a depiction of the Prussian Eagle. The residents objected to this, so the name was changed to that of the area where the fiercest fighting was taking place at the time, namely Belgium.

The two pubs around the green, the George and the Belgian Arms feature in the beer race at the annual Village Fayre held on the first Saturday in June. This is organised by the Memorial Hall Committee to raise funds to improve the facilities of the Hall which was built as a tribute to those from Holyport who fell in the Second World War. There is a War Memorial to the fallen of both wars adjacent to the pond.

Development has taken place beyond the green with three housing estates and various infilling. The population has more than trebled since the 1960s but despite this the heart of the village has retained its charm.

# Hurley 🌿

The ancient village of Hurley is halfway between London and Oxford, being 55 miles from both by river. It has been occupied since the Bronze Age.

Domesday Book (1086) records a church at Hurley, a manor with 25 villeins, 12 cottagers, 10 serfs, 19 ploughs, a mill, 2 fisheries, 20 acres of meadow, a wood for swine and about 120 acres of arable land. William the Conqueror removed the Saxon owner Esgar and conferred the property upon the Norman Baron Geoffrey de Mandeville. In 1976 the villagers bought this ancient lordship of the manor for £2,500. A wall plaque and a hand-inscribed book record the story and names of subscribers.

There are three noteworthy mansions in the village. Manor House and Ladye Place (both now divided into separate freeholds) and Hurley House. Hurley House is 17th century and probably built as a dower house to the original Ladye Place, down by the river. Ladye Place belonged to the Lovelaces but was pulled down in 1837, having failed to find a buyer. In its crypt, all that remains today, the 1688 Glorious Revolution was plotted by Lord John Lovelace, to place on the throne of England the Prince of Orange and his Stuart consort, as William III and Mary.

Adjacent to Hurley House, in the High Street, are three 17th century almshouses, in the trusteeship of Hurley Church Estate. In 1969 they were completely restored at a cost of £5,000.

Some two miles from the village is the old mansion house of Hall Place, now the Berkshire College of Agriculture. Hurley Farms Ltd., covering the land between the river and the main Henley-Maidenhead road, is owned and farmed by the Burfitt family, of whom three generations live in the village. Of the six pubs, the most interesting is the Dewdrop on Ashley Hill, founded for the use of the Windsor Forest foresters; and the Old Bell. The latter was built in 1187 as the guesthouse of Hurley Priory. It has since risen in the social scale from a village inn to a hotel-restaurant.

The Priory was founded by de Mandeville for a cell of monks from the Benedictine Abbey at Westminister in 1086. and endowed with the avowsons of many of the surrounding churches. The remains of the Priory, dissolved by Henry VIII in 1536, centre round the church. The original Cloisters and monks' dormitories can be identified by the stone stringing and blocked-up windows and doors. The modern houses probably mark the original lay-out. The enormous Tithe Barn, converted into a private residence in 1950, and the unusually well preserved dovecote date from the mid-13th century, and show to some extent the wealth of the Priory.

Hurley is a magnet for visitors at all seasons of the year with its open-air swimming facilities and ancient history. In winter, members of the London Angling Association arrive in five or six coaches in the grey dawn, to spend the whole day, like Jeremy Fisher, in the mud by the river, each under his huge green or black umbrella.

# Hurst

When the Vikings had an encampment at Reading, over 1,000 years ago, the land surrounding the village we now call Hurst was part of the great forest of Windsor. The Saxon king Ethelred and his brother Alfred tried to attack the Viking stronghold but were driven back through the forest; they retreated to the marshy meadows on the eastern banks of the river Loddon. The Saxons called those meadows Whistley. The name Hurst came into use much later.

Abingdon Abbey, which had been founded before the Vikings estab-lished themselves at Reading, needed supplies of food and materials to maintain the community. The Saxon kings endowed it and other religi-ous houses with lands that were to form manors. One of those manors was at Whistley which King Edgar granted to Abingdon Abbey in the year 968 AD.

When the Normans compiled the Domesday Book in 1086, they duly recorded that the manor at Whistley belonged to Abingdon. It was shown to have a mill, a fishery, some land that was used for crops, and some woodland for pigs. Over the years oak trees were felled and sent down the river Loddon and Thames, some to make choir stalls for the Abbey. And fish, mainly eels, were transported in large numbers to the Abbot's kitchens.

The people at Whistley had established their own church by the year 1084. First it was a simple wooden structure, but later stout Norman pil-lars of limestone were erected to support a more substantial building, and they are still to be seen in the church.

It was the Dean of Salisbury's scribe who first used the word Hurst. He recorded the Dean's visits here in the 13th century and wrote down 'the chapel at Herst, dedicated to St. Nicholas'. The word 'hurst' means a wooden hill and he used it to identify the church which served Whistley. Over the centuries, Hurst has become the name of the area.

During the Civil War, the Harrisons of Hurst House lost most of their wealth supporting Charles I. The unfortunate king is said to have played on Hurst Bowling Green in more peaceful times. In those days the parish of Hurst was much larger than it is now. Then it encompassed Twyford, Winnersh, Sindlesham, Bearwood and Newland. Twyford was formed into a separate parish in the last century, as were parts of Winnersh, Sindlesham and Bearwood. Another boundary which disappeared then was an old county boundary. For centuries, part of Berkshire was regarded as being in Wiltshire. This curious situation came about because the Earls of Salisbury regarded the land they owned here as part of their holdings in Amesbury. So, for legal reasons, part of Twyford, Hurst and Wokingham were atttached to Wiltshire.

In the 19th century Hurst was primarily an agricultural village. Osiers were grown on the banks of the river Loddon and either made into baskets locally or sent to the markets in London. The river abounded with eels, pike, roach, dace, gudgeon, tench and carp, and it supplied water for the mills at Sandford and Whistley. Whistley mill was used to manufacture paper. There were blacksmiths at Wards Cross, Davis Street and Dunt Lane, and a wheelwright's shop in Davis Street.

A brewery once existed in School Road and there were numerous pubs, beer sellers and drinking houses. Two of the oldest inns are the Castle and the Green Man. The Castle was once called the Church House and the rents from it helped to support the church. Later it became known as the Bunch of Grapes. Three other notable inns which are now just a memory were the Crown, the Barley Corn and the Half Way House.

Since the days when the heaths, moors and commons were enclosed, the railways and motorways have arrived, and the land which was cleared of forest to make way for agriculture, is now providing sites for building, gravel workings and a country park. It might be that Hurst's role in the future is to provide recreation, and a patch of green, in the middle of what seems to be the inevitable urbanisation of this part of Berkshire.

# Inkpen

'Inkpen, what a delightful name' everyone says, 'I wonder how it originated'. It is of Saxon origin. 'Pen' was a Saxon word meaning stockade or enclosure, and 'Inga' was the chief who owned it. Some of the large fields have Saxon associations, especially the one called Haycroft, the name given to a communal hayfield.

The village lies in the extreme south west of Berkshire and most of the visitors who come are looking for Inkpen Beacon, well known as the highest Chalk Hill in England (975 ft). The Beacon is crowned by Walbury Camp believed to date from the Iron Age. The long barrow on

*INKPEN*

the hill west of the Camp was the burial place of Inkpen's earliest inhabitants.

Founder of the church was Roger De Ingpen whose effigy now rests on the right hand side of the altar. Its style is so much like that of an effigy of known date in Salisbury Cathedral that it can be attributed to that period 1220-1250. There were Butlers at the church from 1700-1933. In the time of Henry Dobree Butler, the last of the family, the church was greatly restored and enriched by many treasures. When this greatly loved rector died, the memorial to him was the oak lych-gate made in the village by employees of the local sawmills. The rafters were cleft in the traditional style and the adze used instead of the plane.

The Gibbet – a landmark for miles – was first erected on the hilltop site in 1676 when George Broomham of Combe and Dorothy Newman of Inkpen were hanged for the murder of the man's wife and son. It was the only time it was used. The original gibbet rotted away, a second was struck by lightning, the third lasted until 1949, when it came down in a gale. The hill looked bare and unfamiliar without a gibbet and so by popular request and public subscription a new one was erected. This was made from a 50 ft. 150 year old tree from the Fens Lower Inkpen and made at the sawmills. It has been vandalised, repaired and replaced three times.

In 1948 a film *The Black Legend,* telling the story of the murders was written, produced and directed by Alan Cooke and John Schlesinger with local people in the cast.

Although the downs and the gibbet dominate the village, there are many lanes and houses with fascinating names. Along Weavers Lane there is Puddle Wharf Cottage that carried on a Silk and Blanket business; and Weavers where baskets were made. The Rope Walk and Hell Corner, a coveted corner of ground which up to the 20th century was an important gypsy meeting ground. Bell Lane has no bell; Bottom Lane was part of an old drove road going out towards Salisbury and has the Wansdyke left and right crossing to Prosperous. William Cobbett rode this way to visit Jethro Tull of *Horse Hoeing Husbandry* fame.

Inkpen's best known craft was pottery up to the early 20th century. Local clay was used and labourers were given the name of Inkpen Yellow Legs. The heavier type of pottery was made – bread crocks, flower pots and pitchers. But there was a potter in the village about 2000 BC. In a sand-pit near Totterdown an early beaker was discovered which is the tallest ever found in the British Isles. There was also an unusual bowl standing on four feet. These unique treasures are in Newbury Museum.

There used to be three blacksmith's shops, four public houses, several smallholdings, with milk delivered or collected daily, and several small shops selling groceries. Now it has two public houses, one general store including post office and milk brought into the village every other day.

A small cross in a brick wall tells where a labourer died from cold and exposure in the Great Snowstorm of 1881 when within one hundred yards of his home.

Although Inkpen is a rambling village and there have been some alterations – the sawmills have given way to a small industrial complex – it still retains a great deal of charm with some lovely walks and really is worth visiting.

# Kintbury

Located between Newbury and Hungerford, Kintbury stands on the south side of the Kennet Valley.

Agriculture was, and still is, the main industry in the area, although chalk was dug at many small quarries in preparation for whiting. Until recently there was a small whiting industry and two brick and tile factories. These have now gone, leaving only disused chalk quarries and the name and buildings of Kiln Farm. The village had three water mills and one silk mill in the early 19th century.

The effects of the Industrial Revolution in agriculture were felt in Kintbury, and in 1830 the village momentarily acquired a little wider notoriety. Agricultural machinery was introduced into West Berkshire, and this was accompanied by a serious outbreak of rioting, rick-burning and the destruction of new machinery. A detachment of Grenadier Guards was sent from London to help local Yeomanry, led by Lord Craven, Lord Dundas and Captain Houblon, to quell the riots. The party assembled in Newbury then marched on Kintbury, and the ringleaders were arrested to the number of 100. Most of them were found in the Blue Bell public house, which was the rioters' headquarters. One man was executed at Reading, some were transported and many more imprisoned.

The earliest known settlement at Kintbury is the Saxon burial ground near the school. This is assumed to be the 'Holy Place' referred to by a Saxon lord of the district in A.D. 93. In the Domesday Book the name is Cynetanbyrig and lists a mill on the river Kennet as being worth 4s. or 20p. The original village was sited above the flood level of the Kennet near the present church, which dates from the 12th century with many later additions and alterations. The tower and Norman doorway work survived these alterations. In the church are some fine 18th century monuments, including one to Sir Jennett Raymond by Scheemakers.

During the 14th to 16th centuries, Kintbury village was the main settlement of the Hundred of Kintbury Eagle, which stretched from Letcombe Regis in the north to Shalbourne in the south, and from Hungerford in the west to Enborne in the east.

The Parish of Kintbury was comprised of seven Manors, the land and lordship of Kintbury Eaton, Templeton, Titcombe held by the sejeanty for keeping one of the King's hawks, Balsdon, Inglewood and Wallingtons and the two detached Manors of Denford and Anvilles. The Manor of Kintbury Amesbury, thenceforth known as Barton Court, was bought by Phillip Jennett, a London brewer; his family and their descendants, the family of Jennett Raymond, held the Manor until 1790, when it passed by descent and marriage to the Dundas family.

In the next 50 years this family provided public life with a well-known Admiral and a Member of Parliament for Berkshire, Charles Dundas, Lord of the Manor of Kintbury, later becoming Lord Amesbury, dying in 1832. The family sold the property to Sir Richard Sutton in 1875 and part of it still belongs to the Sutton Estates.

There is only one traceable village legend, that of the Kintbury Great Bell; and one ghost. The bell legend is that a great storm destroyed the church tower and hurled the bell into the river. A wizard prescribed that it should be recovered by passing a chain through a hook fixed to the head of the bell, and then the chain was to be pulled by twelve white heifers, led in moonlight by twelve maidens arrayed in white with red sashes. No word was to be spoken or the chain would break. All went well until the Kintbury witch cried:

> Here comes the great Kintbury bell
> In spite of all the devils in hell.

This broke the spell, the chain snapped and the bell fell back into the river.

The ghost is Lieutenant Dexter's. He asked to be buried with his sword beside him. This sword is said to rattle when people pass through the churchyard at night.

The Kennet and Avon Canal was opened through Kintbury in 1812, and, thanks to the Kennet and Avon Canal Trust, is once again navigable up to Kintbury and westwards.

# Knowl Hill

Knowl Hill has a population of 700 and is 30 miles from London. The Bath Road (A4) passes through the village. The name is derived from 'The Knolle', a hill on the south side once crowned by a clump of elm trees. Extensive views of the countryside can be seen from here, including Windsor Castle. In 1315 a grant of a piece of land at 'La Cnolle' is mentioned in a charter of St. Mary's Priory, Hurley.

At one time Knowl Hill was part of Windsor Forest. Evidence from excavations show that there was once a Roman settlement here, as much Roman pottery has been found. The Bath stage coach rattled through the village until railways killed the industry. Travellers called at the local inns for rest and refreshment while the horses were changed. The farriers and wheelwrights premises are still in existence, now two cottages. In their front walls the outline of the archways through which the coaches would pass are still visible. It is interesting that a modern garage on the opposite side of the road continues the tradition of serving travellers. A frequent bus service through the village connects London, Maidenhead and Reading.

Knowl Hill is chiefly agricultural but it has a brick and tile industry which has been owned by the same family for over 100 years.

St. Peter's Church was consecrated in 1841, and was designed by J. C. Buckler of Oxford. He was runner-up to Sir Charles Barry in the competition for the design for the Houses of Parliament. The church was enlarged in 1870.

Cricket is a flourishing village sport. It has been played in the same field since 1890. A yearly Steam Rally has been held in the village since 1970, originally organised to raise funds to build a new Village Hall, completed in 1974.

When the dreaded Dutch Elm disease hit the country, sadly The Clumps on the 'Knolle' fell victim and the familiar landmark had to be destroyed. The area was thoroughly cleared and re-grassed and now a variety of new saplings are flourishing and in years to come will take the place of the old elms which had stood for centuries before.

There have been one or two changes in the parish affecting the church, and since 1975 Knowl Hill and its neighbouring parish of Littlewick Green have shared a vicar. The old Vicarage in Knowl Hill was sold and is now a private house called The Grange, and until the summer of 1984 the vicarage at Littlewick was the residence of the priest of both parishes. However, it was becoming uneconomical to keep up a large old fashioned house any longer and a more modern house was found for the vicar and his family in Knowl Hill, which, in keeping with modern thought brings him in much closer proximity with his parishioners.

The Old Bath Road has gone through yet another change in the last 10 years, and a dual carriageway runs through the village to take the ever increasing traffic. An iron bridge now spans the road from the junior school entrance on the south side so that children living across the road can go to and from school in safety.

# Lambourn 🐑

Lambourn is situated in the Lambourn valley, virtually at the source of the river, and at the edge of the Berkshire chalk downs. At the north west extremity of the county, the village is within a few miles of the Oxfordshire, Wiltshire and Gloucestershire borders. The name of the village is thought to have originated from the sheep on the downs, and the stream in which they were dipped (the Scottish word burn is still used to mean stream).

The first mention of Lambourn in historical records was around the time of Alfred the Great. It has even been suggested that he was born in Lambourn, and he certainly owned land which was left to his wife. The numerous ancient barrows close by are proof of much earlier settlement of the area, as are finds of Roman pottery in the vicinity.

Norman invaders later made their presence felt, and indeed the nave of St Michael and All Angels Church is 12th century Norman. By the 13th century Lambourn had assumed some importance, and a charter

*view from hill overlooking LAMBOURN.*

was granted to allow a market and two sheep fairs a year to be held. The fairs were held on Edwards Hill on ground now owned by the C. of E. school. For hundreds of years Lambourn's prosperity was based on sheep rearing, to which the downland was eminently suited.

The parish survived the upheavals of the Reformation without serious incident. Both the Isbury Almshouses and the Hardretts Almshouses were allowed to continue.

The Earls of Craven were responsible for the creation of Ashdown Park close by, and by the beginning of the 18th century they were holding regular race and hare coursing meetings.

The village's importance as a centre of the horse racing industry today grew from these beginnings, the downlands proving as suitable for gallops as they had been for sheep rearing. Some of the country's best known flat and national hunt trainers are based in Lambourn a mile away. Consequently the village can also number top jockeys among its residents.

Today the livelihoods of many villagers are connected with horse racing, either directly working in stables, or indirectly providing allied equipment and services. Recent housebuilding has, however, meant an influx of people who commute to Newbury, Reading and even London. Other local industry is largely based at the wartime airfield of Membury, 2 miles above the village, and close to the M4 London/Bristol motorway. Agriculture is now of more importance than sheeprearing at surrounding farms.

It is ironic that Lambourn is attracting stable lads and girls from all over Britain when many other village communities are struggling for survival. Indeed, congestion on the roads has necessitated the creation of horse paths around the village to allow the circumnavigation of built up areas on the way to the gallops.

The principal building in Lambourn is the ancient Parish Church of St Michael and All Angels. It is a most imposing village church with its Perpendicular tower, fine stained glass windows and neat churchyard. The lychgate connecting the churchyard to the Market Square is an attractive and welcoming entrance, erected as a memorial to William Jousiffe, a well known Victorian racehorse trainer.

Inside the church, the chancel and sanctuary were added to the nave during the 14th and 15th centuries. The Chapel of St Katherine, housing the tomb of Sir Thomas Essex, is bounded on the west side by a 14th century arch. The Chapel also contains the Parish Stocks which had stood in the Market Place in front of the church, the 17th century font and the parish chest.

Some of the tombstones have been cleared from the yard, but there is still a quaint inscription on one to John Carter, the last man to be hanged for arson in England. According to the message he set fire to Lambourn. Fortunately much of it remains intact!

Another landmark of the village is the lovely Market Cross in the Square, erected around the time that Henry VI granted the charter for the market and fairs. The cross has recently been restored and looks most impressive.

Across the land by the side of the church there are still traces of the cobblestones that once covered all the village streets. This land leads to the almshouses founded by John Isbury in 1502 and largely rebuilt by Henry Hippesley in 1852. The houses were further modernised in 1956 to make homes for 8 almsmen.

Beyond this is the sarsen wall around Lambourn Place, once the manor house home of the Essex family and several generations of Hippesleys, but now the site of a modern housing estate.

Lambourn may not be the most picturesque Berkshire Village, but it is certainly an attractive and interesting one.

# Langley 🌿

With the change in county boundaries in the early 1970s Langley, already brought into the borough of Slough in 1931, was moved into Berkshire.

Before the war the village was almost wholly agricultural, consisting of a number of farms stretching over a large area from the railway on the north to the Bath Road on the south. These were worked by well-known farming families: Seymour, Major, Emmett and Lobjoit to name some, and employed many men. Others worked in the brickfields adjacent to the Grand Union Canal, where London Stock bricks were made, and some were in the service of the last Squire of Langley, the late Sir Robert Harvey, who lived at Langley Park and owned the beautiful parkland surrounding it and the fine tract of woodlands to the north known as Black Park. After Sir Robert's death in 1931 the estate became the property of the Buckinghamshire County Council, and now both Langley Park and Black Park are open to the public.

Though the population of the village at that time was quite small, all the essential shops were to hand – butchers, a bakery, a post office with sweetshop and newsagents' business, a Co-operative grocery and drapery store, a cobbler, a chemist, hardware store and a printer, and a blacksmith who, of course, was a vital craftsman in an agricultural community. At the centre of the village was Langley Hall, at that time the home of the Actors' Orphanage, and every year the children put on, in their own Bijou Theatre a superb Christmas Pantomime, which delighted everybody, and people came from miles around to see it. The local Flower Show, an important annual event in the village, was held in the beautiful grounds of the Hall, also cricket matches between the boys ' team and a team of famous actors used to be played. Sadly for Langley, the children of the Orphanage moved further out into the country just before the outbreak of war, but fortunately the Hall, a listed building, has been beautifully restored and is now used by the Wilkinson Sword Company for offices. The grounds which surrounded the Hall are now completely built on, and on the site now stands Langley College, Longcroft Day Centre and Residential Home, a Community Centre and a depot for British Telecom.

The old village schools still stand – Horesmoor Green Infants School is now a Youth Club, and the old Central School, lately used as a centre for handicapped people, is now closed. The old Gospel Mission Hall is now a furniture emporium and a new Free Church has been built on the L.C.C. estate. The 12th century parish church of St. Mary's remains in its old-world setting, with beautifully restored almshouses, the Kedermisters to the south and the Seymours to the north. The old Red Lion Inn stands opposite the church gate. St. Mary's church contains the famous Kedermister Pew and Library – the latter unique as an example of an early 17th century church library.

During the war industry had encroached upon the village, notably the Hawker Aircraft company, and when hostilities ended in 1945, it was not long before Langley was chosen to be one of the places to develop for rehousing Londoners who had been made homeless by the war. This happened in the early 1950s and many old houses and cottages were demolished, and farmland done away with to make way for new housing estates which included houses, shops, schools and churches. Later on a very good library and a medical centre were built.

With the close proximity of London Airport, the industry of Slough and its much increased population Langley is no longer a rural area although its centre around the Harrow Inn, with Memorial field opposite, is always referred to as 'the village'. An excellent shopping centre is now there, known as the Harrow Market. Until thirty years ago there was a village pond, but this has since been filled in.

With the many changes which have taken place over the years, Langley has lost most of its old identity, but because of its modern development and the availability of work in the area, it supports a thriving community.

# Leckhampstead

One of the most pleasing places in the downlands, the village sits high above the Wantage to Newbury Road and is divided into three distinct areas – the main village centred on a small green – Thicket and Hill Green.

The original Saxon church dedicated to St. Edmund was demolished in 1860 but items that were saved for the present church of St. James were a Jacobean Pulpit, a 13th century font and the altar rails. The site of the old church is now part of the lovely gardens surrounding Chapel Farm. The Methodist Chapel is still in use in Thicket and is the venue each April for a Daffodil Rally attended by friends of the chapel from a large area. The former Wesleyan Chapel is now a private house.

The old manor house at Hill Green – an attractive 16th century thatched house is now known as Yew Tree Cottage and a farm house built 200 years later in the main part of the village is now known as The Manor.

There are a number of attractive thatched cottages and other houses listed as 'buildings of architectural or historical interest'. An unusual War Memorial is a clock with hands made of bayonets, machine–gun ammunition marks the minutes and the Roman numerals are rifle ammuniton. Shell cases rest on staddle stones surrounding the memorial, and the chain linking the stones belonged to a battleship which fought at the Battle of Jutland.

The village school which was built in 1875 and closed in 1961 has been converted into a Countryside Centre, where Youth Organisations can stay for short periods in conjunction with the centre at Pangbourne and was officially opened by H.R.H. the Duke of Gloucester in October 1982.

*Leckhampstead. Church of St. James. (By S. S. Tenfon. 1856).*

The Village Hall which was built in 1910 and run by a Trust of local people is in regular use particularly by the W.I. and the Art Group, as well as providing a centre for various social functions during the year. During the First World War it was used as a temporary hospital and in the Second World War it was the base for the Home Guard.

At the beginning of the century the village was almost self-supporting, with an undertaker, three tailors, boot-makers and repairer, three carpenters, builder and decorator, wheelwright; agricultural engineer, bread-baked in the old bake house and the Blacksmith. Now the smithy is converted into a private house known as Blundys after the last blacksmith. The shop was closed in the 1970s, but a small Post Office is still open for a few items and is much appreciated especially by the older residents.

The outstanding feature of the village has always been its setting in beautiful downland countryside. Unfortunately as in many areas great numbers of elms had to be felled because of Dutch Elm Disease but the Parish Council and local landowners are busily planting new trees for future generations to enjoy.

# Littlewick Green 🌿

Littlewick Green was recognised as a Common by the White Waltham Enclosure Act of 1807, but the name first appears about the year 1050. A Roman settlement was discovered by aerial photography in a field known as Black Vere. Archaeologists followed up this lead and unearthed Roman relics, proving that Littlewick Green has a long, though perhaps not a spectacular, history.

The visitor will be impressed by the serenity of the extensive village green, although it is not 200 yards from the traffic rushing along the A4 Bath Road. The Green is surrounded by thatched cottages, mellow brick houses, the village church, the village hall and, appropriately enough, an inn, the Cricketers, in the shade of an old walnut tree.

The church was built in 1887 by Fanny Ellis, primarily to provide a burial ground at Littlewick. For generations the coffins were carried down the bridle path leading to White Waltham, to be interred in the churchyard there. The church possesses a treasure of great interest. It is a 15th century tempora painting copied by an unknown artist, which was found in the coach house of the Southern Electricity Board's Headquarters at Woolley Hall. Woolley Hall was the home of George Dunn from 1886 until his death in 1912. He was an expert on four different subjects: astronomy, arboriculture (the trees he planted are a feature of the Hall), horology and old books. His library was sold at Sotheby's after his death for £32,000. It was said that George Dunn suffered from a broken romance. On the morning before his wedding day, his bride-to-be ran off with his brother. The wedding breakfast, which was laid ready, was left untouched all his life.

Formerly, a Fair called the 'Hope Benefit' was held on bank holidays. Donkeys, brought from the New Forest could be bought for £1. Ashley Hill dominates the local scene, and gives rise to the weather rhyme:

> When Ashley Hill begins to smoke
> Then Shottesbrooke begins to soak.

Shottesbrooke, just south of the village, is famous for its fine 14th century church, inspired by Salisbury Cathedral, with its beautiful slender spire rising from the centre of the cruciform design. Sir William Trussell built it, and the story goes that he was 'a worthy old knight addicted to drinking'. He nearly died of his excesses, but recovered by taking 'water drenches and water stupes; water gruels and water soups', to everyone's amazement. His wife, a pious lady, so troubled his conscience and tortured his soul that, on his recovery

'An oath he sware,
To his lady fair,
'By the cross on my shield
A church I'll build',
And therefore the deuce a form
Is so fit as the cruciform.
And the patron saint that I find the aptest
Is that holiest water-saint, John the Baptist!'
(From the Berkshire Book of Song and Ryhme).

Another tale concerns the local smith. On the completion of the church in 1337, he climbed the spire to affix the weather vane. On arriving at the top, he demanded a pot of ale with which to drink the health of the king. The ale was delivered to him, but unfortunately his sense of balance was not equal to his excess of loyalty, and he fell to his death. His grave, the first in the churchyard, was dug where he landed, and on his tombstone was inscribed the two 'O's, all he uttered as he fell!

Ivor Novello, who lived at Red Roofs, was another personality who found the tranquillity of Littlewick Green to his taste, and it was here that he wrote his lovely musical plays, amongst them *King's Rhapsody* and *Perchance to Dream*. Happily, the tradition of the theatre is still being kept alive at his old home by Mrs. Keston Bloom, who runs a theatre school of a very high standard.

Sadly, the village is now bereft of its only shop, which was a grocery, provisions and post office combined; and also its much loved village school, founded in 1873 by a Miss Ann Cherry of the 'Cherry's Charity', a local benefactress. Before this beautifully preserved church school was built, the children of the Littlewick area had to walk to White Waltham School, a distance of some three miles away. This heritage was not given up without a very tough fight by all concerned.

On a happier note, the village Women's Institute has thrived and grown since its changeover from afternoon to evening meetings, and, given concerted effort, should go from strength to strength.

# Mortimer

Mortimer is a long village of about 4,000 inhabitants which extends from the common on a wooded plateau, one and a half miles down The Street to the station, a listed building which has been carefully restored. The common is a good shopping centre and a meal can be obtained at any of the several public houses. There is a very up-to-date doctors' surgery. The Village Hall is very well patronized. There is a pick-your-own-fruit farm in pleasant surroundings with refreshments and a children's play area.

People have lived in the area since pre-Roman times. The village of Stratfield was given by William the Conqueror to one of his supporters, Ralf de Mortimer. The present Great and Little Parks were established by the Mortimer family in 1230 and they became farms at the time of Henry VIII when the manor reverted to the Crown. Henry gave them successively to five of his wives – Katharine of Aragon, Anne Boleyn, Jane Seymour, Catherine Howard and Katherine Parr. Why poor Anne of Cleves was left out is not known! The present Lord of the Manor is William Benyon.

There are two churches. The first, St. Mary's, an attractive Victorian building, was erected on the site of former churches and contains a Saxon tombstone dated 994 AD which reads:

> 'On 8th before Kalends of October Aegalward
> son of Kypping was laid in this place.
> Blessed be he who prays for his Soul
> Toki wrote me.'

This inscription pinpoints one year in the very early history of the village, for it was in 994 AD that Aegalward is mentioned in the *Anglo-Saxon Chronicle*. Aethelward, or Aegalward, was an historian, first translator of the *Chronicle*, consequently a man of influence. Kypping, his father, was Lord of the Manor of Mortimer. Toki, who apparently erected the stone, was a wealthy courtier in the reign of Canute, who was proclaimed King of England in 1017 and who divided the country into the four earldoms of Northumbria, East Anglia, Mercia and Wessex. His reign, lasting until 1035, was one of peace and prosperity, so no doubt Toki took advantage of the lull in hostilities to put up a worthy monument to this learned man of the previous century.

The first village church was burnt down during the Danish invasion, possibly in 871 AD. A second church was built on the same site and added to over the years, and the present church was built over the foundations of the two earlier ones in 1869.

St. John's Church, which is used more often, was built on the common at the expense of Richard Benyon in 1881 as a Chapel of Ease to save the long walk down the hill. It has a pleasant and welcoming interior.

There has always been support for the Methodist Church which is reflected in the new chapel recently built.

Highways and commons in the parish tell a clear story of by-gone days and outdated customs. Welshman's Road was the path along which the Welsh drovers trudged behind their small, tough ponies and shaggy cattle, arriving for the Mortimer Horse and Welsh Cattle Fairs in November and in May. Horse Fairs abounded in the early days, and at the larger fairs as many as 45,000 animals would come under the hammer at the same time. The fairs were the big events of the year for country folk, and a usually quiet village could be transformed overnight into a medley of colour, noise, hard bargaining, entertainment and excitement.

Goodboys Lane was called after a family of that unusual name who were freeholders in 1540. A road was cut in 1805-6 near the old windmill ... the sails no longer creak in the wind but Windmill Road is still there. The Forehead, leading to Beech Hill, was known in 1512 as Fair Mead or Front Meadow. Butlers Lane recalls Thomas Botiller, who owned the land in 1467. Five Oakes, originally Five Oak Glade, crops up in 16th century documents. Gibbet Piece recalls a darker side of life – the execution of two young men in 1787, for the murder of the village carrier. Their bodies remained, hung in chains, as an awful warning until old Madame Brocas of Wokefield had them taken down. Those very chains, made by local blacksmith Mr. Davis, are now in Reading Museum.

The local Fire Service gets many calls, especially in the summer, to woodland fires. They have a popular 2-day horse jumping charity event each year on the Fairground, which is also traditionally bound to provide facilities for visiting fairs and circuses. It is not unknown to find llamas, zebras, camels and even an elephant grazing happily in the centre of the village for the odd day or two.

# Mortimer West End

Although this village is inside the Hampshire boundary, it has been for centuries a tithing of the Berkshire village of Stratfield Mortimer, and therefore linked to the Royal County.

The parish Church of St. Saviour was built and endowed by the Benyon family in 1856. It has some fine stained-glass including a benedicite window depicting the four seasons. James Lawes, the shepherd who inspired W. H. Hudson's book, A Shepherd's Life, is buried in the churchyard. Although he had spent his working life in Wiltshire he retired to his son's cottage in Soke Road.

Two local men, John Mulford and John Whitburn, founded a Congregational Chapel in 1798. Although it was well supported for over a hundred years, it is now falling into decay.

There is no longer a village school; it was closed in 1928 but the converted building remains as a private house.

The parish has a treasure which many of its inhabitants have never seen as it was completely neglected for hundreds of years. This is the Roman amphitheatre on the southern boundary which was just a tall, oval embankment surrounded by a tangle of shrubs until 1979. It is now being excavated with the intention of eventually opening it to the public. It is exciting to see the emergence of the ancient shape, the banks seating an audience of 3,000 and the disclosure of two apsed recesses in the southern and northern bank, probably shrines to propitiate the gods. This place has the magic property of sending all its visitors' thoughts back 2,000 years and evoking the Roman past.

Near to the amphitheatre is a cottage showing its 'cruck' construction, while in the village is another half timbered cottage near to the 17th century Red Lion public house. The name of the Turners Arms reflects the principle occupation of the villagers in the past, when Mortimer West End was part of one of the largest wood working areas in England. The crafts of besom making, bowl turning, charcoal burning, bark stripping and hurdle making are no longer practised, but there are still a few men who can tell of their old skills.

Much of the parish is still woodland and common, although large parts are under threat for gravel extraction. Deer can sometimes be seen and Burnt Common has several plants of ecological interest. Today, the woods are greatly enjoyed by walkers, horse riders and visiting students.

# Oakley Green

Oakley Green starts, according to the name plates erected by the District Council a year or so ago, a few hundred yards from the Braywood Memorial Hall down Oakley Green Road, placing Braywood Cricket Club in Fifield. It stretches the whole length of Oakley Green Road, (B3024) until it joins the A308, with a short diversion at the Nags Head towards Dedworth. Although limited to this stretch of road, there are many houses set back along unmade roads, so that Oakley Green has a greater depth than at first appears.

The first part of Oakley Green (coming from Fifield) is considered by the inhabitants not really to be in Oakley Green but in Braywood and many of the properties have Braywood in their name. Although the powers-that-be have given the people of Braywood addresses in Oakley Green, Windsor, they have Maidenhead telephone numbers.

The houses on Oakley Green Road are a mixture of old and new, but it is often difficult to decide which are the genuinely old houses as many new ones are built in a traditional style. One house, Clairvaux, which appears to be very old and looks as though it should have church associations, is in fact fairly modern.

Many houses in Oakley Green stand well back from the road and are reached by long drives or are down unmade roads which are hard on a car's suspension. One of the former is Willow Farm, once the home of Michael Sadleir, the author of *Fanny by Gaslight*. One of the latter was Nightingale Cottage, up Tarbay Lane (an unmade road a little before the Nag's Head). Here lived for many years Dr Esther Rickards, a noted lady doctor and in later life, a breeder of spaniels and a widely acclaimed Dog Show Judge. After her death, the villagers of Oakley Green and Fifield raised money for a memorial to her, and placed a seat outside Braywood School with a memorial plate. Unfortunately, the seat was stolen. The seat now outside Braywood School was provided from the Council Lottery Fund, but a new memorial plate has been added.

There is one shop, two public houses and two nurseries in Oakley Green. To many locals the shop, the Oakley Green Stores, is still known as 'West's'. The West family ran the shop for many years and served almost everybody in the district. Mr West would visit his customers once a week to receive their orders and collect the money for last week's meat and groceries. Deliveries were three times a week. Some customers never set foot inside the shop.

Oakley Green now ends at Fairacre Farm, and the Army houses built on Broom Farm look for their leisure and shopping towards Dedworth and Windsor, although the new school, Alexander Primary, built mainly for the Army children, is located in Oakley Green.

Returning to Oakley Green Road, this continues until it reaches the A308 and there are a few interesting old houses along this stretch, one curiously called Pooh Cottage. Bishops Lodge is now the Cardinal Clinic, but was the home at one time of Sir Benjamin Rycroft, the famous eye surgeon.

The A308 has recently been realigned, cutting The Willows off from Oakley Green. It is doubtful if these (The Willows, Willows Garden Centre, Willows Caravans and Willows Marina) were really part of Oakley Green, but in their cul-de-sac made from the old A308 (Maidenhead Road) they are now quite separate from the village.

# Owlsmoor

Owlsmoor is situated between Sandhurst, Broadmoor and Crowthorne, close to the Berkshire and Surrey borders. It was originally a very small village, with none of the amenities that most of us take completely for granted. There were no shops, and roads were rough with potholes and puddles abounding. Neither was it on a bus route – in fact, it was truly rural! The population was about 700.

Its oldest building is Linda Cottage, in the Owlsmoor Road, which to this day boasts a small well in the front garden. Miss Bridge, the present occupier, who has lived there since 1959, says that this well was at one time the only regular supply of water. Of course, this is no longer the case! On the outside wall of this same cottage is the Sun Alliance plaque, which company the public had to contact in cases of fire, long before the advent of the Fire Service as we know it today.

According to the 1981 Census figures, the population then was some 6,427. Today there are approximately some 7,000 people living in the area. With the introduction of new houses came an increased need for shops, and the Owlsmoor development now has six, comprising a newsagents with sub post office, chemist, butcher, hardware, grocery and launderette, and more may well be in the pipeline. The introduction of a surgery in the village was another step forward, as was the advent of a dispensing chemist. Alder Valley Bus Services from Reading and Bracknell now call regularly, and there is even an early morning bus to London.

Perhaps Owlsmoor is unique in that it does not possess any public house as such, although these are to be found in nearby Sandhurst and Crowthorne.

The one and only church, St. George's, is quite a small one, but nevertheless a big improvement on the original which was known as the Tin Church because of its construction. Owlsmoor was transferred from Crowthorne Parish to the Ecclesiastical Parish of Sandhurst in 1973. In 1982 its vicar, the Rev. Geoffrey Peace, started work with a view to the setting up of the new C. of E. Parish of Owlsmoor. It is hoped that this will be established soon. This will mean that Owlsmoor Parish will be independent and have the same status as all other parishes in England, with its own geographical area, its own Vicar, Churchwardens and Parochial Church Council and be responsible for its own financial affairs. It is hoped that St. George's will be made a Parish Church – a decision which rests with the Church Commissioners.

In 1982 the Owlsmoor Community Centre was opened, and in September 1985 the new Sandhurst Sport & Leisure Centre will open in the Owlsmoor Road, adjacent to Sandhurst School.

# Padworth 🦉

'Why Padworth?' was the question posed in the campaign to save the village school from closure in 1981. It epitomised the frustration felt in

114

this two-tier community. Top Padworth and bottom Padworth – separated by the death of the Squire in 1932 – cling firmly to their common identity despite constant attacks from those who wish to extract gravel, to expand the railway sidings, to store aviation fuel or to coat roadstone. A disproportion of the Parish Council's time has to be spent lobbying the very authorities who – most imagine – are there to defend the quality of life and the landscape of this part of the Kennet Valley.

'Turn from the city's poisoned air
And dwell with me a little where
The Kennet, gently flowing, speeds
His scent of green and bruised reeds
And water-mints that root in mud,
Cordial and faint; or where his flood
Breaks in a low perpetual roar
Beneath the weir, abrupt and hoar
With ragged foam and trembling spray
Whose perfume damps the hottest day
With cool invisible sweet breath.'

With these words Richard Aldington, the poet, novelist – and probably the most controversial man of letters of the twentieth century – opened his poem, *The Berkshire Kennet* in which he expressed the pastoral tranquility of his surroundings here at Padworth in the 1920s. Aldington however, is better remembered for his biting satire and it is in his 1931 novel, *The Colonel's Daughter*, that – with poignant irony – he predicts the present anguish. He feared for Padworth after the then forseeable death of the Squire.

Major Christopher William Darby Griffith – Major Darby as he is still remembered with affection by those who knew him – was the last squire of Padworth. On the anniversary of Armistice Day in 1932 he was found dead at Padworth House. He had shot himself. He was the last of his line. Lord Roundway, his cousin – from Roundway Park, at Devizes – had little need of the Padworth Estate he thereby inherited and Padworth House, its contents and surroundings were soon separated. The value of this often thoughtlessly dismissed parkland – itself once so central to the history and geography of the village – now lies beneath its broad acres. Both D. H. Lawrence and T. S. Eliot have walked these water meadows; Eliot was later to describe Padworth as a paradise. Neither, though, could have foreseen that the extraction of gravel from these same meadows would one day threaten to drive a wedge between those who live up on the Common from the canalside community down in the valley.

Padworth House was rebuilt in 1769 to the design of John Hobcroft, a student of Robert Adam, and the park is reputed to be by Capability Brown. The House was built for Christopher Griffith who, in 1759 married Catherine, the daughter of Sir William St. Quentin, fourth Baronet of Scampston Hall in Yorkshire. It was largely on Catherine's insistence that the Lower Lodge to the estate was to be an echo of the hunting lodge which may still be seen in the grounds of her former home. Christopher Griffith – a portrait of whom, by Gainsborough, may be seen in Reading Art Gallery collection – hardly had time to enjoy his new home for he died in 1776 and was buried in the church.

A unique glimpse of the past was afforded in 1982 when, as a result of the extensive works undertaken in the church to eradicate dry rot, the removal of the affected floor revealed the Darby Griffith vault. The coffins of Christopher's ancestors were to be seen piled on top of one another at the eastern end; but right in front of those who chose to look were the coffins of Christopher and Catherine. Both were clad in brown velvet studded and decorated in brass which, in the stillness of the tomb, had remained almost unblemished.

Major Darby, though, is buried in the later family vault outside the church – on the north side. An act of Parliament prohibited any further burial inside a church after 1850. It is believed that loneliness contributed to his suicide which is a tragedy in view of the hundreds of estate workers and friends who crowded into the churchyard for his last journey.

# Pangbourne

Pangbourne is a favoured residential and holiday resort on the junction of the Thames and Pang rivers. Approaching the village from Streatley, the Thames, and Pangbourne reach in particular, is of unsurpassed beauty.

The south branch of the Ridgeway, via Upper Basildon, dropped down into the valley at Pangbourne, where the Thames could be crossed, and there must have been a ford, then a rough bridge at that spot since very early times. The Roman Road from Silchester (Calleva Atrebatum) to Dorchester ran through the parish, where Neolithic, Roman and Saxon remains have been discovered. Interesting finds were made on Shooter's Hill when the railway line was cut in 1839, namely, 40 coins of silver, gold and brass dating AD 69 to 383, and many skeletons.

The Pangbourne sign, which is an attraction to visitors, was erected in Station Road in 1961. It shows Beorhtwulf, with the Charter, and a

Saxon ship, over the name of the village. Kenneth Grahame's book, and the symbolic willows, add a modern touch to the design.

Beorhtwulf, King of Mercia, who was put to flight at Canterbury by the marauding Danes in 851 AD granted land, in a Charter dated 843 AD to the parish church of St. James the Less. Rebuilt in 1868, leaving the existing brick tower built in 1718, the church houses a Jacobean pulpit and a large collection of hatchments of the Breedon family. Lord Nelson's favourite bo'sun, Tom Carter, lived in Pangbourne and is buried in the churchyard.

Church cottage, west of the churchyard, was the home of Kenneth Grahame, author of *The Wind in the Willows*, who undoubtedly found inspiration for his classic as he wandered along the ever-changing but always peaceful riverside.

Opposite the church is a row of well-preserved Tudor and 17th century cottages, and next to them the former village smithy.

Berkshire County Council has designated the centre of the village as a conservation area, under the Civic Amenities Act. The area includes High Street, the Square, and the area immediately around the church.

The fine red brick 18th century house, Bere Court, is situated in the south-west of the parish. A former building on the site was originally a country residence and Chapel of the Abbots of Reading. Later this passed to Sir Francis Englefield, and in 1596 it was bought by Sir John Davies. In 1671 the property passed to John Breedon, who was a great benefactor to the village, and who built and endowed the Breedon School, part of which still stands on the Reading Road. The Breedon Trust still exists to educate boys of the parish.

Pangbourne College adjoins Bere Court land, standing on the hill about a mile from the village. It was founded by Sir Thomas Lane Devitt and his son Philip in 1917 to educate and train boys for the Royal and Merchant Navies. The founders stipulated, however, that the education provided was to be suitable for any boy who subsequently decided not to take up a career at sea. The College owns 100 yards of river Thames frontage, and boathouses and craft of all sizes.

A small area of common land, and the old cattle pound, are to be found near Pangbourne College, on the Yattendon Road.

A stretch of riverside, known as Pangbourne Meadow, lying to the east of Whitchurch Bridge, is owned by the parish, having been purchased by voluntary contributions in the 1930s. The adjoining portion of the meadow was purchased by the National Trust and the whole meadow is controlled by the Parish Council.

# Peasemore

Peasemore lies to the north-west of Chieveley and has the ancient sheep drove road, the Green Lane to the Ridgeway, as its eastern boundary. A Stone Age axe head found in the orchard of Princes Farm makes it conceivable that the village could have been inhabited since the Stone Age. Its original name was Praximer but there have been many variations over the centuries.

It appeared in the Domesday Book with three Manor Houses, though one of these moved to the ownership of Beedon upon the marriage of the owner's daughter. The remaining two Manors came into the hands of Henry VIII, who ran them both as one. The first of these still bears the name of Peasemore Manor and was once owned by Thomas Chaucer. The second was Gidley and this was owned by the Hatt family. Hatt is one of the first names on the church register and is of Saxon origin; only one member of this great family remains in Peasemore.

In the 13th century two pieces of land were given to the Priory of Poughley, the first to Peasemore House, which was an annexe to the Priory and formerly known as Priorside; the second piece was Priors

*Peasemore - General view of the village with the church.*

Wood, which then covered about 100 acres of land. Dutch elm disease has caused the temporary disappearance of Priors Copse, which extended to a mere three acres by this time, but this area has been completely replanted with indigenous trees. At the Dissolution of the Monastries Peasemore House was given to Cardinal Wolsey and when he was empeached it fell to the Abbot of Westminster, who subsequently sold it to a John Carlton.

The old church of St. Paeda was of Norman construction but was demolished during the 19th century. The tower on the existing church of St. Barnabas was built by Coward and dates back to about 1730, although the rest of the church was built during the last century. It does, however, boast a nice peal of six bells – possibly one of the best in the county.

In the mid-17th century a fire started at Drakes Farm destroying all the thatched cottages in the centre of the village, the church barns and rectory. A fine 17th century thatched barn survives at Peasemore House and there are a number of flint and brick buildings, a few downland cob buildings and two granaries on staddle stones to be seen, one in the village and one at nearby Hill Green.

In the past Peasemore was a busy little place; the woollen mills, which served Jack O'Newbury, were destroyed in the fire, and more recently the village blacksmith, two shops, the school, the post office and bus service have gone – but there are positive signs of new enterprise. This has always been predominantly a centre of downland agriculture but with the decrease in the number of people employed on the land there is a danger that Peasemore might join the ranks of other dormitory villages. One new 'industry' is the recent development of a racehorse training establishment with its own all-weather gallop.

It is hoped that there will be active encouragement for other traditional rural industries in the future, providing local employment and topics for discussion in the Fox and Hounds.

# Pinkneys Green

Pinkneys Green derives its name from the Norman Knight, Ghilo de Pinkney, who was granted lands in the Maidenhead area as reward for supporting William the Conqueror. Many Pinkneys have been lords of the manor, the last being Catherine Pinkney, mother of the illegitimate Peregrine Hoby, who was adopted as heir to the Hoby estates in Bisham.

A dictionary definition of a village as 'a settlement of huts round a track of land to which all had common rights of cultivation' describes Pinkneys Green exactly. The 'huts' are now well built residences. When the growth of Maidenhead and the trunk roads threatened the district, the National Trust took over the guardianship of Maidenhead Thicket, known to locals as 'The Common'. Within living memory, flocks of sheep owned by the local inhabitants grazed there. There is still a house called Shepherd's Standing built on land where once the shepherds met to pick out their flocks.

Maidenhead Thicket was first known by its present name in the 13th century when it was called Maidenheath or Maiden-hythe. In the days of coaching, highwaymen hid in this wild and uncultivated part and robbed the travellers. There is a record as early as 1255 that trees and brushwood were cut back to make the road safer. The Vicar of Hurley is said to have received extra pay for braving the dangers of the Thicket on his way to take services at Maidenhead. 1838 was the year when the Great Western Railway was opened up between Paddington and Maidenhead, destroying for ever the isolation of Pinkneys Green.

When building threatened an area, the Archaeological and Historical Societies excavated sites, discovering all kinds of medieval and prehistoric objects. As recently as 1964 excavations in an area known as 'Camley' unearthed a potter's field with eleven kilns, four of which have been carefully examined. A variety of interesting domestic pottery shards have also been found. Other digs have revealed shards of Belgic origin and even a Palaeolithic hand axe. Robin Hood's Arbour was found on an exavation in 1960 to have been an enclosure for animals rather than of military origin and proved to date from the period AD 1-500.

The Maidenhead Brick and Tile Company's kilns were functioning at Pinkneys Green until a few years ago. At one time they were owned by Mr Norman Cooper who built the remarkable Queen Anne House on Castle Hill, Maidenhead (unfortunately now demolished), as a demonstration of his virtuosity as a brick and tile maker. The brick works themselves were considered an interesting example of industrial archaeology.

Local names suggest links with the past, such as 'The Old Saxon Road' aligning with Malders Lane, which passes through the old Brick and Tile Company's yard. A Magistrates' Court House once existed at the Bath Road end of the long Courthouse Road, and the Pond House commemorates the Reading Road that is marked on the old maps of the Bath Road.

Pinkneys Green has another claim to fame in that it was the actual birthplace of the Girl Guide movement, the first Troop being formed here by Miss Baden-Powell in 1910.

# Priestwood 🪶

Priestwood was the first Neighbourhood Centre of Bracknell New Town to be developed. Nine such centres have been planned, each with its own community centre, church, shops, schools, public house, play spaces and open rural area. Although Priestwood may not be considered technically a village, the rural spirit and interest remains. After all, Priestwood began in the wooded S.W. section of the parish of Warfield, with a tributary of the Kennet, the Bull Brook, passing through it, fed by Warfield waters.

Today Priestwood is proud of its New Town amenities but has managed to keep its undulating contours and many well-established trees. There is now an attractive riverside walk to Binfield along the Bull. At first we were sad to see farms taken over and Priestwood Common woodlands bulldozed out of existence, but when the pleasant houses with their pretty gardens and wide, well-grassed spaces emerged, we were reconciled to our loss, especially when we saw erstwhile London children playing so healthily and safely in their new surroundings. The growth of neighbourliness has been encouraged by the shopping centre and the church, with its delicate fibreglass spire. St. Andrew's is an exciting new design allowing a spacious uncluttered nave where the altar is wholly visible and the priest is one with his congregation, and not segregated as in older churches.

Bracknell Street grew from a small settlement where paths crossed in Windsor Forest, into a sleepy but prosperous community of about 5,000 inhabitants. Horse fairs were held in April, August and October all through the 18th and 19th centuries when bull-baiting was popular. This sport was forbidden after 1835. The October Fair was also a Hiring Fair where anyone from a cook to a farm labourer announced their skills for hire. The cooks wore a red ribbon and carried a basting spoon, and the housemaids put a blue ribbon and carried a broom. From these fairs sprang the present Cattle and Produce Market. The largest egg market in the South of England founded in 1870 is a Bracknell speciality.

When the Windsor Forest Turnpike Trust was formed in 1759, Bracknell boasted several hostelries for the London stage coaches. Two of the turnpike milestones, proclaiming the distance from Hyde Park Corner, are still to be seen. The Red Lion Inn was one of the original coaching inns, the first stop after the rather dangerous drive from Wokingham through Priestwood Common.

Today, Priestwood is threatened by further development on its Binfield and Warfield borders, on what is pleasant agricultural land.

# Purley 🦢

Purley is a split-level village, cut in two by the Western Region line of British Rail and the Reading/Oxford Road (A329) which runs parallel to it. The nearest railway station is Tilehurst, a mile distant in the east, and to the west are Pangbourne and other Thames-side villages. Four narrow red brick bridges cross the railway, taking you from the lower to the upper level. The river Thames curves round the northern and eastern boundaries, through Mapledurham Lock with its colourful flowerbeds in the warmer months. From here can be seen the wooded hills of the Chilterns on the opposite bank and the boats travelling upstream the 33 miles to Oxford or possibly all the 78 miles downstream to London.

The name Purley has been variously spelt as Porlaa, Porlei etc. and is said to mean 'a clearing in the woods for snipe and bittern' rather than an earlier suggestion of 'land of the pear trees'.

Actually Purley Village – the original Purley Street – is a mere quarter of a mile of pretty old cottages and the infants school, with Purley Lodge at the west end. In the 18th century John George Liebenrood, a Dutch merchant and local benefactor, who married a Purley girl, lived in this house, rumoured to have connections with Reading Abbey. In 1872 the Rector of Purley, Rev. Richard Palmer, generously financed the brick and flint school building for fifty-five children (specified to be of 'the labouring, manufacturing and other poorer classes of Purley'). His sister gave approximately three-quarters of an acre on which plot were 'two messuages (houses) together with gardens and orchards and the schoolhouse and buildings'.

The path leading onwards to the church of St. Mary the Virgin is now a road of modern dwellings, with a boat marina. The church, for a long time isolated from the village, is again surrounded by houses, and like so many others was extensively restored in the 1870s by G. E. Street, to conform with the approved architecture of that time. In 1983 a hexagonal lantern-roofed north aisle, with knapped flint exterior walls, was added to accommodate the growing population, also to serve as a church hall.

Purley Magna manor house was once close to the church but about 1800 the Storer family, Lords of the Manor at that time, built Purley Park, a fine mansion in the classical style on higher, dryer ground, today a home for handicapped men.

On the western side, standing well back from the main road, is Purley Hall, previously known as Hyde Hall and said to date from 1609. The boundaries of Sulham, Whitchurch and Purley meet in the dining room. The Hyde family was much persecuted for its Catholic beliefs.

The mortgaged estate was sold to Francis Hawes of the 'South Sea Bubble' scandal in 1720. The Wilder family bought it in 1773 and held it for nearly 200 years. During that time Warren Hastings rented the house while he prepared his defence against impeachment. His ghost, or that of his wife, is reputed to haunt the house. This side of Purley is shielded by a large area of beech and conifer plantations, maintained by the Forestry Commission, which provide secluded walks and the habitat of muntjac, fallow deer and other wild-life.

The population of Purley remained less than 200 until 1900, when numbers increased dramatically, especially after the influx of refugees from the London blitz of the Second World War. Many remained permanently in their holiday homes on the Purley Park River Estate. The population has risen in the last decade to about 4,000.

We have three shops – two general stores (one housing a post office) and a newsagents/sweetshop. The upper part of Purley, mostly residential, includes the recreation ground and sports pavilion, providing facilities for football, netball, cricket and tennis, with a thriving social club. There are no public houses in Purley. In addition to the infants school there is a primary school (Long Lane) and a very nice hall, built by villagers as a memorial to those killed in the Second World War – this during the day houses the play group.

Bordering the river are three fertile farms – Scraces Farm, Home Farm and Westbury Farm, which includes a thriving vineyard, one of the largest in England and now open to the public.

Like so many Thames-side villages, urbanisation and heavy vehicular traffic has blurred the old village outlines but every effort has been made to preserve trees, of which there are many noble beeches and the venerable oak in Long Lane. It is questionable whether this was ever part of the western boundary of Windsor Great Forest, as village tradition claims. New planting continues. In an endeavour to further the village atmosphere there are plans to hold a Purley Fayre each summer, hoping to bring together all the various groups for a day of fun.

# Remenham

The village of Remenham probably derives its name from the Saxon meaning 'home of the ravens' or, alternatively, from the Remi – a Celtic tribe that roamed and hunted in the area. There are many traces of Roman occupation and evidence that it thrived as a Saxon community until the arrival of the Normans in the 11th century.

It is mentioned in Domesday Book and in the Charters of Westminster Abbey dated 1075. The great horseshoe loop of the Thames between

LYCH GATE. ST. NICHOLAS CHURCH.

REMENHAM.

124

Hurley and Wargrave forms its boundary, including the Marsh and Hambleden locks. This parish boundary is an ancient demarcation, for 2,000 years ago it formed the southern frontier of the Kingdom of Cunobelinus – Shakespeare's King Cymbeline. Between the two locks lies the famous Henley Reach, the longest straight stretch of river on the Upper Thames. It is here that the Henley Royal Regatta takes place every year, as it has done since 1839. The course stretches from Temple Island, with its intriguing 18th century temple in the Greek manner, to the finish one mile and five hundred and seventy yards upstream. It is, in fact, entirely within the parish of Remenham that this venerable rowing event takes place, and during its four days of competition the village plays host to many thousands of visitors from all parts of the world. Two old-established clubs, the Leander and Remenham Club, are sited on the Berkshire bank of Henley Reach – the Leander Club being the senior rowing club in the world.

To the south of the A423 trunk road lies the great estate of Park Place. In 1719, when only a farmhouse, it was bought by Lord Archibald Hamilton, son of the 3rd Duke of Hamilton, who enlarged it and subsequently sold it to H. R. H. Frederick, Prince of Wales who resided there for fifteen years. In 1752 it was purchased by General Conway who added many remarkable and eccentric features to the estate. He commissioned the 'Rugged Arch Bridge' now called Conway's Bridge, built with stones from the ruins of Reading Abbey, which carries – albeit precariously – the main Henley to Wargrave road. Also on the estate is to be found a Druids Temple, or more probably a Celtic burial place, transported in its entirety from Jersey as a gift from the people of that island upon his retirement as Governor.

Park Place also boasts the upper part of the original Wren steeple from St. Bride's Church, Fleet Street. It was erected by a later owner on the highest point of the grounds as an obelisk commemorating the accession of Queen Victoria to the throne in 1837. A notable enterprise of General Conway's period of ownership was his cultivation of lavender on a commercial scale, and construction of ovens and stills for distilling scent. These stills had an additional use, as the local historian R. D. Burnell has pointed out in his book *The Henley Regatta,* in providing a welcome supply of local potato 'gin'. Finally, among his many legacies are Remenham's distinctive Lombardy poplars, the first to have been planted in England. Since 1971 the mansion has served as a local authority board school for boys with special needs.

To the north a group of cottages, Remenham Farm – once the Manor Farm, and the old rectory cluster round the church of St. Nicholas. This is all that remains of the once thriving centre of the village which never recovered from the 17th century disaster when the entire population was wiped out by the plague. The church, in its present form, dates from only 1870 but rests upon Saxon and Norman foundations and has a recorded history of more than a thousand years.

A mile further downstream, at the extremity of the parish, lies the hamlet of Aston once the landing for the Hambleden ferry. During the Civil War, Parliamentarians and Royalists fought a bitter battle here and remains of iron cannon were, until recently, to be found under the crest of the hill by Culham Court. Culham Court itself is the other great estate of the parish centring upon a splendid house also with its royal associations, for the story is told that when George III was entertained there hot rolls from the monarch's favourite baker in London were brought, wrapped in flannel to keep them warm, by relays of horseman!

In the last few decades Remenham, like so many English villages, has had to struggle to maintain its identity. It has been deprived of its shops, its post office, its school and, most recently, its own rectory.

Nevertheless, its residents preserve a pride in its past, a keen sense of present conservation and a concern for its future through an active Parish Council, Parochial Church Council and its flourishing Women's Institute.

# Riseley

Life in the small village of Riseley changed radically for its inhabitants with the opening of the Swallowfield by-pass in Spring 1981. Before that time, and upon the completion of the M4 motorway, heavy container lorries and other traffic had thundered through the village, barely negotiating the narrow bends of the notorious A33. And what had once been a country road, through the middle of a small village, now became the major link for all traffic going south and south-west.

But then, after years during which various schemes to relieve the situation had been considered and rejected, and when one half of the village hardly knew the other half, separated as they were from each other by this continual stream of vehicles, rural peace once more descended upon Riseley.

People could stand and gossip by the roadside, as they do in all small villages. Mothers no longer feared for the safety of their children as they set off on their bicycles to call on their friends, or just played the running, jumping and skipping games which children everywhere enjoy. Indeed, for the first few weeks after the opening of the new by-pass, it was the sound of children's voices echoing about the village of which one suddenly became aware. And the older villagers, reminiscing about the days of their own childhood, were reminded of how they had been

*Riseley Village · had enjoyed Maypole dancing on the village green ....*

able to play whip and top up and down the road, and had enjoyed maypole dancing on the village green.

Once again, Riseley has a village green and a new Village Hall, both meeting places for a village which at last begins to feel itself as a whole community, and not just a piece of ribbon development along a very busy and dangerous trunk road.

# Ruscombe &#x1F33F;

About half a million years ago, an ancient Thames flowed eastwards over the gravel of Sonning Golf Links to Ruscombe, where it turned north. Many Stone Age flint implements have been collected from the gravel pits of Ruscombe Hill, and the present highway through the village was the old Saxon road.

The first recorded history occurs in the foundation charter of the Cathedral of old Sarum in 1091. Among the original endowments is listed 'the church of Sunning (Sonning) with the tythes and other property thereto belonging, and ten hides of land in Rothescamp (Ruscombe)'.

The eastern part of the parish, known as the 'Lakes', was once a marshy swamp, flooded in winter, providing perch, pike and eel in abundance for the fishermen, and withes for the baskets were woven by industrious villagers. In 1820 the upper part of the Broadwater Stream was carried away by the Bray Cut, thus draining the lake. The land was enclosured and cultivated.

The Church of Saint James the Great, made of flint, has a long history, but the chancel is all that remains of the old structure. The nave and tower were rebuilt in 1863-9. An ancient yew tree stands outside the main door, and a patch of rough grass with a few elms is all that remains of the village green. The 400 year old Church Cottage is said to be the original Chaplain's House, but is no longer church property. Of the same date is the shooting and fishing lodge where George I was reputed to pause for a meal when out for a day's sport from Windsor.

William Penn, famous as the founder of Pennsylvania and a Quaker, lived in the parish from 1710 until his death in 1718. He used to drive through Twyford, in a coach and four on his way to Friends' Meetings in Reading. The house he lived in was pulled down in 1830, probably Ruscombe House which was in the field opposite Southbury Farm. The original bakehouse and dairy buildings were finally demolished a few years ago, revealing an unsuspected stairway and attic room. Legend says that this was a highwayman's hideout. Penn's name lives on in the Rural District Council Estate of Pennfields.

The old pump in London Road, used to lay the dust on roads, was restored in 1984.

# St. Sebastians

There is no village of St. Sebastians, it is simply part of the large straggling parish of Wokingham Without and lies mostly along each side of Nine Mile Ride, in a kind of no-mansland between Crowthorne and Wokingham.

At one time the area was all part of the Great Forest of Windsor and since poverty was rife and forest laws severe – a man could be hanged for killing a deer even if his family was near to starvation – the people were lawless and heathen.

The situation became so bad that about the middle of the 19th century, a Wokingham lawyer wrote to the Dean of Sarum appealing to him to help remedy the spiritual destitution of the area. He wrote 'It lies in a wild and remote district and contains a population exclusively labourers or broomdashers who stand in need of regular pastoral superintendence, the want of which must be attended with the growth of irreligion, vice and immorality'. Not a very pretty picture!

The only occupation open to the people at the time was that of broomdashers – cutting twigs in the forest and making them up into brooms or besoms. These were then sold either in Reading or as far afield as Bristol.

The first attempt to bring Christianity to St. Sebastians was made by a young man – a Baptist – who worked at the Heelas store in Wokingham, and who held occasional services there. Eventually, in 1864, the Dean of Sarum decided that something more must be done and a chapel of ease to All Saint's church in Wokingham was built. In 1871, St. Sebastians church was separated from All Saints and the first vicar, The Reverend Hugh Redmond Morres, was appointed.

One of the most attractive large houses is Heathlands, once the home of Mr William Howard Palmer a member of the famous Reading biscuit firm of Huntley and Palmer. The Palmer family took a great interest in the well being of their workpeople and their families and in 1870 contributed to the building of the St. Sebastians primary school, still a thriving school today. Heathlands has now been turned into flats and the stable block houses a riding school.

As a memorial to the men who were killed in the Great War, the Palmer family built the St. Sebastians Memorial Hall. This has now been taken over by the Wokingham Without Parish Council and activities include a play school, Women's Institute meetings, senior citizens' meetings, scottish dancing, dog training, wine club meetings as well as the occasional wedding or coming-of-age parties.

The St. Sebastians Women's Institute was started in February 1925 by Mrs Howard Palmer as an educational and social activity for the women of the then still somewhat remote area.

The two public houses are the Crooked Billet, about 150 years old and the Who'd a tho't it, considerably older. There is a good story to account for the rather strange name of the latter. It is this – one day the First Duke of Wellington and his followers were returning to Stratfield Saye after a hard day's hunting in the forest when they came upon a clearing with a few houses. Hot and thirsty after the chase the Duke sent one of his servants to enquire if they might be given water for themselves and their horses. To the Duke's great surprise, after the horses were watered, he and his men were offered ale brewed in one of the houses. He is said to have exclaimed 'By Gad, who would have thought it' and the present name of the pub, thought to be built on the site of the old alehouse, is a corruption of his remark. The old inn sign showed the duke and his men riding into the clearing, but the present sign shows astronauts walking on the moon and suddenly coming upon a large bottle of beer. Who would have thought it?

In a section of Forestry Commission woodland – Gorrick Wood – is the site of an ancient well, the water of which was supposed to have possessed great healing powers, especially for eye diseases. Queen Elizabeth I is said to have visited this well several times.

An old roman road, known locally as The Devil's Highway, runs through the parish – part of it was dug up during the building of one of the housing estates and a large stone, named the Wulwyn Stone, was unearthed. It stands today near the place where it was found.

There used to be a sub post office cum shop with a telephone kiosk but these have now disappeared. At Heathlands Country Market is a much more modern development, a 'pick your own' and farm shop together with a plant nursery and a 'catch your own fish' tank. This is extremely popular especially in the soft fruit season.

St. Sebastians is now an up to date, flourishing community – a long way from the era of the broomdashers.

# Sandhurst

Sandhurst, Berkshire, is just separated from Hampshire by the river Blackwater and from Surrey by the Wish Stream which flows through the grounds of the Royal Military Academy.

Sandhurst is a name of Saxon origin – hurst meaning a 'wooded eminence' and Sand referring to the type of soil. In those ancient times, a few peasant huts clustered together in a sheltered dell surrounded by moorland and the only possible industry was the cutting of turves. During the reign of Henry VIII, the breeding of sheep was introduced in the area known as Sheep Rayles (now Snaprails), and slowly the population began to increase.

George III attended the first Army manoeurves that took place on the rough heathland towards Easthampstead in 1792, and the obvious advantages of the area for peacetime Army training led to the building of the Royal Military College in 1812, now known as the Royal Military Academy, following its amalgamation with the Royal Military Academy, Woolwich. The R.M.A. is the centre for training officers for the British Army, and until recently the grounds were open to the public, but for security reasons this is no longer possible, and permission must be sought to enter the grounds, to see the Chapel and the College buildings. The coming of the military to the area was followed by the Enclosures Act of 1816, and the building locally of Wellington College and Broadmoor Hospital led to an influx of people and a demand for housing which is still persisting!

In the reign of James I there were 29 houses – there are now over 3,500 homes, even excluding Owlsmoor which as a result of recent boundary changes is now administered by the Sandhurst Town Council. Situated between the M3 and M4 Motorways, and within easy driving distance of London Airport, there is constant pressure to release land for housing, which leads to heavy use of local roads. Sandhurst has over 40 acres of recreational land including a pond, in the centre of the village. 80 acres of Edgbarrow Woods form a country park between Sandhurst and Crowthorne, and Ambarrow Woods are National Trust lands. There are eleven public houses, (but the Temperance Hall has long since been converted to a private house!) also a social club and a Community Hall. A well-used day centre for the elderly and a new public library are situated in the centre of the village. There are four primary and a comprehensive school, plus Eagle House, a prep. school for Wellington College. Also one railway station but no police station.

The earliest mention of a church in Sandhurst is 1220, but the present Parish Church was built by G. E. Street in 1853. It has a tall Surrey-style tower and a shingled spire. Nothing remains of the original church.

Most of the large houses and estates have either been converted into flats or developed as housing estates, and Rackstraw Farm, one of the oldest buildings in the village is now a very busy licensed restaurant.

Sandhurst is under pressure of constant change, but the Richard Bannister Charity founded in 1417 from a gift of 15½ acres of land and understood to be the oldest charity in Berkshire, is still dispensed annually by the local trustees, half of the income going to Crowthorne and the other half to Sandhurst Day Centre Welfare.

# Shaw-cum-Donnington

The two villages of Shaw and Donnington stand less than a mile apart, united in one parish and linked by the river Lambourn on the north side of Newbury.

Donnington village, although without a church, is less scattered and developed than its neighbour. The older houses here cluster together at the foot of the hill, beside the bridges and below the imposing ruins of Donnington Castle. This castle, of which only the gatehouse now remains, is famous for the part it played when defended by Sir John Boys in the Battle of Newbury during the Civil War.

Of great interest also is Donnington Hospital. A delightful group of almshouses sit around a courtyard, and with tall twisted chimneys indicating the building date of 1602. Newer almshouses for women at Abberbury Close were built in 1938 in Tudor style. Another interesting building is Donnington Priory, founded in 1360. This house later became the home of Thomas Hughes, author of *Tom Brown's School*

DONNINGTON CASTLE

*Days* and has recently been restored by a leading firm of auctioneers to become their headquarters and salerooms.

Shaw village, linked to Newbury by modern housing has the impressive Elizabethan Shaw House and its church standing side by side. Shaw House is now a mixed comprehensive school. The pretty church, although Norman in style and with a Norman font, was built in 1842 replacing an earlier church. Nearby stands Shaw Mill, the scene of bread riots in 1766. This has now been restored to attractive residential use.

Sporting interests are well catered for in Shaw-cum-Donnington, with cricket, international motor cross events and a very new public golf course.

Shaw-cum-Donnington is a lovely parish to explore. A favourite place for picnics is the Snelsmore Country Park, recently improved by local conservation groups. It is one of the largest heathlands in southern England, and within easy walking distance of Donnington Castle.

# Shinfield

Shinfield lies three miles south of Reading and is bounded by the river Loddon to the south and east, Grazeley to the west, and Spencers Wood to the south. The earliest settlement was in Saxon times, Domesday Book stating that the King held 'Selingfelde in demesne'. The Loddon provided drinking water, valuable fisheries and power for a mill.

William the Conqueror gave the Manors of Shinfield and Swallow-field to William FitzOsbern, Lord of Breteuil in Normandy and Earl of Hereford, who founded St. Mary's Church about 1070. A list of Vicars, inside the church, goes back to 1280. The advowson of the church was granted in 1289 to the Bishop of Hereford, and remains with the Dean and Chapter of Hereford to this day. In 1312 Edward II and the Bishop of Hereford were shooting deer in the Shinfield part of Windsor Forest, and the Bishop asked the King for assistance in rebuilding his cathedral. Later the Bishop made such a good shot at a deer that Edward agreed to give him the tithes of Shinfield and Swallowfield.

The old Manor House, probably dating from the 16th century was on the main Shinfield Road. In 1792, when repairs were done to a chimney, a Cartulary (a book in which were made copies of deeds of properties relating to Reading Abbey) was found in a blocked-up room. Probably hidden at the time of the Dissolution of the Abbey in 1537, it is now in the British Museum.

An extract from *The Wonders of the Universe*, 1727, reads:

'... My Lord Cromwell, after his success at Dorchester, did bring his forces to Caversham to cross the river, but learning that bodies of Royalists were forming in Reading and in the country beyond, he did dispatch his troops to engage them – which troops did per-sue them to Shinfield and beyond – a body of the enemy having taken refuge in the Parish Church. Cannon were brought up and used, the tower being reduced ...'

*(circa* 1644)

By 1661 the tower had been restored and three of the six bells installed to celebrate the restoration of the monarchy.

In an extensive restoration of the church carried out in 1855 by Sir George Gilbert Scott, the chancel was extended and a tiled floor laid. The brasses in the floor were probably not removed at this time, and in 1936 a subsidence near the font revealed, under the tiles, the Mitford brass. This commemorates the parents of Mary Mitford, who lived at Three Mile Cross, 1820 to 1850, and who described life in Shinfield in the classic, *Our Village.*

As a memorial to those killed in the war and as a thanksgiving for peace, the Shinfield Recreation and Sports Association decided, in 1947, to lease a field for 99 years from the National Insitute for Research in Dairying, for use as a recreational field. Each year a carnival is held. The proceeds go towards upkeep of the field which provides tennis courts, cricket and football pitches, and a children's corner.

The N.I.R.D. bought the manor, formerly the old rectory next to the church, in 1920. An old cedar tree in the manor grounds is known as Katharine's Tree. Legend has it that it was planted by Katharine of Aragon, given the manors of Shinfield and Swallowfield by Henry VIII. In 1985 the N.I.R.D. ceased to exist, the animal scientists joined the Grasslands Research Institute at Hurley, and a new Food Institute was formed at Shinfield.

In 1951 the Shinfield Festival began in a very small way, but has proved so successful that each year sees a greater interest and increase in entries.

St. Mary's Church celebrated its 900th Anniversary in 1971, and every organisation in the village was invited to participate, resulting in ten days of activities and enjoyment such as Shinfield could hardly have known before. Similar activities were held again in 1974/5, to raise money for the restoration of the bells, which were rehung in 1976.

The rural aspect of Shinfield has changed since 1971 which saw the opening of the M4 motorway. Parts of the Lower Earley Development to the north of the motorway come within the parish of Shinfield. A new feature of the skyline is Berkshire County Council's office block opened by the Queen in 1982.

The village has benefited by a new Parish Hall, which replaced the old Community Centre in 1983, and is used by both the Shinfield (afternoon) and Pound Green (evening) Women's Institutes.

# Silchester 🕮

Long before Silchester became the thriving Roman city which its name suggests, it was the important British town of Calleva Atrebatum. The name derives from the tribe of the Atrebates, whose kings ruled much of Southern England. Visitors to Silchester now can follow the perimeter of the Roman city by tracing the remains of the wall which enclosed this important centre and the gateways leading to London, Winchester and Old Sarum can still be seen. In the period between 1864 - 1892 the whole area was extensively excavated, displaying evidence of roads on a grid system and many very large and important buildings, chief of these being the Forum with the Basilica. Sadly, the ground had to be filled in again and it reverted to farmland, the lines of the former road system showing clearly in aerial photographs in the shading of the crops grown there.

In recent years more work has been done by a team of people led by Dr. Michael Fulford of the Archaeological Department at Reading University. Their gaily coloured tents add life to the summer scene.

New evidence has been discovered of way of life in this Roman civilian town, for it was never a garrison, and the ruins of the Amphitheatre which lies outside the wall near the East Gate have also been uncovered. The majority of the finds from the 19th century excavations are in Reading Museum but there is an interesting display of maps and replicas in the small museum in the village.

Just inside the Roman Wall at its eastern side stands the beautiful church of St. Mary the Virgin. This is near the spot where the remains were found within the Roman City of what is thought to be the earliest known urban Christian church anywhere north of the Alps. The earliest part of the present building dates from about 1180 and was added to by succeeding Lords of the Manor. There are some very early frescoes on the walls at the east end. When Oliver Cromwell's soldiers were desecrating so many churches, local legend has it that the original glass from the windows was removed and hidden somewhere for safe-keeping. Unfortunately legend does not recall where – so the parishioners of Silchester are still hoping to discover it intact!!! Certainly the carved chancel screen was buried in a dung heap at nearby Manor Farm and not restored to the church until early in the 19th century. This presented some difficulties to a local craftsman who was asked to repair the screen recently – how to match oak which has spent some years buried in a dung heap? Luckily he succeeded.

There is a tablet on a wall in the church recording the gift by a Mr. Hyde in 1671, of four acres of valuable land to the poor of the parish. Hydes Charity still exists and is administered by trustees from the parish and the name is remembered in Hydes Platt, a small estate of houses in the village.

Although Silchester's history goes back to pre-Roman times it is by no means an old fashioned village. In the Middle Ages the village moved from the Roman city area to the Pound, where cattle were impounded when allowed to stray. Pound House was the pub, and Pound Cottage was the home of the Pound Keeper. There was also a smithy and a bakery near the corner. On its western boundary is situated what is probably the present hub of the place, Silchester Common. This 160 acres of Heathland and wooded areas, with parts designated as a Site of Special Scientific Interest, with rare plants, butterflies and birds. There are two playing fields for cricket and football, one of which is used by Silchester Church of England Primary School. Also on the edge of the Common is the Methodist Chapel and, close to the playing field, stand the post office and shop, the local inn, the Calleva Arms and the Village Hall. The hall is the centre of numerous activities throughout the year.

In 1978 the present Duke of Wellington, who as Lord of the Manor owned the Common and several farms in the area, put them up for sale. The villagers were, naturally, very concerned about the future of the Common, but their worries were ended by the great generosity of Mr John Cook. Having bought the property Mr Cook presented the Common to the Parish Council for the people of Silchester for all time in memory of his father Mr Sidney Cook who once owned a farm nearby. At the handing over ceremony Mr Cook broke a twig from an oak tree growing on the Common and presented it to Lady Atkinson, Chairman of the Parish Council. This followed an ancient custom when many people were unable to read or write and signified the legal transfer of land.

Although nearby towns have experienced rapid development and the village is only 15 minutes drive from both the M3 and M4, Silchester still enjoys a rural environment and peaceful setting.

# Sonning

Turn off the busy A4 down Sonning Lane, and at once you sense the magic ... whether it's the green tunnel of summer trees, the glowing tints of autumn, arching bare branches or glittering frost of winter, the peace is there.

Perhaps Dick Turpin felt the same sudden lightness of heart when, after a 'hold-up' on the Bath Road, he galloped down the lane heading for his aunt's cottage. Tradition has it that, reaching the village, off he leapt (well-trained Black Bess making her way to the underground stable below the cottage) and raced through the churchyard, over the bridge into Oxfordshire. There he'd lie-up till the hue and cry had died down and he could join Bess. The cottage in time became The Dog, one of many inns in Sonning; it is now, with its neighbour, a private house called, of course, Turpins.

It is difficult to realize today, wandering around this small, peaceful village, that a thousand years ago it was the nerve centre of one of the largest parishes in Wessex, stretching from Sonning Common to Sandhurst. It boasted, in the 10th and 11th centuries, its own Saxon Bishops, three of whom became Archbishops of Canterbury; and from the 11th to 16th century the Bishops and Deans of Salisbury regularly visited their own vast residences here. This enormous estate was handed over to the Church in the 7th century, and was very much on the map when Reading was but a huddle of huts hugging the banks of the Kennet. Sonning's importance declined because it was not a good administrative centre for such a vast diocese; later there was the growth and rivalry of Reading Abbey.

SONNING. THE DEANERY (LUTYENS)

Domesday Book records 'Osmund Bishop of Sarisberie holds Soninges in demesne, in right of his Bishopric'. The Bishops' rambling palace lay alongside the church, looking on to the river and the water meadows beyond.

In 1574 the manor of Sonning was given to the Crown, later passing to private families, Barker and Rich chief among them. Another ghostly visitor, as the church clock strikes midnight, is a willowy Miss Rich, who allegedly floats over the ancient flint wall in Sonning Lane.

Beautiful St. Andrew's Church, much restored in 1852 by the perhaps over zealous Victorians, has interesting brasses and monuments; and if walls could talk, what tales they'd have to tell! One Vicar had a habit of striding through the village with bared sword; another in the 1570s displeased his wardens by putting a new seat for his wife '... in an unmeet

137

place', and allowing his cattle to run wild in the graveyard. Grave-robbing was prevalent in the last century, the bodies being sold to unscrupulous doctors for research. One such medical gentleman from Reading was in the habit of dining with Sonning's vicar while his confederates were at work just over the wall!

The Thames is islanded through Sonning, and the weir plays an important part in flood control. The rare Loddon Lily grows in the woods by the lock, itself famous for its flower garden which has many times earned the coveted 'garden award'. Sonning used to be centre of operations of Thames Navigation. Here lived the General Surveyor, and under his personal supervision was carried out constructive works from Lechlade to Staines, including the erection of pound-locks to replace the old flash-locks. A large, heavily laden barge needed the combined efforts of 50 to 80 men to negotiate it up through a flash-lock, and these 'scuffle-hunters' were the terror of the neighbourhood. In 1773 wages of men making the towpath were 1s. 6d. per day; when working in the water, gin was provided!

The mill, rebuilt many times and operating its own fleet of barges, ceased to work, for the first time since Saxon days, in 1969. It has now been converted into a unique, picturesque theatre and restaurant, keeping its original character, incorporating the mill wheel, etc. It attracts many visitors from far and wide. The audience can stroll round the beautiful grounds beside the river, during the interval, and relax to sound of running water.

Behind the ancient Deanery wall is a fine house, designed by Lutyens in 1899, standing just above the site of the old Deanery House. After various alterations, the present owner is in the process of restoring the house and gardens to their original state.

Sonning boasts its own Fire Station, manned by volunteers, and a thriving Working Men's Club. The Best-kept Village plaque has often graced the 'hall'.

The village is anxious to preserve its identity, and lives in the present as well as treasuring its past. In the Middle Ages it was a place of pilgrimage, and today, despite the traffic, modern pilgrims can still enjoy the peace and beauty of its ancient streets and riverside walks.

# Speen 🌿

On the road west just out of the large town of Newbury, is the village of Speen. At first sight just a village cut in half by the A4, Speen has a history way back beyond the Romans, because it was a settlement and hill fort for the early Britons and equalled by few other places for its rare

138

archaeological association with the Celtic period, pottery and bronze spearheads having been dug up on Speen Moor. Such natural advantages led to the Romans selecting this site for the station they called 'Spinae'. It is also rare that the modern name of a place resembles that which it bore in Roman times, and Speen is a remarkable exception. It stood at the crossroads of all the Roman roads in this area. Saxons and Normans left their mark here too, with Manor Houses and parts of St. Mary the Virgin, Speen's ancient church.

The next period of history where we find Speen playing an important part was the Civil War. There were two battles of Newbury during the period of strife between the Royalists and the Roundheads, and the second battle was fought at Speen Hill. During the Georgian era the nobility braved the bad roads and the highwaymen to take the waters at Bath. The Bath Road or A4 went right through Speen and the coaching inn, The Castle, stood at edge of the village and Royalty is said to have slept there. As time went on and traffic increased, Newbury had a by-pass but the A4 still ran through Speen. Lorries grew bigger and speed limits were set. Then one day the M4 was opened and Speen returned to comparative quiet on the roads.

Now let us take a walk around Speen and look for signs of this ancient history. Take the Old Bath Road out of Newbury and you come to the start of Speen Lane. Look across the road at a Georgian building, once the coaching inn, now three houses known as Castle Houses. Right on the corner stands a stone monument to commemorate the second battle of Newbury during the Civil War. A little over twenty years ago, Speen Lane was still a lane with a few large old houses and a Jacobean house that became an hotel. These have gone, but the modern houses fit in well with the old lane. As we walk along, we can see that the houses on the left have a marvellous view over the Kennet Valley with the River Kennet bordering Speen Moor, where the Celtic pottery and bronze spearheads were found. Rare flowers and water birds can be found here. Further on we cross the deep cutting of the old railway. Dr Beeching put paid to that piece of railway. The only turning to the left takes us down to the church, past the Sextons Cottage, and pausing to lean on a gate and admire the view over ploughed fields, the Kennet and Avon Canal in the valley, and the hills away in the distance.

Then we see the church, nestling in the trees. St. Mary the Virgin is the product of three churches on this site, each leaving its mark, the Saxon, Norman and 13th century, and much is retained, despite Victorian restoration.

Out of the churchyard through the lych-gate and up the grassy path, we find Our Lady Well, so named as dedication to the Blessed Virgin, the ancient church being under her special protection. The water was a spring of pure water held to have special healing powers for sore eyes, rickets, and measles. It is known locally as a Wishing Well, and it is said a ghost has been seen. We are back in Speen Lane and passing a 400 year old farm and barn. We are almost at the end of Speen Lane, with its beautiful old houses, and finally the Village Hall and the War Memorial. The Victorian Village Hall built in 1886, sees many activities within its walls. The playgroup, the W.I., kung fu and many social occasions.

We have come out on to the A4 at the far end of the village, so let us turn back along the main road and complete our circle, past the village store and post office. On the corner of the turning on the left, is an old Toll House. The road is Station Road but there is now no station and the level crossing gates have long gone, but that is the entrance to an excellent playing field. Opposite the Toll House is the oldest pub the Hare and Hounds, and further down the road on the edge of the village is the modern pub, the Starting Gate, a good name as many well known jockeys live in Speen. To complete our circle we arrive at the primary school.

The route we have just taken has changed very little over the years, with the exception of some modern houses at the beginning of Speen Lane. Speen has spread slightly on the northern side of the A4, but not much, and it remains an interesting place to visit and to live in.

# Spencers Wood ✍

Travelling south from Reading, Spencers Wood is approached by a hill, on the brow of which stands Queen Anne period Hill House, adorned at the driveway by a hawthorn bush 'so dainty and white' mentioned in Mary Mitford's classic *Our Village*. A few steps on a beerhouse stood, the Royal Berkshire Brewery's the Cricketers (now Arden House) which later became a butcher's shop, proudly displaying until the shop closed recently an order from Queen Victoria, headed 'Osborne House, I.O.W.' and dated 1888. The order requested '36 lbs sirloin at 9d per lb' to be obtained from Shaw Farm. Behind the building are the remains of a school where pupils paid one penny per day for tuition.

Next along our route was the Salmon family home, fronted by a beautiful hedge of red May trees; a lovely old oak beamed residence, alas, now gone. We now reach St Michael's church, donated by the Hunter family of Beech Hill, a neighbouring village, and built in 1908. The village hall, donated in memory of a member of the above family, was built by local men – Messrs Wheeler, Cox, Aldridge etc. Miss Hunter, a very gracious lady, is recently deceased.

Behind the church stood three or four Elizabethan cottages; one, restored, still remains. Nearby at one time stood a lock-up for local miscreants, sometimes used as an overnight stop to house prisoners on their way to the Reading courts.

The recreation ground was given by Captain Cobham of Shinfield. This was once rough with gorse, and in springtime was spangled with harebells. Horses and goats were tethered there, and sometimes a travelling fair would pull in and their music could be heard in the village as children enjoyed their rides on the roundabouts. Cricket was played and in the 1920s Messrs Lowe, Double and Merry were keen and strong batsmen. Today the recreation ground has a well-kept square and still a keen side, and for children there is an improved play area.

We now pass 'Eastrop', one of several Victorian houses, once the home of Mr Kenneth Salmon, the church architect, and Miss Queenie who was the church organist at that time. Mr Wheeler the builder of the church, lived in a thatched cottage (like many others, gone) alongside Jack Hobbs the butchers, which remains to this day a butcher's shop. Stanbury, a stately home which was owned by a Mr Alfrey, was often the meeting place of the South Berks Hounds, a spectacular sight as they proceeded along Wellington Drive, which still remains a lovely drive flanked on either side by a unique plantation of Wellingtonia firs, a sequoia conifer named after the Iron Duke. Stanbury park now houses a small residential estate, and the old 'weathercock cottages' no longer remain. Mr Alfrey donated the Church of England school, now a flourishing library, and a few of the old pupils still live in the village.

From 1890 until 1960 the village smithy was run by the Double family, and Mr C. Double & Sons all held the country championships. The building now houses a small light engineering company. Milestone Cottage still stands, and the old milestone 'Reading 4 miles – Basingstoke 12 miles' is still clear to read. This cottage was once an inn called Four Mile House and the Southampton coaches made a stop to refresh passengers and horses after the dusty journey. A straight-through village which is adorned by a pond on which the swans nested, and at which the horses quenched their thirst, and nearby a swing gate gives access to the common where a windmill pumped water. An old roman road in bygone days led to the brick kiln, where clay from the common was used to make bricks with which to build many of the local houses. Opposite this pond at the beginning of the century the local horsedrawn fire brigade was housed.

Our hairdresser's shop, 'The Old Bakery' was exactly what the name implies; Mr Clements was our first horsedrawn baker, and is still remembered by a few residents; a close in a housing development in the village bears his name. Now almost at the end of the village a saddlers, Webbs, stood and what was Cordery's garage is today a small industrial estate. The first village bus was gas fuelled, and was followed by 'Pride of the valley' – Reading 6d return, and weekly half a crown.

We are at end of our village. Goodbye to old days, but memories remain and Spencers Wood is still a happy place, full of good people, old residents, and new.

# Stanford Dingley 🦚

Stanford Dingley one of Berkshire's most beautiful villages, has a lovely setting in the valley of the Pang. It is as attractive as its name, the first part of which it owes to William de Stanford, in 1224 Lord of the Manor, and the second to Richard Dyneley, mentioned in 1428 as the son of William Dyneley, Esquire, of the Bodyguard to Henry VI.

The village can be justly proud of its old buildings, its mill was first mentioned in the Domesday Book. It has a 15th century coaching inn, several scheduled buildings, and numerous attractive houses and cottages. Two outstanding are the Old Rectory, a splendid Georgian house of mellow red brick, with attractive dormer windows, and the Garden House of a slightly later period.

The church is dedicated to St. Denys. Few churches in England bear his name. Legend has it that he was martyred in Paris during the 3rd century by beheading. He is said to have picked up his severed head, and walked away with it. Where he put it down he was buried and a church built to St. Denys. He has always been portrayed decapitated in medieval art, his head in his hands, and is indeed so represented on the lectern in Stanford Dingley church.

The charming and picturesque church, screened by Spanish chestnut trees, has a wealth of interest. Certainly a Saxon church was standing here before the Conquest. The present form is largely the result of building about 1200; but parts of the original masonry are contained in the walls at the west end of the Nave. The font is plain, probably Norman, the roof is finely timbered, and a splendid 13th century door, with contemporary ironwork, is plainly part of the original scheme. Restoration work in 1870 revealed wall paintings and some frescoes, which date from the 13th century.

No self-respecting English village is without at least one ancient inn. Stanford Dingley can boast of two splendid ones. The Bull, an old 15th century coaching inn with a wealth of old beams, is famous locally for the game played there – 'Ring the Bull' – the object being to swing a ring suspended from the ceiling by a cord on to a horn; certainly a game of some antiquity. The Boot Inn, though not so old, is reputedly haunted by a man who hanged himself in its orchard. Doors are said to close mysteriously at times; and speaking of ghosts – the Old Rectory is said to have one, and a shrouded women is said to walk in Jennets Wood at midnight.

Notable sons of the village were Thomas Teasdale, who made a fortune in the parish as a clothier, and later founded Pembroke College, Oxford. John Lyford, Citizen and Merchant Taylor of London, lord of the very ancient manor of Rushdens in the village, whose family also distinguished themselves as weavers and merchants in the clothing trade. Dr. Richard Valpy, Headmaster of Reading School from 1781, who had the Stanford Dingley advowson, and made his brother rector. Three other Valpys also served the parish. Another village worthy, Thomas Smith, became a factor to the Turkey merchants, died in Constantinople in 1623 leaving £20 to purchase a piece of land towards the maintenance of the church.

Throughout the ages industries have thrived in Stanford Dingley. Alongside the brick and weatherboard mill (mentioned in Domesday records) was the tannery, one of the oldest industries in Berkshire, based originally on ample supplies of oak bark. The former smithy, adjacent to its minute cottage, can be found in the centre of the village opposite the Bull Inn. More recently there was a bottle factory near the bridge, and its products are occasionally found in the gardens close by.

# Stockcross

'The old order changeth, giving place to new'. This adage could well be applied to the village of Stockcross, north of the A4 Bath Road, and about 2½ miles from Newbury. At first sight, it does look very much the same, but there have been a great many changes. The main road through the village, Ermin Street, is now what is known as a 'haul road' to the M4 some six miles away, and the volume of traffic has increased tremendously.

High technology has crept into the area too, with Benham House, a beautiful Georgian residence, built in 1175 under the direction of Henry Holland, being sold to Norsk Data, a Norwegian computer company. The gardens of the house were laid out by 'Capability Brown', and it was the home of the Sutton family for many years. Most of the retired people living in the village spent their working lives at Benham, either in the house, the garden or on the farm. They still live in the houses built for them, of brick and timber, at the turn of the century, by the Sutton Estate, to replace the older ones, which were then pulled down.

The village is a strange mix of architecture , with a few very old thatched houses remaining, reputed to be about 300 years old, and about half-a-dozen still called the 'new' houses, but built within the last twenty years.

Stockcross has a very garden-minded community, and that, together with the well-kept churchyard, has helped it to win the Best Kept Village competition on more than one occasion.

The Church of St. John, though not old, (the foundation stone was laid in 1838) is a very beautiful building, admired by many. Much of the interior fabric owes a great deal to D. N. (later Sir Ninian) Comper, whose work can also be seen in Westminster Abbey and Southwark Cathedral. The church was paid for originally by the Rev. H. Majendie, a most worthy and philanthropic gentleman, who was vicar of Speen for 50 years. He also was a prime mover in bringing education to Stockcross, when a school was built in about 1830, in the centre of the village. Needless to say, this building was eventually outgrown, and a new school was built in 1964.

As well as being great benefactors of the church, the Sutton family built a Working Men's Club in about 1874-75, now known as the Sutton Hall; this remains very much in use by, among others, the Billiards Club, the Women's Institute and the Silver Threads.

So, the village has a church, a school, a hall, three pubs and, fortunately, a post office/shop.

# Streatley  ⚬⚮

In the Goring Gap between the River Thames and the Downs lies the lovely village of Streatley, favourite riverside port of call for innumerable small boats and weekend sightseers. The Swan Inn, plushy and popular, lies along the towpath beside the weir, gay with flowers, ducks and swans. Above it the road bridge leads over to Goring and Oxfordshire.

The old wooden bridge with toll-gate for carts, toll-house and pedestrian gate was replaced in 1923.

About 900 people live in Streatley, in handsome old houses and cottages grouped around the bridge and church, and some excellent modern houses on the A329, which cuts through the village below the well-wooded downs.

In the early part of this century the brewing family of Morrell owned three-quarters of Streatley, in land, woods and farms. A beautiful William and Mary house in the High Street was their home.

Another fine house of the same period is the residence of a local doctor, and an Elizabethan farmhouse, once Place Manor Farm, is supposed to be haunted by a lady in white!

The Norman church of St. Mary is attractively set among trees behind the Swan Inn and off the main road; it was extensively restored in Victorian times.

Higher up on the A329 is the old Bull Inn, a good black and white building of considerable charm, and once a coaching inn for the Royal Mail coach to Oxford.

A modern addition to Streatley's many attractions is a famous cheese shop selling a wonderful variety of cheese from all over the country.

The land around Streatley rises steeply on both sides of the river, with fine views and noble trees ... its natural setting is as beautiful as any in Berkshire, and on a fine sunny day admiring visitors converge on it from all corners of the world.

# Sulham & Tidmarsh

Sulham and Tidmarsh are two pretty villages in the Pang valley about a mile south of Pangbourne. Sulham, sheltered by a fine ridge of beechwoods, is still very quiet, consisting of a few attractive old houses and cottages strung out along a narrow country lane. Tidmarsh has always been busier. The road running through it was a turnpike road in coaching days, and the old toll cottage can still be seen a short distance from the ancient Greyhound Inn and the village forge. Today the road is the A340, linking the A329 from Oxford with the A4 and the M4, and carrying a growing volume of traffic. The straight stretch which speeds motorists on their way south of Tidmarsh was built in 1855 by Mr Benyon of Englefield to replace the old twisting route through the hamlet of North Street to Theale.

The Pang valley, abundantly wooded and watered, has been a farming area for centuries. During construction of the M4 in 1970 the remains of a Romano-British villa and farmhouse were discovered near Maidenhatch Farm in Tidmarsh. Nunhide Farm in Sulham dates back to Domesday. There was a vineyard in Tidmarsh in the 13th century, by which time there was a mill, probably on the same site as the mill which only ceased to grind corn early in the present century. A rabbit warren was recorded in Tidmarsh in the 17th century, when James I granted the lord of the manor the right to keep deer, rabbits and pheasants.

St Lawrence's Church at Tidmarsh was begun in the 12th century and has a 13th century apsidal chancel. It has been well restored and retains its Norman font and south doorway. Sulham's 13th century church was pulled down but replaced in 1838 by the Reverend John Wilder with the present flint and stone church, with its tall spire and brilliantly coloured lancet windows. The Wilders were principal landowners in Sulham for over 300 years and members of the family served as rector.

John Wilder, rector 1836-92, also built several of the pretty thatched cottages (one of which was the Post Office until the 1960s), the village school (opened 1837, rebuilt 1892, closed 1970), and the round brick tower near Nunhide Farm known as Wilder's Folly.

In Tidmarsh Robert Hopkins of the Manor House built a school for 45 children in 1856. It was closed about 1905, but the tiny school house survives, as does Sulham school, as a private residence. During the past 50 years most of the old occupations have died out, and strangers have moved into the villages. Tidmarsh Mill House was let by the miller as far back as the 1920s, when Lytton Strachey, the essayist and biographer, lived there. Gamekeepers no longer inhabit the old keeper's cottages, which newcomers have bought and modernised; as they have many of the other old dwellings, including the former Tidmarsh bakery in the row of brick cottages opposite the Greyhound. But the forge, derelict for some years, has been reopened, and the fire glows again for the making of decorative wrought ironwork and fireplaces. Several new houses have been built in the spaces between the old.

Farming and forestry are still the main occupations; and there are now also a breeze block factory, a stud, boarding kennels and riding stables. Tidmarsh has a small village hall; the county mobile library stops at the Greyhound once a fortnight, and there is a weekly bus into Reading.

# Sulhamstead

Sulhamstead is an oval-shaped, scattered village, three miles across and twice as long, stretching from Burghfield Common northwards across the Bath Road, up to the wooded ridge of Englefield. The present parish comprises the two ancient parishes of Sulhamstead Abbots and Sulhamstead Bannister.

The lovely parish church of St. Mary's dates from about 1220 but it is thought that an earlier church must have existed on this site as the font is at least a century older, which links it with the foundation of the abbey of Reading. It was originally dedicated to St. Bartholomew, then came the Black Death and the villagers, perhaps in a 'last ditch' desperate plea for mercy, re-dedicated their church to the Mother of Our Lord and it became St. Mary's. Visitors are entertained by a memorial tablet in the chancel to Robert Fenn 1816 - 1912 who hybridised and improved the potato for which he was awarded the Victorian Medal of Honour. Some distance away at Sulhamstead Bannister, the burial ground remains of two former churches. St. Michael's the most recent, was demolished in 1966 and some of the flints were used in the new vestry at St. Mary's.

Early in the 18th century the lord of the manor Daniel May built Sulhamstead House, a white ionic porticoed house looking over the Kennet valley. The house and land was left to his descendants until 1910. During the Second World War it became an RAF Training School and is now the Thames Valley Police Training College. The garden boasts a 600 year old Cedar of Lebanon.

The village is fortunate in having a number of other beautiful and interesting houses and gardens, among them Folly Farm, a fine example of a Lutyens house; the Old Rectory – a William and Mary house – and Tyle Mill – originally a corn mill, all of which regularly open their gardens to the public.

The only remaining inn, the Three Kings Jack's Booth, on the Bath Road, was once a busy coaching inn, and there are many differing stories concerning its name. The most likely links it with Jack of Newbury, the wealthy cloth merchant, who undoubtedly would have spent a lot of time travelling the Bath Road to and from London. Another suggests that the inn was used as a boxing booth for entertainment by a

St Mary's Church
Sulhamstead Abbots

local man called Jack and an early map shows a small hamlet called Jack's Booth. The Three Kings are presumably of biblical origin.

The Kennet and Avon Canal now cleared from Reading to Sulhamstead Lock, provides moorings for many pleasure craft and westwards towards Ufton Nervet it becomes a fisherman's paradise.

Unfortunately much of the natural beauty of the area has been marred by the erection of pylons and the extraction of gravel, but it is hoped that nature will eventually do her valuable work and camouflage these scars.

# Sunningdale

Sunningdale is a rather straggling area, the older village clustered round the church, and the newer part across the fields about a mile away, which grew around the London Road and the station.

Despite the boundary changes of 1974 the area was left unchanged, and the county boundary still divides the two parts and means that Sunningdale is administered by two county, three district and three parish councils.

The name is probably Saxon in origin, meaning 'the home of Sunna's people' and the land where the village grew was largely a marshy waste, part of Windsor Forest which formerly stretched from Windsor to Basingstoke. Evidence of early occupation was shown in the discovery of several Bronze Age barrows. One, excavated in 1901, contained fragments of twenty-three cinerary urns, some of which are now in Reading Museum.

Throughout history, the main highway to the south west has passed through Sunningdale. The Roman Road from London to Silchester, known locally as the Devil's Highway, crossed the river at Staines, ran through the site of Virginia Water, Fort Belvedere and Coworth, then skirted the field behind Church Road, along the edge of the Recreation Ground and thence to Bagshot. Later the turnpike road from London, still marked by milestones, followed roughly the same route though, running to the east of the village. Within living memory, a thatched turnpike cottage stood at the corner of Broomhall Lane and the London road, across from the Chequers Inn. About a mile away, along the London Road towards Coworth is the Red Lion Inn, which with the Chequers are old coaching inns, still in business today. In the 18th century these roads through a wild and desolate Windsor Forest and Bagshot Heath made the area an ideal hunting ground for highwaymen. William Davis, Claude Duval, Captain Snow and Parson Darby are all known to have carried out their infamous deeds in this vicinity. It seems

148

that the village is still keeping the tradition of being near the main high-way, as the M3 Motorway now crosses Chobham Common just over the Surrey border.

In 1828 a Baptist Chapel was built in the village but it was not until 1840 that a church was built in Sunningdale, on the site of an old gravel pit. Until then the villlage had been part of the parish of Old Windsor, although separated by six or seven miles of forest. Soon Holy Trinity Church was not big enough for the increasing population and was rebuilt in celebration of Queen Victoria's Golden Jubilee in 1887. The vicar at this time was Rev. Raffles Flint, nephew of Sir Stamford Raffles. Sadly, the Congregational Church, which celebrated its centenary in 1965, closed about eight years ago.

Holy Trinity Primary School was built in 1842 on land given by St. John's College, Cambridge. It provided education for all ages until Charter School, now comprehensive, opened in 1958, covering secondary education for the area.

Coworth was occupied as far back as Saxon times, but the present mansion was built about 1800, the last private owner being Lord Derby. Coworth Park Farm is an excellent example of a Tudor farmhouse, the front being virtually unchanged since it was built.

Fort Belvedere was built as a folly in 1755 by the 2nd Duke of Cumberland, and enlarged and used as a hunting lodge by George IV. The ruins in the grounds, which we can see from the shore of Virginia Water, are part of an ancient temple transported here from Leptis Magna, near Tripoli. Queen Victoria was a frequent visitor and a royal salute was fired annually on her birthday from the guns mounted outside the house. Edward VIII, when Prince of Wales, made his home here and modernised the interior. It was here that the abdication order was signed, and afterwards the King left through Coworth Park grounds in order to avoid the press and publicity.

There are several other large houses in the district, some still private residences, but many taken over for other purposes. Sunningdale Park is used as the Civil Service College, Charters by De Beers Ltd., and Coworth Park has been developed as offices. Shrubs Hill Place is a private school, though part is still occupied by the Verona Fathers. Others, such as Dale Lodge, and Broomfield Park, have been demolished but their names are remembered in the modern estates built on the sites.

The few shops in the village centre have declined in number but there is a good selection near the station. There are two pubs, the Nag's Head and the Royal Oak, as well as those mentioned on the London Road.

The district is well known for its proximity to Ascot race course, which was founded by Queen Anne, and has Sunningdale golf course, which is the venue for many international meetings. Sunningdale

Ladies Golf Club is the oldest ladies golf club in the country.

There are many magnificent trees in the area, some of which are quite rare specimens, and in the early summer the many coloured rhododendrons and azaleas in the gardens are a breath taking sight.

# Sunninghill

Sunninghill is not a picturesque village with thatched roofs, village green, manor house and smithy, although it had all these in the past. It lies 200 feet above sea level, about six miles from Windsor, in a wooded area with light heathland soil. The area was once part of a Royal hunting forest which ran south of the Thames, and many roads nearby are still called 'rides'.

The Saxon tribe which lived here before the Norman Conquest were called the Sonnynes, hence Sonninghill and Sonningdale, and the daughter of the tribal chief, called Isabella, became abbess of a nunnery at Broomhall. In a little clearing where two rides cross, a church was built for the foresters or verderers. It was built in 890 AD and was replaced in the 12th century by a Norman church called St. Michael and All Angels. The nuns of Broomhall were given the church by King John in the first year of his reign and held it until all monastries and nunneries were dissolved by Henry VIII, when it was taken over by St. John's, Cambridge, who hold it still. It was enlarged and altered in the 19th century and an original Norman arch removed at this time, was later discovered built into a garden wall. This restored arch and a very ancient yew tree are probably the oldest sights in Sunninghill.

On the highest ground, surrounded by patches of bogland and dense forest, large houses began to be built. John and Joan de Sunninghill lived in the manor at Silwood Park in 1362 and since then the area has been a favourite place for large estates and well known names. Rumour has it that Nell Gwynne had a lodge there.

The founding of Ascot racecourse by Queen Anne and the popularity of the chalybete wells, which rivalled Bath in the 18th century, resulted in more houses being built and gradually the little cottages of the people serving them began to cluster south of the road to Ascot.

The Windsor Forest Enclosure Act in 1813 meant much hardship for the people. They could no longer wander freely to cut turf and wood for fuel and a man could be hanged for catching a hare to feed his children. The building of the South Western Railway from London to Wokingham in the 1850s, which passed through the village, made a big difference and many houses carry the dates of the more substantial brick houses built during the next forty years.

A mission hall was built in 1880 and both it, and the Salvation Army suffered from the attentions of a group known as the Skeleton Army. These, paid by the brewers to stop the spread of the tea-total movement in the Non-Conformist churches, broke up meetings with fights, window-breaking and other activities such as releasing pigeons sprinkled with pepper through the windows. Later, this same building became a Music Hall and the inhabitants of Sunninghill were able to see London artistes like Little Tich and Albert Chevalier. The building became a Methodist Church, which it still is.

The village gained from the generosity of the land owners. One bought the land and had the first public school built, another the Reading Rooms, which now houses the village library. A fine village hall was built in memory of Thomas Cordes, who had lived at Silwood Park. One of the earliest rural cinemas, which still survives, was owned by Captain Brooke and his mother Her Highness, the Ranee of Sarawak not only laid the foundation stone but sometimes played the piano to accompany the early films.

In the 1950s and 60s there was another upsurge of new building, when St. Michael's school was enlarged, many of the open spaces and fields were filled with new houses, big houses were altered into flats or demolished and their gardens made into estates.

Some of the largest houses, where great house parties had gathered for Royal Ascot race-meetings, Henley and polo, became hotels, nursing homes, training centres for large firms or, in the case of the manor house, Silwood Park, part of Imperial College.

Now there is a little light industry in the village, but most people work in London, Slough, Bracknell or Heathrow. There are about thirty shops, a bank, post office, a primary and large comprehensive school and some small offices. The law-abiding citizens of present-day Sunninghill live among the few remaining trees of the old hunting glades and the newer birches, pines and rhododendrons, with only the odd fox or squirrel to remind them of past days.

# Swallowfield

Swallowfield, six miles south of Reading, is a large parish of 400 acres which includes Riseley and Farley Hill. A section of the Roman road from Silchester to London, now called The Devil's Highway, runs along its southern boundary. The whole district was once part of Windsor Forest and it still contains a good deal of woodland. The name of the village is derived from an old German word meaning 'rushing water' – an earlier name for the river Blackwater – one of three rivers which flows through the parish. The population is about 2,000 and is increasing; many new homes are going up.

There is plenty of social life – A Dramatic Society, a Horticultural Society which is 100 years old in this year of 1984, two W.I.s, a Youth Club, a Fishing Club, a Churchwomen's Fellowship, Scouts, Guides, etc.

The old Manor House, now known as Swallowfield Park, has a long recorded history. A Norman lord, Sir John le Dispenser, one of its earliest owners, in 1256 built All Saints Church in a corner of his park.

The estate has been owned by many distinguished families over the centuries and many notable people have been guests at their house. The names of some are written over doors upstairs – King Charles II, Queen Anne and John Evelyn are amongst these; other famous names are in the Visitors' Book – Henry James, Lord Curzon and Randolph Churchill for instance. Several of the Russells were interested in literature and they numbered amongst their friends and visitors Dickens, Thackeray, Charles Kingsley, Wilkie Collins, Ruskin and Mary Mitford. This lady, who wrote *Our Village* and much else, lived for some years in a cottage in Swallowfield and died there in 1855. She probably got most of her material for her stories of country life at Three Mile Cross, where she lived before, and from Shinfield, but she makes passing references to Swallowfield, especially to its Parish Church, near which she is

Swallowfield Park
BDT.

buried. Her grave is often visited by admirers of her writings. The house and surrounding grounds were sold to the Country Houses Association in 1964 – a body which buys and conserves large houses of historical and architectural interest and provides accommodation for retired and semi-retired people. The public rooms and grounds are open to the public from 2 - 5 p.m. on Wednesdays and Thursdays during the summer months. The greater part of the old manor property – the fields and woods and farm buildings – was bought by the Hon. P. M. Samuel of Farley Hall. One of the barns was in 1983 made into a private residence and its occupant owns the old Dovecot – a listed building.

During the 1970s the usually quiet life at the Park was enlivened by visits from T.V. crews who used the mansion and its grounds as the back-cloth for incidents in films. How exciting it was to see Dr. Who driving his old fashioned car about. A much less enjoyable excitement came to the village in 1982 when a whirlwind blew many tiles off roofs and knocked down chimneys, fences and green houses. Fortunately no-one was hurt although one W.I. member had a narrow escape when bricks fell through the ceiling onto the bed where she lay. There are still no street lights in Swallowfield village but there is less traffic passing through since the Swallowfield by-pass was opened; this benefits householders in or near the road to Reading. There is an interesting moated 16th century house here, 'Sheepbridge Court' which is itself a listed building, while its moat is an Ancient Monument. The house was added to in the 17th century and has attractive unusual windows and brickwork.

To the east of the village, Farley Hill, a pleasant, well wooded district, relieves the flatness of the rest of the parish. It has its own church, St. John the Baptist's – an attractive red brick building about one hundred years old, the Victory Hall, a Junior School and several fine old houses. Farley Castle, formerly the home of the explorer, Mr Mitchell Hedges, was bought in 1958 by Miss Woolley and adapted for use as a school for handicapped children of good ability. Splendid work is done at Hephaistos School; some of the pupils later gain high degrees and good posts. Farley Court has been made into flats: Charles Kingsley lived there for a time while vicar of Eversley. Farley Hall is a handsome Queen Anne house.

# Thatcham 🦮

Even with the recent spread of new houses, bringing its population to a still rising 17,000, Thatcham preserves the heart of the old village at its centre.

St. Mary's Church stands in a quiet area of trees, a high brick wall sheltering it by the alleyway on the north side; a low wall bordering the remainder of the churchyard and its tombs. Saxons first built a church on this site, of which nothing remains; the first stone building being constructed about 1141, its Norman doorway still preserved at the south side. Restorations and additions have been carried out through the years, including a recent church hall, and in 1970, two new bells completed one of the few ten bell peals in Berkshire, which rings out on Sundays and festive days, and when visiting teams of ringers call at the tower.

Beyond the eastern end of the church, past a row of small cottages, is the Broadway Green. At its corner, the stump of the old butter cross still marks the site of a flourishing market where, in the 12th century, Newbury men, jealous of its success, attacked the stalls. There is no market now and the green, with its small trees, rose beds and seats, is flanked by two supermarkets and other shops. Traffic passes constantly. The stocks, where Mrs. Barfield, the Thatcham historian's wife and schoolteacher, sheltered an offender from the rain with her umbrella, have disappeared. At weekends, local charities still set up stalls and hold small fetes.

Where the Broadway joins the Bath road at its northern end, stands the King's Head. This was one of Thatcham's old coaching inns and much of the early building and stables is still visible. It was due to its owner, Miss Fromont, who feared losing the coaching trade and who owned areas of land to the south of Thatcham that, when the railway came, it was only permitted to be built a mile away from the village.

The narrow High Street which turns off at this end of the Broadway, was once part of the old Bath road, but has been bypassed for some time. The crooked lines of various roofs over its shops and still narrow pavements show the character of an old village street, although new frontages and windows have been added.

Beside the post office, Church Lane turns off the High street back towards St. Mary's church, passing on its way, the old British school which was opened in 1847 and acts now as a hall for the United Reformed Church next door.

The Kennet comprehensive school is now available for local children, as well as several junior schools, among them Francis Baily along the Bath road, named after the famous astronomer born in 1774.

The direct route to the railway is along Station road from the southern end of the Broadway, but it is still possible to walk through the new houses on the Moors estate, over the railway line, across the fields and down the Kennet and Avon canal to the station.

This corner of Thatcham has its own character. The river Kennet, always full of swans here, curves towards Chamberhouse Farm, the house built on the site of the old Chamberhouse manor, once called a castle and surrounded by a moat, (the name coming from Roger de Chambre).

The Swan Inn was once used by bargemen taking loads of meal, flour, coal, timber, iron and other heavy goods between Newbury and Reading, or from Bristol and Bath to London. Tables are still set out in its garden and it is full of visitors in the summer time.

A lane runs beside the railway track by the site of the old Chamberhouse Mill, dating back to the early 15th century, and which produced flour until 1967. Further along at Colthrop mills, the paper making industry flourished from 1805 when Fourdrinier, a Frenchman who invented paper making machinery, converted the old fulling mill to paper making. Now a sprawl of new industry grows outwards along the Bath road towards Woolhampton.

The canal itself will become busy again with pleasure boats when the locks are cleared within the next few years between Reading and Newbury, and eventually to Bath.

At the western end of Thatcham, the old rubbish tip is being reclaimed and landscaped into a leisure park. A nature reserve lies along the footpath below this, beside the reed beds, home of the reed and sedge warbler. The gravel pits nearby have filled with water. Some of these belong to Thatcham and Newbury anglers. Swans and wild water birds come and go. It was near here that the first signs of habitation in Thatcham were found, with evidence of a Mesolithic site, and here where future residents may spend their spare time.

# Theale

The Parish of Theale situated in the Kennet valley, extends as far east towards Reading as the Burghfield Road, the land being taken up with new housing estates; but it is separated from the actual village by the M4 motorway. The A4 Bath Road, which was a coaching route from London to Bath is no longer in use as a main road and a by-pass takes most of the larger traffic away from Theale.

Theale can claim to be one of the earliest villages in the area, probably with continuous occupation for at least 2,500 years. During excavations for railway ballast in the last century, between The Green and the railway, many items of historical interest were found, including pottery, tools and ancient burials. From these it was possible to assume that there had been a settlement in Theale from the early Iron Age, (700 BC), through the Saxon and Roman periods to the present day. Theale was the head of a Hundred, or administrative district, and as such was a place of importance throughout medieval times.

The Theale area was also the site of at least two battles, one between the Saxons and the Danes at the Battle of Englefield in 871 AD is said to have taken place at a spot called 'Play Platt' (the battleground). During the Civil War, the Earl of Essex was attacked by Prince Rupert with a thousand musketeers and cavalry, and many casualties resulted.

Until 1832 Theale was a tithing of Tilehurst. Dr. Martin Routh was the Rector of Tilehurst from 1810, Tilehurst being the largest parish in Berkshire at the time. In 1832 his sister, Mrs Sophia Sheppard, donated funds for a church to be built in Theale and dedicated to The Holy Trinity. She died in 1848 and her cenotaph is situated on the north side of the chancel. It shows the lady engraved in brass, attired in a long gown and with her head veiled; at her feet lies a dog.

In 1913 a Congregational Church (now renamed United Reform) was built on land formerly occupied by an old tudor tavern named the Angel and donated by William Cumber, farmer and alderman. A Hall of Memory was built in 1920 to house the Sunday School and Old Conrade's Club, but has since been replaced by a new hall named after its donor John Cumber, son of William, and Justice of the Peace.

The Roman Catholic Church of St Luke has been built during the last 20 years.

The village once brewed its own beer, the name of Blatch's Brewery being well known in the area. The buildings which remain the same are now used for other purposes. Theale has many pubs compared with its population. In the old coaching days there were many more which gave it the nickname of 'Little Sodom'. There are six in the main street of the village now, but within living memory the Angel and the Castle were also situated in the High Street. The 14th century building which is now the Old Lamb Motel was the original Lamb Inn, the present one being built at the beginning of the 19th century, and taking its name from the original one which was for many years known as the Old Lamb Teahouse. As a Motel the Old Lamb has retained its thatched roof and ship's timbers. A fine open fireplace and the original beer cellars are still there. Scratched on one of the leaded window panes is the date 1704.

Theale Grammar School was built in 1963 and is now a very good comprehensive school known as Theale Green School. The primary C of E school has had some very fine new buildings added. Both schools can boast of excellent swimming pools and the comprehensive school is used by the community and district for evening classes, sports such as tennis, squash and badminton, are also in great demand.

The old Parish Room is no longer used for village functions, as a new Village Hall and Social Club was built some six years ago by the war-

156

time Welcome Home Fund for service men and women of the village, public loans and collections, also local government grants. These buildings have been enlarged during the last two years.

Theale Village has grown with modern housing estates on either side of the main thoroughfare, and industrial units to the south, probably because of its close proximity to the motorway and the railway. In 1901 the population of Theale was under 1,000, in 1984 it is possibly around 3,000. The future of Theale seems to be one of further industrial development and its consequent housing accommodation.

# Tilehurst

The name Tilehurst comes from the old Tigel meaning Tile and Hurst meaning a wooded hill, so Tilehurst was a wooded hill where tiles were made. Alas today we have no kilns, the last one being closed then pulled down and is now a housing estate called The Potteries.

No history of Tilehurst would be complete without the mention of the 'Berkshire Lady', Frances Kendrick. She was a very high spirited girl so determined to marry the man she fell in love with, that she anonymously challenged him to a duel in Calcot woods. When Benjamin Child, the gentleman in question appeared at the appointed place he was a little put out to find that his opponent was a woman, and to add to his dismay Frances informed him that he must either fight or marry her. He was in a tight corner as he could not fight a woman, but if he refused he would be a laughing stock. They were married in 1706, and lived at Tilehurst Manor.

Tilehurst had many watering places and wells and ponds at one time. One such place is the Sheep Wash in Armour Hill. Many caused concern and had to be covered because of their unclean condition and several wells were taken out of use. A better water supply was provided by the Water Orders Confirmation Act of 1894. The present water tower in Park Lane was constructed in 1931-2 and is a very good land mark which can be seen from many miles around.

In School Road in 1910 there was an old forge with a shed adjoining which was used for the shooting of unwanted horses and ponies. They were then put into a cart with the help of a pulley-chain and drum and taken away, today in this place stands some modern shops and a bank.

St Michaels church is first mentioned as a gift to Reading Abbey in a charter of the Bishop of Salisbury from 1189-1193. The present church is of fairly recent construction with the exception of the south aisle which dates from the 13th century. The tower was built in 1737 and the spire added when the church was rebuilt in 1854-6. The church houses the Vanlore tomb which is very elaborate and is thought to be the work of William Wright of Charing Cross who died in 1652. The Epitaph reads:

> 'When thou has read the name Here lies Vanlore
> Thou need'st no story to inform thee more'.

An interesting charity is the Poors Land Charity. Land was left in the time of George II to the Lord of the Manor, to the Rector of Tilehurst and to the Overseers of the Parish, 3 parcels of land in all: one next to the Workhouse, land on Kentwood Common and land on Kent wood common near Harmoor. These lands were let out as allotments, or let out as grazing land to tenants on a 21 year lease. The proceeds were to be laid out in coals which were to be distributed to all parishioners whose rent was under £10 per annum. In 1904, 200 families received 4 cwts of coal at the cost of 16 shillings (80 pence) per ton. In 1906, 32 tons of coal costing 18 shillings per ton was distributed to 328 persons in Tilehurst and Theale. During the later years the distribution of coal has ceased for 3 reasons – (1) the high cost of coal   (2) many houses no longer burnt coal   (3) the coal merchants refused to deliver small amounts of 1 or 2 cwts to the various houses. The Charity Commissioners therefore revised the charity to allow the trustees to make financial grants in many different ways to people on need in the ancient Parish of Tilehust.

Mary Lines Alms Houses are let to ladies over sixty years of age who have lived in Tilehurst or Theale. Years ago they had to be Church of England members and must have attended at least one service on a Sunday but these rules no longer apply.

# Tutts Clump

> Tutt's Clump, – the signposts lean persuasively,
> in a rough circle pointing up flinty lanes or
> grass-grown cart tracks. In their midst remains
> only a smooth-turfed eminence, out of the sky
> scooping a shallow segment. No tree nor stump
> but only the signposts now recall Tutt's Clump.
>
> Once there were beech-trees here in a tall ring,
> once the slow cows in summer sought this shade
> or of an evening courting couples strayed
> to plan their future and stood lingering.

And once on a blowy night beneath these trees
stern Colonel Tutt, pious with Bible in hand
and sword at belt, rapped out a curt command
and gave his Parliament horse some brief hours ease.
Yet by those hours he earned long centuries' fame,
sealing the spot with his short vigorous name.

by Peter J. Henniker Heaton

Tutts Clump is a tiny hamlet between Bradfield and Bucklebury, hardly more than a scattering of pretty cottages.

The delightful place name is thought to come from a tree surmounted mound opposite the Traveller's Rest, where a General Tutts rested his horses before the Battle of Newbury during the Civil Wars.

At the same mound St. Birinus is said to have rested on a pilgrimage, and when he stuck his sword into the ground it became alight.

In a steep lane called Rotten Row are several beautiful old black and white cottages; an old village inn called The Slipper is now a private house known as Farthings. It was named by the Temple Thurston family, who were told to 'save their farthings' and they could have a country cottage.

Brick houses in the district have been built of locally made bricks, although the kilns are now disused.

Bradfield Hall, a late 18th century brick house with a clock tower and a good painted ceiling by Adam is mentioned in the section headed Bradfield.

Tutts Clump has a small Methodist Chapel with the foundation stone dated 1879.

# Twyford

Although Twyford did not become an ecclesiastical parish until 1876 (when it was separated from Hurst) it is very much older than is generally supposed. Much of present day Twyford is largely the end product of the successive eras of the coach, the train and the car, but it did exist as a settlement 400 or more years ago. We can cite as evidence John Leland the traveller who wrote in 1538 'Twiford is a praty townlet, at the west end runneth Loden, a praty river and so breketh forth in armes that thereby I passed over four bridges'.

For many centuries the use of land was controlled by the manors. The "township" of Twyford was no exception, having to answer to the Lord of the Manor of Hinton Pipard. The Court rolls of this manor are still available in part and they mention in 1589 the Bull Inn and the Mill, and in 1624 the Bull Inn, Bell Inn, and the Rose and Crown, all in the High Street.

Further evidence of Twyford's early existence is given by a War office document of 1686 listing the number of stablings and beds at public houses in Berkshire. This showed a total of 21 stablings and 29 beds for Twyford. There is also a reference to the Ford at Twyford in an 11th century Anglo-Norman document referring to skirmishes with the Danes in 871 AD.

The road through Twyford, London Road and High Street was part of the London to Bath Road until 1928 when the by-pass, now the A4, was built.

There is little doubt that the origin of the name Twyford is the obvious one – i.e. two fords. The importance of these fords lay in the wool trade which centuries ago was of the greatest economic importance to England.

Polehampton School House in the High Street was erected in 1725 under the will of Captain Edward Polehampton whose name is commemorated in the new Branch Library provided by the Polehampton Charities in 1983. There is a story that on Christmas Eve about the year 1666 a destitute boy named Edward Polehampton was befriended by the landlord of the Rose & Crown inn, who gave him food, clothing and shelter and helped him on his way to London. Edward Polehampton prospered and grew rich. On his death he bequeathed a charity to benefit the poor boys of the village. The present Wee Waif inn on the road to Reading was named after Edward Polehampton.

The pleasant group of almshouses in London Road were built in 1640 by Sir Richard Harrison, Lord of the Manor of Hurst, and later endowed by his grand-daughter Lady Frances Winchcombe.

In recent years much restoration work has been carried out in the High Street notably the 'Old Farm House' Webbs Cottage and buildings adjoining the Bell Inn.

In 1978 High Street, Church Street, and parts of Waltham Road and London Road were designated as a conservation area.

Twyford was the home of Llewellyn Treacher, Antiquarian and Geologist, Captain Coleridge, Victorian Water Colourist and Gordon Stables, prolific author and pioneer of the Caravan Club.

# Ufton Nervet

The present parish of Ufton Nervet was originally two parishes, one called Ufton Richard or Ufton Nervet, the other called Ufton Robert. The name Ufton was already there in Saxon times. It is a common

English place name and means Uffa's town or Uffa's farm. The second part of the name comes from one of the families who ousted the Saxon thanes and gained the land after the Norman Conquest. Ufton (or Offetone) is mentioned in the Domesday Book.

Its parish church was re-built in 1861 by Mr Richard Benyon, but it contains many ancient monuments, including memorials to the Perkins Family of the 16th and 17th centuries. The ivy-covered ruin of the little chapel of Ufton Richard may be seen close to the old Pound and opposite the Dog and Partridge, a 17th century licensed inn which was converted into a private residence several years ago.

At the end of its lovely broad avenue of oaks stands Ufton Court, with its great old barn, outbuildings and cottages, and on the south side its terrace, old walled garden and fishpond. From the 15th century until 1782 the property was owned by the Perkyns (later Perkins) family. it was Lady Elizabeth Marvyn (widow of Sir Richard Perkins and later Sir John Marvyn), who in 1560 bought the Pole Manor Estate and there built around the old medieval manor house, the magnificent Elizabethan building of today. Like many built during the reign of Elizabeth I, the house adopted the popular'E' shaped pattern.

The inside has no less than three priests' hiding-holes for Roman Catholic recusants and on the human side boasts literary connections with Bolingbroke, Steel, Pope and others.

When Elizabeth Marvyn died in 1581 she left to posterity not only Ufton Court, but a bequest to the people of Ufton parish which they enjoy to this day, the Annual Bread Dole. In her will she left a charge upon the estate to provide every year 20 bushels of wheat to be made into bread, 25 ells of canvas and 50 yards of narrow cloth to be distributed to the poor people of Ufton and Padworth each year about the middle of Lent. For 400 years this annual gift has been given according to Lady Marvyn's will, and the records provide a fascinating history of both the good and bad times of the life in the parish.

In 1715 a new young bride arrived at Ufton Court. Arabella Fermor, considered the most beautiful woman in London Society, she had been the cause of society gossip and was reluctantly immortalised as Belinda, the heroine of Pope's long satirical poem, *The Rape of the Lock*.

In 1833 the Ufton Estate was sold to Mr Benyon de Beavoir of Englefield House in whose family it has since remained.

While much has changed, much too has endured; agriculture remains the chief business of the village, although the majority of the residents now work outside the parish. Grimm's Dyke or Ditch, an ancient earthwork can still be found in Ufton woods where there are many walks and rides.

The present village school, known as Sulhamstead and Ufton Nervet

Parochial School, was founded in the late 19th century by the notable Victorian Rector of Ufton – James Fraser. He became a national authority on education and on 'labour relations' in the agricultural industry and was a reformer in his time. He was much favoured by Queen Victoria who sent for him to preach before her at Windsor. The school was modernised in the early 1960s and extended in 1984.

The church of St. Peter's still stands sentinel in a landscape which time and change has treated on the whole gently and remains the focal point for parish life and worship that it has been for countless years.

# Waltham St. Lawrence

Aerial photographs to the north east of Waltham St. Lawrence show traces of an unusual Romano-English temple: Roman and pre-Roman remains can still be found and it is possible the area has been inhabited since neolithic times. The original settlement was destroyed by raiding Saxons in the 7th century.

The church, mentioned in the Domesday Book was part of the first Earl of Essex, Geoffrey de Mandeville's reward for supporting the Conqueror. The Advowson, regarded as a source of income, was passed over to the Prior of Hurley when the Earl decided to found a monastery as an act of piety.

An important family were the Newburys who lived in a moated manor house, Beenhams, and for 400 years ran a printing business in London. They gave to the village the 14th century Bell Inn which stands near the church and Neville Hall. The Lordship of the Manor was bought originally from the See of Winchester and eventually sold to the Neville family in 1608.

During the Civil War the village was deeply divided, with the Neville brothers fighting on opposite sides, and though the principal families were Parliamentarians, the vicar remained a Royalist. According to the Parish Register there were burials of soldiers from both sides, and when Beenhams was demolished in the 19th century it is reputed that the skeleton of a Royalist soldier in full accoutrement was discovered. Sir Thomas Foote, a 17th century Lord Mayor of London, rented the house at one time and set up a charity which still exists. A barn standing near the site of the old manor is said to be the oldest in Berkshire.

In the mid 17th century the population was around 300. Little is known of village activities apart from records of the ringing of the church bells for various accessions, coronations and royal birthdays. When Queen Victoria came to the throne in 1837 the population had risen to around 740. A small brick church was built in Shurlock Row in

1870 – this has a reredos in hand-carved oak on the wall behind the altar. The clock in the small bell-tower was put there after the First World War as a memorial to Mr. Beale who lived in the old manor house (now demolished) which stood next to Manor Farm in Shurlock Row.

By 1931 the population was 1,055. The Second World War brought great changes. Since 1952 over 100 new houses have been built, some being council property, including six semi-detached bungalows for the elderly, and some owner-occupied, thus bringing many newcomers to the village. Barns were converted, old cottages renovated, large houses divided, others extended, and one public house, the Fox and Hounds on the Straight Mile became a private dwelling. By 1981 the population had reached 1,363.

The majority of inhabitants derived their livelihood from surrounding towns or by commuting to London. Very few earn their living from the land as in times past. Of the nine farms in the parish only five remain, the rest having been divided among other estates, and the houses and buildings sold off. The large orchards and nurseries which once flourished have all gone apart from one, selling mainly alpine and rockery plants. In spite of all these changes there remain villagers who can trace their ancestry back many generations. The primary school at West End, built in 1910 to replace the two Church schools still has children whose grandparents were themselves former pupils.

A small but important printing firm, the Cockerel Press, originated in Waltham but is no longer there. Various businesses flourish for a while, then disappear, but there is still a small engineering works, a busy garage for car repairs and sales and smaller concerns mainly of the building, odd jobs and garden supplies kind.

There is plenty of activity in the community with the Silver Band, Women's Institute, Darby and Joan, Pony Club and Play Group. Unfortunately, of the various youth organisations – Cubs, Sea Scouts, Brownies, Guides, Junior and Senior Youth clubs, only the Brownies still meet regularly. A Village Show, run originally by the Women's Institute and now by a Village Committee, is held each summer. Occasionally everyone gets together as they did during Queen Victoria's reign to organise a fete or raise money for the village. In 1977 Queen Elizabeth's Jubilee was celebrated in style and the bell ringers also raised a large sum of money for the strengthening of the church tower and re-tuning of the bells which unfortunately were still away at the bell founders and so could not be rung on this occasion.

One significant change in the appearance of the village has been the loss of all the fine elm trees due to Dutch elm disease. The yew tree planted by the church lych-gate in 1655 was split by a freak storm not long ago but still sprouts new growth – perhaps a symbol of the life of this ancient village.

163

# Warfield 🍃

The ancient Parish of Warfield still lies anxiously in the green belt, to the north of Bracknell New Town, although that green belt has been reduced in recent years, and at the present time there is the threat of development on a large scale, Warfield Street has lost Newhurst Nurseries to the developers and on this site there are now ten new houses and bungalows.

St. Michael's church, still one of the best preserved churches in Berkshire, is now faced with a huge restoration bill for repairs to the exterior of the tower, the west window and the Angelus tower at the east end of the church. One new feature in the church is the magnificent stained glass window designed by Brian Thompson, OBE. The inscription reads 'To the Glory of God, and in loving memory of Amey Butler, 1883-1966'. The badge of the Royal Berkshire Regiment recalls her husband who was killed in the First World War. The sheaf of arrows is a reminder of her six daughters, all of them still alive. The window is of black and gold patterning, a colour scheme frequently used in 15th century buildings. The dedication service was taken by the Rev. Norman Bedford and the address given by the late Rev. Harcourt Trevor. A memorial tablet to the latter, who was vicar of Warfield for eleven years and died in 1978 is in the Chancel.

Warfield recently lost one of its most regular church members, Alfred Nelson May, known affectionately as 'Dan', who was a bellringer for many years, and a sidesman until the time of his death in August, 1984. He was also decorated for his work with the Territorial Army.

Rectory House was once the home of Sir William James Herschel. It was here that he published his book *The Origin of Finger Printing*. His old-age hobby was coloured photography developed on glass – Miss Caroline Herschel, a descendant of the former – who lived in Warfield for many years, has now retired and lives in Bath, where the Herschel Museum has been opened.

Church Farm was the home of Miss Dorothea Herschel, and during the 1920s she taught the village children country dancing and was the power behind almost every event held in the village. Her niece, the late Mrs. Eileen Shorland, the local historian and author of the *Pish* published in 1967, lived at Meadons. There is an oak tree in the churchyard at Warfield planted by Sir William Herschel and beneath this are the ashes of the Herschel family.

There are still five inns or public houses in Warfield, the two oldest being the Three Legged Cross, formally known as the New Inn, and the Cricketers, known locally as the Orchard House, the latter is at Hayley

Green and now is a very popular meeting place for people from outside Warfield, having a barbecue, bistro and large car park. The Three Legged Cross was at one time the home of the Moss family who are the well known local builders.

The Shepherds House Hotel at Moss End was formerly just a beer house and with the Leathern Bottle at Jealotts Hill now enjoys trade from outside the village. The Plough and Harrow stands at the crossroads opposite the Memorial Ground and adjacent to the Brownlow Hall, which was the gift to the village made by Sir Charles Brownlow in 1913. This hall is the meeting place for every organisation in the village.

At the time of Her Majesty the Queen's Silver Jubilee, it was decided that the pedestrian entrance to the Memorial Ground, which houses many of the local events, should be made more imposing. Accordingly, a lych gate, with low brick wall wings was designed and built by James Moss and Sons. One wall bears a stone tablet commemorating the Silver Jubilee, and the other has a stone memorial to the fallen in the two world wars. The money for the entrance was raised over two years by the annual village fete, which is always well supported by Warfield villagers as well as many from the surrounding areas.

Warfield Neighbourhood Association is a new and thriving enterprise and the Warfield Players, a theatrical group, are about to stage their first production.

Warfield Primary School, once in danger of closing, is now the centre of activity with the number of pupils increasing each term, and, with an energetic P.T.A., the school holds its own fete, dances, and Bonfire Night celebrations.

Guides, Brownies and Youth Fellowship, together with Cricket and Football clubs are well supported, and there is also a place for the Senior Citizen's Club and the W.I.

Warfield and District Amenity Society – formed to protect the village from developers – fights on despite ever-increasing threats from developers. Warfield Park, now a modern mobile home estate, has its own residents' association and community centre, complete with shop and launderette. It houses almost one-third of Warfield's population and church services are taken in the Park on Sunday afternoons.

# Wargrave

Madame Tussaud lies buried in Wargrave churchyard. No, not *the* Madame of Waxworks fame, but her daughter-in-law. However, it seems appropriate that a person so closely connected with the originator of all those motionless monarchs should lie here in Wargrave, known to so many royal persons.

William's 1086 survey reports: 'Weregrave ... Edid held it ...' Edid being Edith, Edward the Confessor's Queen. Edward's mother, Queen Emma, was supposed to have lived in the village, the remains of her palace, in Church Street, being finally demolished in 1827.

The A'Bear family is one of the earliest recorded in old deeds, and many properties such as Bear Place, Bear Ash, and Bear Hill bear witness to their influence.

The present white, bow-fronted, early 19th century Manor looks across the river from its fine position and must have been a welcome retreat for George III and his family in 1804. Much of Park Place lies in Wargrave, and General Conway, one-time owner, built the rustic bridge on the Henley road with stones from Reading Abbey.

In the 18th century the extravagant Irish peer, the Earl of Barrymore, came to live just off the the High Street, in a house now known as Barrymore. In 1782 he built an elaborately fitted theatre close to his house, and installed Delphini of Covent Garden as permanent clown. The theatre cost over £60,000 and the first performance in 1791 was a gala night. London actors took the principal roles, and people of all ranks, including George IV, flocked from far and wide, especially in the summer months when a visit to this rural riverside village was well worth the often uncomfortable journey.

The rakish earl was not to enjoy his venture for long; he died suddenly in 1793 as the result of an accident while escorting French prisoners to Dover, and was buried in Wargrave Church chancel on a Sunday, so that his creditors could not seize his body and hold it for his debts. He had squandered £300,000 on theatrical and sporting activites, and his home was sold up and the theatre was pulled down.

Wargrave's greatest benefactor was Mrs Henrietta Smith, who lived in a house called Woodclyffe, which she left to be a convalescent home. She donated the Woodclyffe Hall in the High Street, where most public functions take place, in memory of her husband, being opened with ceremony in 1900. £1,500 was endowed for its upkeep, and a village clock was added to the front in 1970, from an endowment by the late Irvine Rankin. This generous lady also provided almshouses, allotments, a hostel (on the site of Queen Emma's palace), a recreation ground, and electric light in the church and Mission Hall.

Lavender Cottage, still standing above the Henley road, was for over 100 years home to Zachary Allnutt, the lavender grower, and his family. The 40 acres of lavender, on both sides of the road, must have sweetened the air for some distance around, before it ended up in the not so fragrant streets of London. You can still enter the cool, dark cellars under the cottage, but the stills and apparatus for making the essence and lavender water no longer stand there.

The Bull Inn and White Hart were both popular halts for the coaches that had turned off the busy Bath Road; the newer St. George and Dragon is probably better known, looking on to the Thames, and with its celebrated sign. Now kept inside the inn, it was painted by Royal Academicians G. D. Leslie and J. Hodgson, with St. George on one side fighting the Dragon, and on the other downing a welcome tankard of beer after his efforts!

Whitsunday, 1914, was a black day in the story of Wargrave. On that day, one of the foremost Feast Days of the church, a militant group of Suffragettes set fire to St. Mary's and partly destroyed the ancient building, apart from the Norman tower heightened with Tudor bricks. Some ancient chalk arches were saved, and later rebuilt in the north wall, but the fine Jacobean pulpit and all the memorials were reduced to ashes. The church plate was snatched from the flames, as were the old registers dating from 1537, and including such fascinating village names as Pocket, Knife, Rolls, Butter, and Sally Lunn.

The new church, built as closely as possible to the old plans, was reopened in 1916, and one wonders whether the congregation could have imagined, on that wartime Sunday, when women were still without the vote, the sort of life their grand-daughters would be living in Wargrave and elsewhere half a century on.

# Wash Common

Wash Common on the west of Newbury is really part of the old market town, but lies on higher ground, on the open heath land between the Kennet and Enborne valleys, and has some of the feeling of a separate village.

It was on this sparsely populated tableland that the first battle of Newbury was fought in 1643, and many of the older streets of Wash Common have names that link them with their turbulent past. Essex Street, Charles Street, Stuart Road, Battery End, Cary Close and Falkland Road are all reminders of those unhappy days.

The Falkland Memorial at the junction of Essex Street and Andover Road commemorates that Lord Falkland who lost his life in the battle. His body was carried to Falkland Farm, and local legend says that his ghost still haunts the place. It was here also that Sir Jacob Astley, fighting on the King's side, prayed his famous little prayer: "O Lord, I may be very busy today, I may forget Thee, but please do Thou not forget me".

The great oaks that once grew on Wash Common were widely used for building, and it is claimed that 16th century ships which fought the Spanish Armada contained Berkshire oak from these heathlands. It is sure that the original wooden bridge in Northbrook Street, Newbury, was sturdily constructed from local trees.

Today the whole district is purely residential, with a number of schools, churches, social clubs and a lively community spirit.

# Welford 🦢

The Lambourn Valley has no more attractive village than Welford, built round the splendid Queen Anne mansion, Welford Park. The parish, which spreads over 5,000 acres with the small population of 750 people, includes the village of Wickham and the hamlets Hoe Benham, Easton and Weston.

The Roman Ermin Street passes through the parish, and coins and pottery have been found locally. In 686 AD the Saxon King of Wessex, Caedwalla, granted Welford and Wickham to the Monastery of Abingdon.

The M4 motorway now divides Welford from Wickham, and the old bridges over the Lambourn River are now dwarfed by the massive flyover carrying the great road.

Welford Park, set in beautifully wooded parklands, with deer park, swift-flowing river and drifts of snow-drops, bluebells and daffodils in their seasons, was built in 1702 by the famous architect, Thomas Archer.

An earlier house had been a hunting lodge of Henry VIII until 1546, when it was granted to Sir Thomas Parry, faithful Treasurer of the household of Princess Elizabeth during her stormy girlhood. This house was later sold to Sir Francis Jones, a Lord Mayor of London.

The Archer family lived in their grand new house until 1770, when the heiress Susannah Archer married Jacob Houblon, and their son took the name of Archer-Houblon. This family remained at Welford Park until 1954, when the present owner inherited it from her uncle.

The lovely little church of St. Gregory stands near the great house, and was very much rebuilt by the Rev. W. Nicholson in 1852-55. Much of the fabric was retained in the new building, including the rare round tower with octagonal spire ... the Victorian restorers carefully marked every stone and faithfully placed it in its right place in the new church.

# West Ilsley 🌿

West Ilsley is a small well-wooded village nestling within a fold of Berkshire Downs. It hardly reveals itself until the last minute of approach from whatever direction.

It is bounded on two sides by anciently important roads – the Ridgeway and Old Street. On the North side is the Ridgeway, a track which may have been used by Neolithic man and was certainly in use in the Bronze Age. On the West side is Old Street which runs south at right angles from the Ridgeway. This appears to have been a Roman road and near it is said to have been a Roman town known locally as Old Newbury. Just outside the parish boundary north of the village, is Schutchamer Knob which, in times past, was a market of great importance. The ancient name was Cwichelmshleaw, which means the hill of Cwichelm, who was a Saxon King. The free men of each Hundred came once a month to a Moot to deal with crime, law suits and taxes under the Reeve.

At the time of Domesday West Ilsley was part of the Hundred of Compton, known then as Nachedorne, on the Hundred of the Naked Thorne. It is interesting to note that Alfred's battle of Ashdown against the Danes was fought around a single thorn tree of some importance.

It is believed that a church has stood here since the 12th century. It was restored in the 17th century and much restored and enlarged in the middle of the last century. At one time there was, in the west wall, a singers' gallery which bore the royal coat of arms, and occasionally the village band. This gallery was removed when the church was restored in the mid 1800s. The sole remaining article of furniture from the past is the pulpit which is made up of Jacobean oak panels.

Two very distinguished clerics should be mentioned. In 1616 Marcus Antonio de Dominis, Archbishop of Spalato (now split) fled to this country and was received by James I who appointed him Master of the Savoy, Dean of Windsor and Rector of West Ilsley. He was a scientist of some distinction whose explanation of rainbows has been described as 'the most valuable of all earlier contributions to the scientific explanation of rainbows'. In 1622 De Dominis publicly recanted all he had written against the Papacy and James I not unreasonably deprived him of his benefices and ordered him out of the kingdom. He returned to Rome and was later imprisoned in the Castle of St Angelo. He died in his cell in 1624 or 1625. Later his body was dug up and publicly burned with all his writings.

Dr Godfrey Goodman succeeded to the living in 1619. During the Civil War he entertained Charles I at West Ilsley Rectory on the night of

Friday November 8th 1644. He paid dearly for his loyalty to the King as in 1646 the Committee for the County of Berkshire ordered 'that the rectore and ye profits thereof be sequestered and the Humphrey Newbury officiate as rector'.

The Civil War brought much hardship to the Community. A local farmer wrote, 'we cannot enjoy our land because the armies on both sides be so near to us consuming the profit of our grounds. Taxes are so hard we are not able to pay'. On August 12th 1645 a general meeting was held on the downs between Wantage and Ilsley and a humble petition drawn up to bring to the notice of King and Parliament their unhappy plight. The only result of this petition was that the High Constable of Reading was sent to prison for promoting the meeting.

There are several interesting houses in the village. The present Hodcott House was built in the 1820s and succeeded one believed to have been built by Indigo Jones. The present racing establishment is situated at Hodcott; among the owners of famous horses is the Queen who takes a great interest in flat racing. West Ilsley House is another interesting building the date of which is not known but here the Morland family established a brewery which flourished over a number of years. There were two breweries in the village at that time which provided work for more people and the population increased. Manor Farm has an ancient barn which can be seen from the road and is sometimes referred to as Tithe Barn. It is now tiled but is said formerly to have been thatched. Parts of the farmhouse are clearly very old – perhaps late Tudor. Rowles Farm was at one time held by the Head family. It derives its present name from Mr William Rowles who came to the village in the 1840s.

The school which was built in 1870 ceased to be used in 1966, the primary school at East Ilsley is used for both villages and the school and the school house are now dwelling houses.

The Blacksmiths shop has now disappeared and the baker's ovens are no longer used.

Quite a number of modern houses and bungalows have sprung up over the last decade or so. The village has been designated a Conservation Area so we look forward to the future with some hope.

# Wickham ✑

In the village of Wickham is a particularly interesting church dedicated to St. Swithun, with a Saxon tower and tremendously thick walls of flint and mortar. The tower had been used as a beacon and was once separated from the church, but that zealous restorer, the Rev. W. Nicholson, rebuilt the nave and sanctuary and incorporated the old tower in the new church.

Perhaps the busy gentleman's most original contibution to St. Swithun's is the famous Elephant Chapel. The interior roof is of carved oak, there are eight angels in the nave carved in lime wood, and eight splendid papier mâché elephants in the north aisle. Mr. Nicholson brought three elephants from the Paris Exhibition of 1862 and set them up as examples of Fortitude, Docility and Strength for all to admire. He regarded them as just as appropriate as angels in his church. Later, five copies were made in this country, bringing the full troupe up to eight.

Two pew ends in the centre aisle were designed by Sir George Gilbert Scott, and the font cover was brought from New Zealand. The font near the door is very ancient, and was dug up near the church early this century.

The village, in which there are thatched cottages as well as houses, old and new, also has a Village Hall, a general shop with post office, a primary school and hostelry. The original part of the Inn is said to be 16th century and when re-thatched in 1984 its name The Five Bells was woven into the ridge.

# Old Windsor

Old Windsor has always been proud of its ancient status: in the Domesday Book it was described as the third largest town in Berkshire. The Saxon kings had a palace here, and six Natural Assemblies were held here between 1070 and 1106, as were also a number of Ecclesiastical Assemblies which decided details of the government of the Church of England.

It was while staying in Old Windsor that William the Conqueror saw the site on which he built his castle at New Windsor; and subsequently the wooden Saxon palace fell into disuse and remnants now remain only underground.

As New Windsor flourished, Old Windsor became a small village, and few old buildings now remain. Of these, the church, rebuilt in 1220, is the most important.

In the 18th century, Old Windsor became a popular residential area for people with connections with the Castle, and the Tapestry Hall was built, to house a tapestry weaving works, employing immigrant Flemish workers. At this time the school was built, and the workhouse, which is now Old Windsor Hospital.

A great deal of building took place after the Second World War, and this has continued, resulting in the growth of the population to about 6,000. Thus, there is a very lively community, which supports many flourishing sporting, social, artistic and youth societies and clubs. Above all, it is a really pleasant and friendly place in which to live.

# Windsor Great Park

The Great Park has survived many changes throughout the years; originally a hunting ground for kings, but with the arrival of the Second World War the deer disappeared from the scene. From a place of remoteness at the turn of the century it has now become a hive of activity. Virginia Water and the woodland gardens have attracted large numbers of visitors. Polo on Smith's Lawn, eventing, equestrian and driving competitions and many sponsored walks all add to the variety of attractions going on throughout the year.

It was in 1932 when the W.I. crossed the boundaries of the Great Park to settle beside the historic building of Cumberland Lodge. This had been the home of the Duke of Cumberland, third son of George III and he was well known for his success in breeding race horses. Here, a disused stable building was converted for use as a village hall, since most of the population were living in this area at the time.

The last members of the Royal Family to occupy Cumberland Lodge were H.R.H. Princess Christian (daughter of Queen Victoria) and Prince Christian. He had been Ranger of the Park and had a great influence on the affairs of the Estate.

Changes affecting the Park were on the way during the mid 1930s. Schemes to build houses in and around the Park were started and this created more staff accommodation. Their Royal Highnesses the Duke and Duchess of York were then residing at Royal Lodge. When the Duke of York ascended to the throne as King George VI he continued to spend much time at Royal Lodge whenever public engagements allowed. He encouraged plans to develop a village within the Park which would be central to the Estate and its administration.

When the design of the village was decided it consisted of semi-detached dwellings, each different in character to give a model village effect. Included in the scheme was a sub-post office/general store. Separately, but closely connected with the scheme was to be a social club and sports ground. This stage of the development was completed in 1951 and the King and Queen visited the New Village. His Majesty unveiled a tablet built into the wall of the Post Office commemorating the occasion and the party then inspected the new social club which was named the York Club to honour Their Majesties' interest. The W.I. were now able to use this new building as the venue for their future meetings and activities.

Over the next decade further development continued to increase the size of the residential area of the village. In recent years the red deer have again returned to the Park and although confined to a limited area the public have free access to them.

A prominent feature of the Park seen by visitors worldwide is the equestrian statue of George III on Snow Hill, at the end of the Long Walk. The present avenue replaces an earlier one of elm trees planted in the reign of Charles II and regrettably victims of Dutch Elm disease some years ago. The Copper Horse, as the statue is popularly known, features as a logo in the banner of the Institute.

The Royal Schools built in 1845 for teaching the families of employees was originally two separate schools. Teachers were man and wife who lived in the School house which was the centre of the building. On one side the boys were taught by the master and on the other, the girls were taught by the mistress. In those early days the children wore uniforms and school meals were provided. Queen Victoria showed much interest in the school and its teaching and so has each sovereign since. Today it is a county first school.

The highlight of the year is the Annual Flower Show which brings the Estate people together with their friends from outside and is graced by the presence of H.M. Queen Elizabeth, the Queen Mother. Her Majesty takes her time seeing everything and always shows great interest in the W.I. display and demonstrations. She also presents the prizes.

Windsor Great Park has a long history and is blessed with its full share of beautiful countryside.

# Winkfield ✺

Winkfield is said to be the second largest parish in England and takes in a great arable area of Windsor Forest, with several widely separated hamlets ... North Street, The Plain, Maidens Green, Brock Hill, Winkfield Row and Chavey Down.

With vigilance and a strict enforcement of the Green Belt policy, the village is fighting to keep this corner of Berkshire rural, instead of becoming a dormitory area merging with Bracknell New Town and North Ascot.

There are some fine old buildings and interesting houses to see ... St Mary's Church, dating from the 13th century, the old Court House, now the White Hart inn, the Old Rectory, the Abbey Farm and Abbey Gate House. Also there are the Knights Hall in Winkfield Lane, the old Forge and the Pumproom, plus Handpost Farm, Keepers Cottage and

Tile Cottage at Winkfield Row.

Winkfield Place is now the Constance Spry School which not only has residential students but also runs day courses in the Constance Spry way with cookery, flowers and other domestic arts.

Once farmers and foresters, the people of Winkfield now tend to work in the neighbouring towns or commute to London. For a time there was an interesting Space Age Industry in the village: the Tracking Station in Pigeon House Lane received and recorded information from the various satellites, and passed it on to similar larger stations round the world. This has now closed, and nothing so far has taken its place, but the nearby nurseries continue to flourish.

Two great motorways pass within six miles of Winkfield – the M3 at Bagshot, and the M4 at Maidenhead. Once more the village is threatened with extensive housing development – a continuation, virtually of Bracknell New Town.

# Winnersh ༄

Winnersh, today lying halfway between Wokingham and Reading on the A329, and adjacent to the river Loddon, one of the main tributaries of the Thames, originated as a Saxon settlement. The name Winnersh is believed to be of Celtic origin. In Norman times it became part of Windsor Forest, a wild heathland occupied by unfriendly gypsies and highwaymen. The appalling state of the trackways and roads led to the authorisation in 1759 of the Windsor Forest Turnpike, two of the gates being situated in Winnersh. Law and order was a problem, so the Forest Association was formed in 1830 for the policing of the forest, in particular for the detection of arson which was prevalent in those days.

Throughout the Middle Ages and almost to modern times the present Parish of Winnersh was sparsely populated and was a Liberty (partly autonomous) of the adjacent Parish of Hurst. The few dwellings were farm cottages or houses spread thinly along the old main road from Sonning to Wokingham. Incorporated in the present parish is the village of Sindlesham, a name of obvious Saxon origin. The mill at Sindlesham is mentioned in the Domesday Book and is still standing.

New impetus was given to the area in 1816 when John Walter II, son of the founder of the *Times* newspaper bought 400 acres of forest land from the Crown. He built a Georgian mansion called Bearwood. John Walter III extended the Estate to 3000 acres, demolished the Georgian house and built the present grandiose mansion to accommodate his family of thirteen children. By it he built the Model Estate of Sindlesham with a church, pub, school, dower house, bake house,

workers' club and cottages, shop and a farm. To the right of the entrance he planted the beautiful rhododendron drive which stretches to
the next village of Barkham, and to the left he gave a field for recreation
especially cricket. To this day an idea originated by the same John Walter is carried on when the cricket team from the *Times* meets the team
from the estate workers of the mansion in the annual match played out
on the village green known as King George's Field. In 1911 John Walter
V sold the estate in lots, but continued to live in the mansion.

In the 1840s a railway was constructed between Reading and
Guildford, which now extends to Gatwick airport, and, later, a branch-
line to Waterloo and this passed through the village making it accessible
by road and rail.

March 1928 saw the founding of the Sindlesham and Winnersh W.I.
at a meeting at St Catherines Lodge, Dower House of Bearwood Mansion, under the chairmanship of Mrs Block. The years following the
Second World War saw Winnersh engulf Sindlesham and the W.I. was
renamed Winnersh. During the First World War the Mansion House
became a Canadian hospital, then an orphanage for the Merchant Navy
and today is Bearwood College. The Walter Dynasty was at an end, but
Sindlesham Village Estate remains almost unaltered and is part of the
main village of Winnersh.

There remain in the village magnificent oaks now under preservation
order and half-timbered houses from the hunting days of the forest.
The unique Loddon Lily still flourishes on the river banks and foxes and
badgers abound. A bonus from the M4 motorway excavation has
resulted in a Country Park called Dinton Pastures giving beautiful
recreational facilities to the area.

Churches are well represented in Winnersh. The Church of St. Mary
the Virgin is comparatively modern, the foundation stone being laid on
June 27th 1965 by the Right Reverend Eric Knell, the Lord Bishop of
Reading.

# Woodley 🐿️

Present day Woodley lies between the main roads from Reading to
Wokingham on one side, and Reading to Maidenhead on the other, and
has developed into a sprawling, thickly populated (33,000 approx) area,
on land which until very recently was farmed. We probably owe this to
the proximity of an M4 motorway intersection, and thus a swift passage
to London.

However, the village first began to emerge in the 18th century as a
series of 'Greens' or settlements lying on the routes to other villages or

important buildings such as Sandford Mill, which was mentioned in the Domesday Book. It still stands, though very few of the other original houses remain and have to be sought for amidst present day housing estates. By the end of the 19th century another separate area emerged, known as Cobblers City – still referred to as 'the City'. The inhabitants of this group appear to have been independent of agriculture and developed other trades, and some even went into Reading for work.

At the turn of the 18th century much help came from the Palmer family who lived in nearby Sonning, but interested themselves in the welfare of their Woodley tenants (for they owned most of the land), and in others scattered throughout the Greens and Cobblers City. It was Robert Palmer who in 1871 built and endowed the church of St. John the Evangelist, together with a school. Both buildings are very attractive examples of their period and are in active use.

The other important 18th century landowner was Henry Addington, who was Prime Minister for a time. His house, Woodley Lodge, lay in the Manor of Bullmarsh, now called Bulmershe, and although the house is demolished, a small fragment of the orangery remains in the Bulmershe Teachers Training College. A Mr. Jones Wheble purchased the estate in 1801, where his decendants lived for some years, but the only remnant left now is the beautiful Bulmershe Court which was one of the old farmhouses. It is difficult to date, but parts of it are Elizabethan and well restored in that manner. It is said to house a ghost, but of whom is not known. Part of the estate contained a large heath famous for revels and traditional games held there largely for the enjoyment of Reading people. Nowadays there is a Sports Centre also enjoyed by Reading people!

The village hall, called the Coronation Hall as it was built in the year of our Queen's Coronation (1953) was officially opened in 1956 by the late Sir Douglas Bader who was a member of the Woodley Aerodrome Flying Club in pre-war days. It is strategically placed in the Memorial Recreation Ground which commemorates the dead of the First World War. Many sports activities and a yearly carnival in aid of charity, thrive there.

A shopping centre incorporating a modern Chequers Inn stands on the site of an old coaching inn on a route through Windsor Forest. The Bull and Chequers remains at Woodley Green, and Lands End still stands on the route to Sandford. Another modern public house, the Good Companions caters for the needs of Wheelers Green.

# Woolhampton ✤

Woolhampton appears at first sight to be a village in two parts; Upper Woolhampton, built on a southern spur of the Berkshire Downs, and Woolhampton, following the line of the A4 road and the river Kennet, originally much larger than it is today.

The name Woolhampton derives from a Saxon warrior, and the village is mentioned in the Domesday Book as Ollavintone, and was Wolhampton in Chaucer's time. In medieval times it would have been part of the Windsor Forest.

In pre-Conquest times Woolhampton was held by Earl Godric, as a gift from Edward the Confessor. Earl Godric was killed at Hastings, and William the Conqueror gifted Woolhampton to one of his followers, Henry Ferrers. In 1159, Robert Ferrers, 2nd Duke of Derby, became a monk, granting the manor of Woolhampton to the Knights of St. John of Jerusalem, or Knights Hospitallers, who became the resident Lords of the Manor. The overlordship was still with the Earls of Derby, who also became Dukes of Lancaster, and when a later Duke became Henry IV, Woolhampton passed to the Crown.

The estate was purchased from the Crown in 1544 at the Dissolution of the Monasteries by a Roman Catholic, William Wollascott, and during the Civil War Woolhampton remained staunchly Royalist, with the Wollascott family facing fines for their loyalty.

In 1757, the Wollascott male line failed, and the estate passed by marriage to the Catholic Earl of Fingal, who owned it until 1786, when all but 7 acres of the estate were sold to John Crewe. The remaining 7 acres are the site of the present-day Douai Abbey and School. A Roman Catholic school has been there since 1855, and in 1903 the Benedictine monks, expelled from France by the Government, established their Abbey and school there.

Woolhampton House was built in the period 1700-1800, on and around the original Manor House. This was the era of road improvement and construction, and the London - Bath road (now the A4) was able to take coaches by about 1700. The Angel Inn goes back further than this in history, but the 18th century saw it flourish as a posting house. The present building is only 50 years old, the old inn being demolished so that the A4 could be widened.

John Crewe's daughter, Anne, married the 3rd Viscount Falmouth, and until 1856 the estate was part of the Falmouth lands. At about this time, the Falmouth Arms, situated on the main A4, was built.

In the mid 19th century, St. Peter's Church was completely Gothicised. The roof and main walls of the old church were retained and the walls encased in flint. The old bell tower was turned into an attractive shingled spire. Next to the church is the village school. The Falmouth family took an interest in it, and Viscountess Falmouth left a legacy to help educate the local children. In 1861, Mr. James Blyth, who purchased the estate in 1856, made a grant of land and buildings to the rector and his successors 'to have and to hold for the education of the children of Woolhampton'. The school is now a Church school with aided status, and Mr. Blyth's successors still live in the village.

The river Kennet is a beautiful focal point of the village. Parts of the river were canalised between 1790 and 1820, forming the Kennet and Avon Canal, which opened up the West Country for the passage of goods by a method far cheaper than the road. The Rowbarge Inn, on the banks of the canal, would have catered for river traffic in the same way that the Angel Inn did for road traffic. It is not known how long the Rowbarge has been an inn, although the building itself is over 400 years old. The most famous patron of the inn was King Edward VII, who would call in after a day at Newbury races. The canal is receiving a new lease of life by the current reclamation of Woolhampton lock, due to be completed in 1985, which will make this section of the canal navigable once again.

The character of the village today is changing from a strictly agricultural community to one where many of the population work outside the village. There has been a gradual disappearance of the traditional village shops, leaving one village store and a post office, in place of the former butcher, baker, hairdresser, cobbler, draper, blacksmith and others. However, there is some local industry moving in; the Water Mill (of which there has been one since 1350) has been restored as offices, as has an old barn in the centre of the village. There are several light engineering operations and family-run concerns which help to keep Woolhampton a thriving village community.

# Wraysbury

Wraysbury, formerly in Buckinghamshire, lies at one of the easternmost points in Berkshire. It is a village on the banks of the river Thames, and is full of history. It was formerly called Wyrardisbury, and an archaeological dig on higher ground where stands the parish church produced Mesolithic and Neolithic flints, and also some Saxon and Roman remains. In times past, although subject to flooding, Wraysbury was strategically placed for river traffic.

In medieval times, Wraysbury was part of the Crown Lands of Windsor, and royal parties would have hunted in the forests. At Ankerwyke, there are the ruins of an ancient priory, and at Place Farm, later known as King John's hunting lodge, can be found one of the best examples of scissor beams in this country.

Magna Carta Island is opposite the village, and it is here that the famous charter is reputed to have been signed. At Magna Carta House there is a stone tablet, found in the river Thames in Victorian times, believed to be the original table on which the signing took place. This stone is now housed in a room in the older part of the house, surrounded by the shields of the Barons of the day.

In the grounds of the burnt-out shell of Ankerwyke House there is an ancient yew tree, under which Henry VIII was believed to have courted Anne Boleyn, and later waited with her successor, Catherine Howard, for the news of her death.

It is not known when the first church was built on the present site of the parish church of St. Andrews, but it is almost certain to have been in Saxon times. Records show that in 1112 the living belonged to the Abbot of St. Peter's in Gloucester. In 1327, in the reign of Edward III, it was given to the Dean and Canons of Windsor, in whose hands it remains today. The Chancery, which is the oldest part of the church, was probably built about the time of the signing of the Magna Carta in 1215. The church has six bells, the oldest of which is dated 1591.

Wraysbury has two railway stations and four inns, the oldest, the George dating back to 1666. There are also several interesting houses and cottages in the village. One house, now known as the Barley Mow was built in Tudor times, and is thought to have been two cottages. By 1600 it became a beer house, known as the Papermakers' Beerhouse. The papermakers worked at the mill in Wraysbury, which had previously been a copper mill; the copper ore came up the Thames on barges and was then taken by horse-drawn transport to the mill. One of the beams in the Barley Mow is reputed to be from one of the barges, and shows the rib marks. The age of some of the beams has been confirmed by experts as being from the Tudor period.

# Yateley ✎

It is disputable whether Yateley should be in this book, as it is actually in Hampshire, with a Surrey postal address – but Yateley W.I.s are affiliated to the Berkshire Federation.

Yateley means Gate into a Clearing, presumably a clearing in Windsor Forest as it once extended this far. There are few ancient remains: only two Stone Age implements have been found, thirty bucket urns from the Bronze Age dug up in an urnfield, and a single Roman coin.

Yateley Manor School now stands on the site of the old Manor, which was called Hall Place. The main house in the parish, however, is Yateley Hall, where the Diggle family lived, and whose memorials were in the church until recently. The Hall is now another of Yateley's schools.

The Geale family were important in Tudor times. They stayed in the area for at least five generations, with Richard's great grandson of the same name, and his family, leasing a mill on the site of Yateley Grange.

Yateley church is mainly of 12th century origin, although incorporating 10th century Saxon work. It is the oldest building in the parish, being dedicated to St. Peter. Unfortunately, a large portion of the church was burnt down by an arsonist in May 1979. As it happened, many of the ancient items were stolen by the arsonist and were later recovered. These included musical instruments which accompanied the hymns in days gone by: a bassoon, two clarinets and a piccolo, now safely in the bank vault. The Victorian Royal arms found its way to the United States, however, and has not been seen since.

The Dog and Partridge was once the Church House, and at one time part of it was used as an almshouse. The pub across the Reading Road, the White Lion, was frequented by the renowned robber and murderer, Charles Peace, whose likeness may be seen in Madame Tussauds. He arrived in Yateley in 1872, and legend has it that he used to sit in the bar, remarking 'I hope they catch that rascal soon'. He rented a cottage in Moulsham Lane, now no longer standing, but he fled when workmen found some of his loot in a hollow tree. He was later caught and hanged in Leeds.

Another villain from Yateley was Parson Darby. He preached on Sundays, but on weekdays he robbed the mail-coach at Hartford Bridge, a popular spot for highwaymen. His stableboy was often puzzled to find his master's horse sweating excessively in the morning, obviously having been ridden hard the night before. Tradition says Darby was fond of the ladies, and in 1841 he was finally betrayed by one, and hanged on Darby Green for robbery and murder.

Col. Thomas Blood of Minley Warren stole the Crown Jewels after knocking down the Keeper of the Tower of London in 1670, only to drop them when his horse stumbled. Somehow he talked his way out of the death penalty, was given a Royal Pardon and his confiscated lands restored to him.

Brandy Bottom may have acquired its name from smuggled casks of brandy being rolled down an incline and hidden under bales of hay at the foot. A less exciting version is that it is really Branding Bottom, where cattle stopped overnight on the way to London, and were branded on their hindquarters.

Yateley, of course, has its village ghost. A spectral coach is said to drive up to a house at full speed, and then disappear. There are some stories of royalty: Prince Arthur, eldest son of Henry VII is reputed to have crossed the river Blackwater at Yateley Mill, on the way to meet his future bride, Katharine of Aragon at Dogmersfield Park. This same mill is said to be where George III sheltered, wet and bedraggled.

Today Yateley is known for its Common, a popular picnic area, and one of the largest in the country. Blackbushe Airport is nearby, where plans for an Aircraft Museum are being carried out, and many Second World War planes may be seen: Spitfires, Junkers JU-52s, a Mustang and even a Lysander.

Yateley Industries is a thriving organisation. Here disabled girls hand-block-print materials with their own designs, and these materials are now known nationally.

Although the village has a partially fluid community, there are still many people with their roots there.

# Yattendon and Frilsham

Here is a really beautiful village, compact, immaculately cared for, and set in lovely wooded country high in the Downs. The centre of Yattendon is built round a wide road, almost a square, where a noble free-standing tree dominates the scene, and is aptly opposite the very attractive Royal Oak inn. Dutch elm disease claimed the old tree and in June 1977 it was replaced by a free-standing oak, planted by Lord Iliffe of Yattendon to commemorate the 25th anniversary of the reign of H.M. Queen Elizabeth II.

The partly moated Manor House stands in a group of fine old buildings along the village street ... the Manor, the Grange, the church, the Rectory and the Malt House, all well worth looking for.

In the days of Henry VIII the Manor House belonged to the Norreys family, who entertained the King and his Queen – Katharine of Aragon, with her lady-in-waiting, Anne Boleyn. According to legend, the young Henry Norreys picked up a handkerchief for Anne, and this set in motion the sad events which led to her death and his execution as one of her lovers.

To many people the name of Yattendon is best known for its association with Robert Bridges. When he was living at the Manor House around 1896, he helped to compile the *Yattendon Hymnal* for which he wrote most of the hymns, fitting them to old tunes. Robert Bridges and his wife Monica also compiled the *Yattendon Psalter*, which is still used

YATTENDON

in the church today. The ashes of Robert and Monica Bridges were placed under the terracotta cross – a memorial to his mother – in the front part of the churchyard.

The church of St. Peter and St. Paul was built about 1450 on an earlier foundation. There is a fine rood screen made by local carvers, and the enterprising members of the village class for copper-work made the copper font ewer and the brass candlestick behind the south door.

A tragedy in 1956 led to the discovery of a number of deep and forgotten wells in old houses around Yattendon. Mrs Faithfull, in the Royal Oak Inn, fell to her death 134 feet in a well that suddenly opened in the floor. Many tons of flint were used to seal up the opening, and other wells were made safe.

Frilsham, an extension of Yattendon with some old cottages and much new housing, has now been separated from Yattendon by the M4 motorway which cuts right through superb unspoiled country and beechwoods. The little church of St. Frideswide, originally Saxon with Norman and later additions, has an almost unique round churchyard, which indicates a pagan origin.

On a beautiful site among the beechwoods is the Frilsham Clubroom and sports ground, with superb views over some of the loveliest unspoilt countryside in Berkshire. Between the villages of Yattendon and Frilsham are some curious and interesting chalk caves. Today sadly they are overgrown and some of them have collapsed.

Take your camera with you when you visit Yattendon and Frilsham ... there is much to delight the discerning eye.

# Interesting People

Addington, Henry: Lord Sidmouth, lived at Earley and was educated at Reading School.

Alwyn, Simon: the immortal Vicar of Bray.

Ashwell, Lena: Lady Simpson the actress, lived at Chieveley until her death.

Bacon, Rev J.M: the hot-air ballooning pioneer lived at Cold Ash.

Bacon, Roger: had an observatory at Sunninghill.

Backhouse, William: lived at Swallowfield and invented a pedometer in 1628.

Baker, Sir Benjamin: builder of the Forth Bridge, lived at Pangbourne.

Bateman, H.M: cartoonist who lived at Curridge.

Benson, Archbishop: was the first headmaster of Wellington College.

Bevin, Aneurin: once lived at Lane End Cottage, Brimpton.

Binyon, Lawrence: poet, is buried at Aldworth.

Blood, Thomas: thief of the Crown Jewels lived near Yateley.

Bramwell-Booth, Misses: daughters of the founder of the Salvation Army, residents of Finchampstead.

Bridges, Robert: poet, is buried at Yattendon.

Canning, George: Prime Minister, stayed at Easthampstead.

Carroll, Lewis: author of *Alice in Wonderland* visited Cranbourne Vicarage.

Camberlain, Mrs Neville: wife of the Prime Minister, lived at West Woodhay.

Cherry-Garrard: Anaractic explorer lived at Denford House, Hungerford.

Coverdale, Miles: first translator of the whole Bible into English, lived at Newbury in 1539.

Cumberland, William, Duke of: victor of Culloden who bred the famous racehorse *Eclipse* at Windsor.

Darby, Parson: the highwayman who lived at Yateley, and was hanged at Frogmore Green

Dashwood, Sir Francis: a founder member of the 'Hellfire Club' lived at Hawley House in the 18th century.

Davies, Barry: sports commentator, is a resident of Datchet.

Davies, David: Rector of Barkham who wrote the standard work on agricultural wages in the 18th century entitled *The Case of Labourers in Husbandry*.

Day, Thomas: the author of *Sandford and Merton* was killed in a riding accident, and is buried at Wargrave.

Dors, Diana: actress, is buried at Sunningdale.

Duval, Claude: highwayman who had a house at Bagshot.

Field, Marshall Earl Alexander of Tunis: lived near Cranbourne and has a chapel dedicated to him at St Peter's church.

Fenton, Elijah: poet, is buried at Eashampstead.

Fermor, Arabella: of Ufton Nervet, was the original Belinda, heroine of *The Rape of the Lock* by Alexander Pope.

Grahame, Kenneth: author of *Wind in the Willows* lived as a child at Cookham Dean, and had a home at Pangbourne.

Grace, W.D: used to play bowls at Hurley.

Gwynne, Nell: lived for a time at Holyport.

Hartley, David: signatory to the Peace Treaty between Great Britain and the

USA in 1783, owned East Shefford.

Hastings, Warren: lived at Purley House from 1788 to 1794, and is reputed to haunt the house.

Herschel, Sir William: the famous astronomer, lived at Datchet.

Hughes, Thomas: author of *Tom Brown's Schooldays* had his home at Donnington Priory.

Langtry, Lillie: lived at Hartley Court, Grazeley for some years before her death.

Laud, Archbishop: secured the Royal Charter for his home town of Reading.

Lawrence, D.H: lived for a time at Hermitage.

Lovelace, Richard: the Romantic poet, lived at Hurley, and was Lord Lieutenant of Berkshire.

Lovelace, John: son of Richard, plotted the downfall of James II at Ladye Place, Hurley.

Mitford, Mary: who wrote *Our Village* is buried at Swallowfield.

Montague, Mrs: the original 'Blue Stocking' lived at Sandleford Priory.

Newbury, John: the first publisher of books especially for children, was born at Waltham St Lawrence.

Norreys, Henry: who lived at the Manor House, Yattendon, was beheaded as one of the lovers of Anne Boleyn.

Novello, Ivor: actor and composer, wrote *Perchance to Dream* while living at Red Roofs, Littlewick Green.

Penn, William: the Quaker who founded Pennsylvania in the USA, was born at Ruscombe.

Pettifer, Julian: the television broadcaster is a resident of Boxford.

Pope, Alexander: the poet, lived at Binfield as a young man.

Powell, Miss Baden: founded the Girl Guide movement at Pinkneys Green in 1910

Sadleir, Michael: author of *Fanny by Gaslight* lived at Willow Farm, Aldworth before her marriage.

Sanger, George: circus owner, was born in Newbury.

Sellwood, Emily: wife of Lord Tennyson, lived at Pibworth House, Aldworth before her marriage.

Sieff, Lord: lives at Brimpton.

Spencer, Sir Stanley: famous 20th century artist, was born at Cookham.

Stair, John: produced the William Pear at Aldermaston.

Strachey, Lytton: the biographer, lived at Tidmarsh House.

Tree, Sir Beerbohm: frequently stayed at Binfield Rectory.

Tull, Jethro: author of *Horse hoeing Husbandry* was born at Basildon.

Turk, John: Swan keeper to Her Majesty the Queen, is a resident of Cookham on Thames.

Walter, John: founder of *The Times* newspaper, lived at Bearwood, Wokingham.

Watt, Watson: the inventor of radar, lived at Datchet.

Wilhelmina, Queen of the Netherlands: lived at Stubbings House, Burchetts Green, as an exile from the Nazi occupation of Holland in the Second World War.

Zetland, Lord: Secretary of State for India in 1939, lived at Snelsmore.

# Notable Monumental Brasses

Basildon    John Clerk and wife
Binfield    Walter de Annefordhe, 1361
Bisham    Brinckhurst family 1581
Brightwalton    John Newman 1517
Burghfield    Nicholas Williams and wife 1568
Compton    Richard Pygott and wife 1520
Cookham    Babham family, and others
Datchet    Hanbery family 1593
Easthampstead    Thomas Berwyk 1443
Hurst    Richard Warde and wife 1574
Kintbury    John Gunter and wife 1626
Lambourn    de Estbury family and others 1406 to 1619
Langley    John Bowser 1608
Remenham    Thomas Maryet 1591, and John Newman 1622
Sandhurst    Richard Geale and wife 1608
Shefford (Little)    John Fetyplace 1524
Sonning    Lawrence Fyton 1434, and others
Stanford Dingley    Margaret Dyneley 1444, and others
Streatley    Thomas Buriton and family 1603
Swallowfield    Christopher Lytkott and family 1544
Tidmarsh    Margaret Wode 1499
Tilehurst    Gauwyn More and family 1469
Upton Nervet    William Smith and wife 1627
Warfield    Humphrey Staverton 1592
White Waltham    Margaret Hille 1445
Welford    John Westlake 1490
Winkfield    Thomas Montague 1630
Wraysbury    John Brecknock 1488, and John Stonor 1512
Yateley    Lawerd family 1517, Rygg family 1532 and others
Yattendon    Algernon Simeon 1924

# Index

Aldermaston   11
Aldworth   12
Arborfield   14
Ashampstead   16
Ashmore Green   17

Barkham   18
Basildon   19
Beech Hill   21
Beenham Valence   22
Binfield   24
Bisham   26
Blackwater (see Hawley)   90
Boveney (see Eton Wick)   76
Boxford   28
Bradfield   30
Bray   32
Braywood   34
Brightwalton   35
Brimpton   36
Bucklebury   38
Burghfield   40
Burchetts Green   42

California   43
Charvil   44
Chavey Down   45
Chazey Heath   47
Cheapside   48
Chieveley   49
Cockpole Green (see
Crazies Hill)   59
Cold Ash   50
Colnbrook   52
Compton   53
Cookham Dean   54
Cookham on Thames   56
Cranbourne   58
Crazies Hill   59
Crowthorne   60
Curridge   61

Datchet   61
Donnington (see
Shaw-cum-Donnington)   131

Earley   64
Eastbury   65
East Garston   67
Easthampstead   68
East Ilsley   69
East Shefford (see
Great Shefford   85
Emmbrook   71
Emmer Green   72
Enborne   73
Englefield   75
Eton Wick   76

Farley Hill (see
Swallowfield)   151
Fifield   78
Finchampstead   80
Frilsham (see Yattendon)   181
Frogmore Green   82

Grazeley Village   83
Great Shefford   85
Greenham   87

Hampstead Norreys   88
Hamstead Marshall (see
Enborne)   73
Hare Hatch   90
Hawley   90
Hermitage   92
Holyport   93
Hurley   95
Hurst   96
Hyde End (see Brimpton)   37

Inkpen   97

Kintbury   99
Knowl Hill   101

Lambourn  102
Langley  104
Leckhampstead  106
Little Shefford (see
Great Shefford)  85
Littlewick Green  108

Mapledurham (see
Chazey Heath)  47
Marlston (see Bucklebury
-cum-Marlston)  38
Mortimer  109
Mortimer West End  111

Nine Mile Ride (see
California)  43

Oakley Green  112
Oare (see Hermitage)  92
Old Windsor  171
Owlsmoor  113

Padworth  114
Pangbourne  116
Peasemore  118
Pinkneys Green  119
Pound Green (see
Shinfield)  132
Priestwood  121
Purley  122

Remenham  123
Riseley  126
Ruscombe  127

St. Sebastians  128
Sandhurst  131
Shaw-cum-Donnington  131
Shefford Woodlands (see
Great Shefford)  85
Shinfield  132
Shottesbrook (see
Littlewick Green)  108

Silchester  134
Sindlesham (see
Winnersh)  174
Sonning  126
South End (see Bradfield)  30
Speen  138
Spencers Wood  140
Stanford Dingley  142
Stockcross  143
Streatley  144
Sulham  145
Sulhamstead  146
Sunningdale  148
Sunninghill  150
Swallowfield  151

Thatcham  153
Theale  155
Tidmarsh (see Sulham)  145
Tilehurst  157
Tutts Clump  158
Twyford  159

Ufton Nervet  160

Waltham St. Lawrence  162
Warfield  164
Wargrave  165
Wash Common  167
Welford  168
West Ilsley  169
Wickham  170
Windsor, Old  171
Windsor Great Park  172
Winkfield  173
Winnersh  174
Woodley  175
Woolhampton  177
Wraysbury  178

Yateley  179
Yattendon  181